Pack Up Your Gloomees in a Great Big Box,

then sit on the lid and laugh!

BARBARA JOHNSON

Pack Up Your Gloomees in a Great Big Box,

then sit on the lid and laugh!

WORD PUBLISHING

Dallas · London · Vancouver · Melbourne

PACK UP YOUR GLOOMEES IN A GREAT BIG BOX, THEN SIT
ON THE LID AND LAUGH

Scripture quotations used in this book are from the following
sources:

The King James Version of the Bible (KJV).
The Amplified Bible (AMP). Copyright © 1965 Zondervan Publish-
ing House. Used by permission.
The Holy Bible, New International Version (NIV). Copyright © 1973,
1978, 1984 International Bible Society. Used by permission of
Zondervan Bible Publishers.
The Living Bible (TLB), copyright 1971 by Tyndale House Publish-
ers, Wheaton, Illinois.
The New American Standard (NASB) © 1960, 1962, 1963, 1968, 1971,
1972, 1973, 1975, 1977 by The Lockman Foundation. Used by
permission.
The New King James Version (NKJV). Copyright © 1979, 1980, 1982,
Thomas Nelson, Inc., Publisher.
The Revised Standard Version of the Bible (RSV), copyrighted 1946,
1952, © 1971, 1973 by the Division of Christian Education of the
National Council of the Churches of Christ in the U.S.A.

Library of Congress Cataloging-in-Publication Data

Johnson, Barbara (Barbara E.)
    Pack up your gloomees in a great big box, then sit on the lid
and laugh / Barbara Johnson.
      p. cm.
    ISBN 0-8499-3364-1
    1. Women—Religious life. 2. Women—Conduct of life. I. Title.
BV4527.J619   1993
248.8'43—dc20   92-42172
                                                   CIP

Printed in the United States of America.

345679 LB 98765

I am so grateful to be able to dedicate this book to Andrew Johnston, my special friend, who so patiently sifted through hundreds of letters for me in preparing the material for this project. His encouragement and continual willingness to help were the special ingredients that allowed this book to be completed.

And not just completed, but finished with joy. Andrew and I laughed together over so many parts of this book, and we had so many chuckles over which letters to put in and which ones to leave out. If you find yourself laughing over anything in the following pages, it's very probable that Andrew and I laughed together over it too.

Andrew is in heaven now, and as I think of him, I can see him with his head thrown back and laughing as he found humor in even the small things.

Memories are so special to me . . . the legacy Andrew left to me in happy memories is priceless. His courage and devotion have been an inspiration to me, and in turn, they allowed this book to be written so that YOU, the reader, will be able to pack up your gloomees in that great big box, then sit on the lid . . . throw back your head . . . and laugh like crazy!

Contents

Acknowledgments

With sincere appreciation, I acknowledge the many people who have shared with me the letters, poems, clippings, articles, and other materials used in the writing of this book. Many of these materials came from supporters of Spatula Ministries, a non-profit organization designed to peel devastated parents off the ceiling with a spatula of love and begin them on the road to recovery.

Diligent effort has been made to identify the author and copyright owner of all material quoted in this book. However, because so many unidentified clippings are sent to me from all over the world, it is sometimes impossible to locate the original source. I would be grateful if readers who know the correct source for items now labeled "Source unknown" would contact me so that proper credit can be given in future printings.

The letters used in this book are based on actual correspondence I've had with hurting parents, but most letters have been edited to protect the writers' identities. In a few special cases I have requested and received permission to use real names and facts, and I thank those writers for sharing so graciously.

Special acknowledgment and grateful thanks also go to the following individuals and companies for these materials:

Some information in chapter 2 is reprinted from GOOD GRIEF by Granger Westberg, copyright © 1962 Fortress Press. Used by permission of Augsburg Fortress.

Also in chapter 2 are letters as seen in a Dear Abby column by Abigail Van Buren. Copyright © 1992 UNIVERSAL PRESS SYNDICATE. Reprinted with permission. All rights reserved.

The cartoon in chapter 2, "I'm perfectly willing to compromise," is adapted from Ashleigh Brilliant Pot-Shot No. 2122. © Ashleigh Brilliant Enterprises, 1981. Used by permission.

The "Sometimes I get so frustrated" baby-photo cartoon in chapter 3 is reprinted with permission of The C.M. Paula Company, 7773 School Road, Cincinnati, Ohio 45249-1590.

The poem "When life drops a pooper," used in chapter 3 is from card number 015337 © Recycled Paper Products, Inc. All rights reserved. Original design by John Richard Allen. Reprinted by permission.

In chapter 4, the "Feel Unloved?" cartoon is copied with permission from an American Greetings card © AGC, Inc.

In chapter 5, Dennis the Menace ® is used by permission of Hank Ketcham and © by North America Syndicate.

Also in chapter 5, a portion of an Ann Landers column is reprinted. Permission has been granted by Ann Landers and Creators Syndicate.

The two cartoons used in chapter 7 are from greeting cards. The "Extra-Strength Deodorant" cartoon is from card number 068111 © Recycled Paper Products, Inc. All rights reserved. Original design by Kevin Pope. Reprinted by permission. The blow-drying porcupine is from card number 240047 © Pawprints. All rights reserved. Original design by Lynn Munsinger. Reprinted by permission.

Introduction

If It's Free, It's Advice;
If You Pay for It, It's Counseling;
If You Can Use Either One, It's a Miracle!

The radio call-in show was going well and I had already fielded several easy-to-handle questions—problems similar to those I had heard before and for which I could offer some practical suggestions that had worked with others.

Then a caller frantically reeled off an incredible barrage of pain and frustration. Her husband was alcoholic. Her son was gay, and her unmarried daughter had just uttered the words every mother fears: "Mom, I'm pregnant."

On top of all *this*, her house had burned, the contractor hired to rebuild it had co-mingled funds, and now creditors were coming from every direction, wanting their money *now*.

Somehow the poor woman managed to say all this in one breath while the talk-show host and I looked at each other in bewilderment. Then she finally stopped and waited for my answer. But I was dumbfounded. What could she do? Where could she go? To whom could she turn?

The pause grew into a pregnant silence. The talk-show host fidgeted as I frantically searched my mind for something that might help this poor woman. How could I possibly solve

1

all her problems with a twenty- or thirty-second speech over the radio? Finally, I blurted out, "GOD ONLY KNOWS!"

There was a moment of shocked silence, then people in the studio audience started tittering. The talk-show host started chuckling, and then even the woman on the other end of the line had to laugh as she realized that my answer, not given flippantly but in real empathy, was true. Only God could know the answer to all those problems!

That's why I have always liked Deuteronomy 29:29, "The secret things belong to the LORD" (NIV). When we are at wit's-end corner, when life is a mystery that seems to have no answer—*only God knows*. Meanwhile, however, we have to cope, grapple, survive—yes, and triumph. That's what this book is about: finding answers when there don't seem to be any, adapting to situations that appear to be hopeless, and accepting people in your life—particularly your loved ones—when they are doing the totally unacceptable.

Can You Fix My Kid?

In fourteen years thousands of parents have come to Spatula Ministries with every conceivable kind of problem. On the first night they attend a Spatula support group, parents typically want to know, "How can I fix my kid?" Soon, however, they realize that isn't the question. The real questions are: "How can I fix myself?" "How can I help my spouse get through this?" "How can we keep our marriage strong so we can deal with what life has brought us?"

And as they continue to share—and to listen—they make some lifesaving discoveries:

They learn about the need to love their wayward children unconditionally. They learn that they can't change their children. *They can only change themselves.*

They also learn how to be rid of their guilt, how to forget the past and look toward a future that is bright with hope.

They learn how to get on with life, how to put their loved ones in God's care—in short, how to let go.

They learn that helping others is a tremendous benefit because, as I have said so often, when you refresh others, you yourself are refreshed.

And somewhere along the way, they learn to laugh again in spite of the painful memories or the ongoing cares. They finally realize they will feel better. It takes time, a great deal of time. It also takes many tears, and it takes a lot of talk—hours and hours of talk. But it does happen. They come in wounded, dazed, and troubled, but after a while they learn how to drain the abscess of pain and begin the healing process.

As I worked on this book, I searched for a word to describe all the STUFF that can happen to us. Words like *problems, troubles,* or *tragedies* just didn't cut it because they were too grim. But then I found it—gloomees. I think you'll admit it's hard to say "gloomees" without at least a hint of a smile.

I believe laughter is the best prescription for pain there is; that's why I titled this book *Pack Up Your Gloomees in a Great Big Box . . . Then Sit on the Lid and Laugh.*

When the gloomees close in, that's the time to see the humorous side of things, not to deny reality but to help make sense out of what is so UNREAL. And sometimes, as you will see in the following chapters, it gets very unreal indeed!

Your Letters Light Up the *Love Line*

Our local Spatula Ministries support group meets once a month in the Southern California area. Over the years, dozens of other branches of Spatula have sprung up and now the Spatula network of caring and love stretches across the country. But as important as our support groups are, they are only part of the total outreach. I spend hours on the telephone each month, talking to parents who may have no support group nearby. In addition, my husband (Gopher Bill) and I publish the *Love Line,* a monthly newsletter that provides help, inspiration, and laughs for thousands of other folks.

Besides the humor, one of the most popular features in the *Love Line* is the letters from parents. Some of these folks have just landed on the ceiling because of unthinkable problems and disaster, and they need a spatula of love to scrape them off and get them back down on their feet. Still others have been coping with pain for quite awhile. In some cases they are drowning, going down for the last time. But others are learning to tread water and even to dog paddle and they want to share their progress with the rest of the Spatula family. I'm often told, "The letters from the other parents are my favorite part of *Love Line*. Keep 'em coming!"

Because letters like these mean so much to folks who are hurting, I've made them a key feature of this book. Sometimes I share my answer to them; others I let speak for themselves with wisdom that is far better than mine. My only problem with sharing these letters is a lack of space; there are so many more I'd like to include.

As you read some of these letters you may want to say, "This *can't* be true! Somebody is putting Barbara on or she is just making this up!" It's possible that someone might write a letter full of fictional problems, but frankly I doubt it. As for making them up, I couldn't begin to imagine all these problems—I don't think anyone could.

Believe me, I don't have to make anything up! I find plenty of it every day in my mailbox or in the voices of those who call on the phone, frantically wanting to talk to someone who will "please listen."

I Don't Claim to Be an Ann or Abby

I hope you don't think this book is going to be Barbara's version of Dear Abby or Ann Landers. An advice columnist I am not! Frankly, I'm a better listener than I am a giver of advice and answers. In the final analysis, God is the only One who knows the answers to anyone's problems. But along the way, He has given us some principles that can and do work. By going through my own refining fire, I have learned a little bit about what helps people when they descend into the inferno of suffering and think there is no way out.

In the following chapters there will be times when I deal with questions one at a time and try to give specific suggestions that might help. In other cases, I may quote several letters and then give a broad answer that's based on my own experience or on input from knowledgeable people I trust. Oh, yes, I'll also be sharing many letters from parents who are coping and who want to help others find their way back to sanity. And behind every answer or suggestion stands the only One who can really help any of us. Truly, *God only knows.*

You should expect to be resistant to some of the answers you find here. You may read things here that you aren't prepared to accept. I wasn't prepared either. In fact, I still haven't found answers to a lot of things. When I learned of my son Larry's homosexuality, I went to a Christian counselor who told me at the very start, "I've had very little success in changing the sexual orientation of homosexuals." I didn't want to hear that. I wanted that doctor to tell me how to fix Larry—fast. Instead, it took months and then years—eleven years in fact—before anything happened. Larry wasn't "fixed," but his heart changed, and, more important, over those years *I* changed. God changed my heart of stone into a "heart of flesh." He gave me the ability to accept, adapt, understand, and, above all, to love unconditionally.

People who know my story ask me how I ever survived learning about Larry's homosexuality and then enduring the lonely estrangement that occurred because I lashed out at him with anger and even hatred. This happened *after* I'd already endured devastating injuries to my husband and the deaths of two sons just as they reached the threshold of adult life. All of these experiences squashed my heart, but out of that came a fragrance in my life that could never have happened without going through the crushing pain. One of my favorite bits of verse says it so well:

THERE IS NO OIL WITHOUT SQUEEZING THE OLIVES,
NO WINE WITHOUT PRESSING THE GRAPES,
NO FRAGRANCE WITHOUT CRUSHING THE FLOWERS,
AND NO REAL *JOY* WITHOUT SORROW.

How did I survive? I tried a lot of things and I learned a lot, mostly by trial and error. And I'm still learning. I try to steer away from the pat answer and the hollow formula. I also avoid the instant solution, the microwave maturity, the quick fix, the heavenly Band-Aid without surgery. That just isn't the way God works. As Jesus said in John 15:2, we need to be pruned, and pruning can be painful.

The bottom line, however, is exactly what I told that desperate lady who called the radio station that night wanting to know how to unravel the mysteries of a life that had overwhelmed her. *God only knows.* The secret things *do* belong to Him. When the gloomees try to strike us down, He always has the answer. And when we seek Him with all our hearts, the gloomees don't have a chance!

We're All in This Together . . .
You're Just in a Little Deeper

Welcome to the Real World

That lady who called the talk show with a life full of problems was one of many I meet all the time—in person, on the phone, or through the mail. While she had more than her share of setbacks, there are folks who experience even greater tragedy.

For example, one mom's recent letter also included a news clipping published several years ago describing her "all-American family," which included her husband, herself, and seven kids ranging in age from eight to nineteen. The article mentioned how both parents stressed spiritual values and how the father, while successful in his job, believed his family was even more important than his career. The article went on to describe the children as polite, bright, articulate, and outstanding students who wanted to please their parents by doing well in their studies. Sundays were family days—church, then dinner with the grandparents. One of the grandmothers was herself a former recipient of an "outstanding mother" award. And to top it off, every year the dad took the whole family on a vacation trip.[1]

Here, indeed, was an example of what a truly God-fearing model family should be like; but just two years after this article appeared in the local newspaper, their trials began. By the time the mother wrote to me, she listed the following blows to her all-American family:

The ninth-grade girl began needing help for depression. Her seventh-grade sister had been hospitalized five times for anorexia and almost died. A sophomore son away at college began to manifest clinical depression. (He ultimately committed suicide.) Another son had shown frightening signs of becoming addicted to alcohol. Finally, the youngest daughter had been diagnosed as having "bipolar disorder." Daily doses of lithium seemed to be helping stabilize her moods. The woman's letter continued:

> My faith has always been the most important thing in my life and my husband has always insisted on the importance of a sense of humor. You have the rare gift of combining both. May God continue to bless your efforts with your spatula of love!

I have a special empathy for these parents because my family, too, was going along in an all-American way before our roof fell in. I also appreciate this woman's emphasis on faith and a sense of humor. It is amazing how overwhelming pain and bitter disappointment bring out the need to laugh. Another mom who wrote to me described it like this:

> A friend gave me your book, *Stick a Geranium In Your Hat and Be Happy.* I read it and laughed out loud. That's something that has been missing from my life—laughter. It felt so good. I have a thirty-year-old daughter—she has been "in the world" since she was a teenager. She was baptized when she was eleven years old. Since her rebellion, there has been a marriage, a child, a divorce, and now a new child is on the

way even though she is not presently married. Drugs, illness, counseling, denial—you know the whole story. This new baby is due March 2. The father is a rock 'n' roll songwriter/house painter. Jesus help us!

Many people who write to me in pain reveal a positive attitude full of faith and trust even when they don't quite understand what's going on. It's as if they know they might as well let a smile be their umbrella—they're going to get soaked anyway. One woman said:

> I have been in a tunnel for a while. Our oldest daughter has three sons, a nine-year-old with leukemia, a seven-year-old with cerebral palsy, and the six-month-old has an appointment at children's hospital this month for tests to see what's wrong—he cannot hold his head up and has trouble seeing.
> We are all believers, but even God's own people travel through dark areas, don't we?

Another mother (I suppose 95 to 98 percent of my mail comes from wives and mothers) wrote to tell how she and her husband drove two and a half hours to where their son lived so they could take him out to dinner. He had already let them know he was gay, and they were devastated. When they got there, the father told his harried and very concerned-looking son, "Your mom was missing you so very much and she wanted to travel to see you to give you a hug."

What they thought might be a terrible encounter turned out to be a time when they could assure their son they loved him very much and that God loves him even more and wants only the best for his life. Their son hoped they could see his "friend" as a roommate—just like the ones he had back in college. They said, no, they still believed his lifestyle was wrong and they would never back down on that, but they would love him as much as they always did. The mother's letter went on to say:

> I don't know if I told you or not, but my oldest daughter had separated from her second husband and moved in with

us. Our second daughter is mentally retarded . . . and now
our youngest son is gay. I can't believe all of this has happened
to us . . . and in the meantime we buried a sister-in-law who
died of a long-time cancer battle. So it is really tough in our
lives at the present. . . .

In Tribulation There Can Still Be Hope

The above letters are only a taste of the thirty or so I receive
almost every day. All these hurting people could probably identify easily with King David, who also knew what it was like to
have life go sour:

> Save me, O God, for the waters are come up to my neck—
> they threaten my life. I sink in deep mire, where there is no
> foothold; I have come into deep waters, where the floods
> overwhelm me. I am weary with my crying; my throat is
> parched; my eyes fail with (hopefully) waiting for my God.
> (Ps. 69:1–3AMP)

I especially like the Amplified Bible translation of verse 3,
which speaks of how David waits "hopefully" for God to act.
Often we find ourselves hoping and waiting, and then hoping
and waiting some more. We experience the tough moments of
life, the moments when we have done all the appropriate
things: We have prayed, we have read the Word, we have taken
our stand, we have put on the armor of God. But nothing
changes. Circumstances remain the same. We have praised God
and rejoiced in the victory He's going to give us, but our depression remains.

In those moments we confess with David that the floodwa-
ters are overwhelming us and yet we still have hope. God will
act, won't He? Our hope may start to fade, and in those moments we must evaluate our faith with hard questions.

Do we have any faith at all?

Do we have enough faith?

Is what faith we have ineffective?

Or could it be that we don't know how to use our faith very well at all?

In times like these, you are in TRIBULATION, an English word taken from the Latin word *tribulum*, "a tool used to thresh grain." Tribulation doesn't refer to having just one blow come down upon you. The thought behind tribulation is that you have had one blow right after another. While you're going through these heavy blows, you may look at others who are enjoying a comforting relationship with the Lord and be tempted to tell them:

> PLEASE SPARE ME THE GHASTLY DETAILS
> OF YOUR HAPPINESS!

When people around us are rejoicing and praising God while we are struggling through deep mire and flood waters, we begin to wonder if something is the matter with us. We begin to feel like second-class Christians. And then the final straw comes if these people who are being blessed and who don't face the problems we do are quick to give us the glib answers: "Just praise the Lord . . . You are just not praising the Lord enough . . . What you need to do is take your stand . . . Just praise the Lord!"

When the flood waters of the cesspool have come up to your very soul, you don't need challenges; you need COMFORT. You need a friend to come alongside and say, "I am hurting with you . . . I am standing with you . . . I am weeping with you. I am undergirding you as best I can. Link your shield of faith with mine and somehow we will make it together."

When Pain Becomes a Permanent Guest

In these troubling times, God is stretching our faith. Twenty years ago Margaret Clarkson wrote a book entitled *Grace Grows Best in Winter*. Her goal was to show that one's trust and faith in God's grace and love grow in the icy, trying times when those cold winds come to chill the soul. As she put it, "the time has arrived when you know that pain has come to you, not as a temporary lodger, but as a permanent guest, perhaps even as master of your house of life."[2] That's how one desperate mother must have felt when she wrote to tell me:

> I look forward to your newsletters and read every word and want to continue getting them; but to tell you the truth, they really don't help much. [Some parents] talk about their children bringing home "friends"—and they have nice little chats? I think I would kill my son, his friends, and myself if he ever brought any of them home.
>
> My son was such a sweet, bright young man . . . He and his two brothers fussed a lot among themselves; they're all so different. But he was always smiling, always so full of joy, and so helpful. Old and young, men and women, EVERY-ONE liked him.
>
> Now he's girlish, effeminate. He isn't disrespectful, just not there. He won't talk. He isn't a part of our family . . . I don't think I can stand it a day, an hour longer. I don't sleep. Then I sleep forty-eight hours or more. I know what other people are going through—that doesn't change what I feel. Besides, I only talk about this one. I've lost two children to death. My daughter lives on the streets with a drug-crazed creep (she brought him here once). My sister-in-law, who I thought was one of my best friends, told me recently that she hated me the day her brother brought me home as his bride and had not changed her mind since (thirty years). . . .
>
> I don't want to be the kind of person everybody hates or who does everything wrong—I don't know how I can be such a failure in so many ways. That isn't all, but it's enough to say I'm not feeling sorry for myself for just one little item; it's for being overwhelmed and not knowing what to do, and for knowing I am this way and not likely to be any different, and for knowing my being this way isn't enough for my children or my family or my husband and his family. . . .
>
> I'm supposed to be old and wise and teaching younger women and others the ways of the Lord—and here my life's falling apart. Sorry—there's just no one else to talk to.

Everybody Has Two Big Questions

No matter what the pain and problems may be like, everybody is looking for the answers to two basic questions: WHY? and HOW? Folks who write to me often ask, "Why me?" "Why us?" "Why our family?" But just as often they also want to know, "How?" "How can I deal with this?" "How do I learn to live with pain?"

I don't have all the answers. Frankly, sometimes I'm not even sure I fully understand the questions. I wish I could always have something to say that would make everything all right right now, but I don't. I do know one thing, though:

WHATEVER COMES TO ANY OF US
IS SENT OR ALLOWED BY GOD.

To some people, that may make God sound weak, uncaring, or even sadistic, but when you're facing the real world it helps to remember that God is in control. He is still at work, even when we feel that our suffering will never end. Like the psalmist commanded, we must "hope . . . in God."[3]

Michael Malloy, director of Christian Counseling Services in Nashville, Tennessee, attended a seminar conducted by Dr. Larry Crabb, a Christian psychologist and author of many excellent books such as *Inside Out*. Malloy was intrigued when Dr. Crabb asked the group, "Do you use God to solve your problems? Or do you use your problems to find God?"

When we use God to solve our problems, we may try following biblical principles we've been told will solve everything. Unfortunately, we can do this and life still has a way of caving in. Then, when the principles don't seem to work, we are in danger of doubting God as well as our own faith. On the other hand, when we "use our problems to find God," we aren't looking for the quick fix or the instant solution; we are learning something about the "theology of suffering." Michael Malloy wrote:

Those who suffer well and keep a passion for God in the midst of their pain are often called saints. I think of two women in my life who had considerable influence—both grandmothers.

One, named Birdie, lost her first family, husband and ten-year-old daughter, in the '20s. She met my granddad about a dozen years later and married him after his divorce—when divorce was really not popular. She was "the other woman" but as I got older and spent time with her after my granddad died, I came to see the beauty of her spirit that overcame the loss of two families—one by death, the other by being shut out by most of our relatives.

The other lady was my Dad's mom, Martha, who lost her husband just before the fourth of July in 1925 in a farming accident. She remarried and had twins, one of whom was damaged at birth but lived until he was 24.

I recall Robert at Grandma's house when I was young. He had to be fed, diapered and seldom left his wheelchair. Grandma cared for him constantly. At other times I recall going with her to clean doctors' offices. When I was in college in nearby Stillwater she would spread a table of food fit for harvest hands on Sunday nights for me and my college roommates. She was always doing something for somebody. . . .

My grandmothers saw things many of us don't see about life. There is a "window" that opens to those who move into suffering in pursuit of God. None of us want to suffer. What we want is out of it—but when it comes we have a choice to let it take us to a high plain or to become cynical, bitter and disillusioned.[4]

When Michael Malloy talks about the "window" that opens to those who move into suffering in pursuit of God, I think of a favorite verse in Hosea where God speaks of transforming our valley of troubles into a "door of hope" (Hos. 2:15 KJV). In the face of any hopeless situation, hope is there, even if we don't feel it. God can take sour, bitter things in our lives and blend them into something that smells and tastes as sweet as honey.

Suffering Is Like Baking a Cake

I like to compare suffering to making a cake. No one sits down, gets out a box of baking powder, eats a big spoonful, and says, "Hmmm, that's good!" And you don't do that with a spoonful of shortening or raw eggs or flour, either. The tribulation and suffering in our lives can be compared with swallowing a spoonful of baking powder or shortening. By themselves these things are distasteful and they turn your stomach. But God takes all of these ingredients, stirs them up, and puts them in His own special oven. He knows just how long to let the cake bake; sometimes it stays in God's oven for YEARS. We get impatient and want to open the oven, thinking *Surely the cake must be done by now.* But not yet, no not yet. What really matters is that the cake is BAKING and the marvelous aroma is filling the house.

I find that people who trust God with their suffering have an invisible something, like the invisible aroma of a freshly baked cake, that draws people to them. As Paul put it, "all things [all the ingredients of pain and suffering] work together for good to them that love God" (Rom. 8:28 KJV).

When we believe that nothing comes to us except through our heavenly Father, then suffering begins to make a little sense to us—not much, I admit, but a little bit, and that's all God needs to work in our lives, just a mustard seed of faith. Then we can see that God is using our pain to work something in us that is redemptive. Every trial or broken relationship goes into God's oven and eventually we begin to "smell" like cake or fresh bread. Even our suffering counts for something!

God Has Plans for Each of Us

The apostle Paul knew something about suffering. He was beaten, whipped, stoned, and shipwrecked. He lived in danger from foes and friends alike, especially the false brothers who betrayed him. He went without sleep, food, and water. And on top of all this, he lay awake many nights agonizing for the churches he had founded, especially when they went astray and fell victim to false teachers. (See 2 Cor. 11:23–29.)

Despite all this, Paul could also say, "But thanks be to God, who always leads us in His triumph in Christ, and manifests through us the sweet aroma of the knowledge of Him in every place" (2 Cor. 2:14 NASB).

You see, God knows what He is doing with each of us. I believe that what He said to the Jews when they were in captivity also applies to believers today when we face "hopeless problems." Through Jeremiah God told them, "For I know the plans that I have for you, . . . plans for welfare and not for calamity to give you a future and a hope" (Jer. 29:11 NASB).

You may be in a tough situation, possibly a real calamity that seems more hopeless than any described in the letters included in this chapter. But if you are trusting God, the word calamity really doesn't apply because calamity, as defined in the dictionary, is "an uncontrolled disaster." And when you are trusting the Lord with your pain, nothing is out of control in your life. After God told the Jews He had plans for their welfare that would give them hope, He went on to say, "Then you will call upon Me and come and pray to Me, and I will listen to you. And you will seek Me and find Me, when you search for Me with all your heart" (Jer. 29:12–13 NASB).

In his editorial on suffering, Michael Malloy also said:

> **Knowing God is everything.** There is nothing more than Him, although throughout our lives we will be tempted to believe in a variety of "set of hoops" doctrines that we must jump through to see God. It ultimately comes down to believing what at this point we cannot see. But we have the assurance that when we have persevered long enough, we will see Him and know Him as He is. And you know what? I think that those who have endured suffering for a time get a sneak preview of the all that is to come.[5]

In this real and broken world we will have suffering, but it's comforting to know that Satan is not in charge. The Lord is faithful, and no matter how bad things get, He protects us from the evil one. We can rest assured that, while Satan is dangerous and deadly, he does not call the shots.

Satan cannot call the shots because he hasn't paid the price of admission. We don't belong to ourselves; we have been bought with the greatest price. Once we realize that, we can rise out of any pit we might fall into in this life. We know that ultimately nothing can harm us because we can always say:

MY ME DOES NOT BELONG TO ME.

Many people who write me feel powerless and over-whelmed, just like the lady who said her life was falling apart and she had no one to talk to. I know how she feels because I felt that way myself. And I know the trap she has fallen into because I fell into it too. We can get so caught up in trying to run on our own steam we forget to ask God to guard our hearts and give us power we do not have in ourselves.

As we cope with the real world, it helps to keep an eternal perspective, not one that can see no farther than today's pain. That's why one of my favorite sayings is:

THE IRON CROWN OF SUFFERING
PRECEDES THE GOLDEN CROWN OF GLORY.

In one of his best-selling books, humorist Robert Fulghum talks about the "Uh-Oh frame of mind." It's a perspective that lets us see life's catastrophes as momentary difficulties rather than horrendous tragedies. As Fulghum puts it, "When you see something as 'Uh-Oh,' you don't have to dial 9-1-1."

When we have the Uh-Oh philosophy of life, we welcome the surprises a day may bring, and instead of pressing the panic button we say, "Here we go again . . . back to the drawing board," and "Has anybody seen Plan B?" Fulghum sums it up by saying, "'Uh-Oh' is more than a momentary reaction to small problems. 'Uh-oh' is an attitude—a perspective on the universe. It is part of an equation that summarizes my view of the conditions of existence:

'Uh-Huh' + 'Oh-Wow' + 'Uh-Oh' + 'Oh, God' = 'Ah-Hah!'"[6]

Obviously, the most important part of Fulghum's equation is "Oh, God." If ever there was an "Uh-Oh" kind of guy, it was the apostle Paul, who said:

That is why we never give up. Though our bodies are dying, our inner strength in the Lord is growing every day. These troubles and sufferings of ours are, after all, quite small and won't last very long. Yet this short time of distress will result in God's richest blessing upon us forever and ever! So we do not look at what we can see right now, the troubles all around us, but we look forward to the joys in heaven which we have not yet seen. The troubles will soon be over, but the joys to come will last forever. (2 Cor. 4:16–18 TLB)

The Fine Art of Burden Casting

No, I have no magic formulas for making pain go away, but I do recommend the following method for burden casting because it is based on Psalm 55:22: "Cast your burden upon the LORD, and He shall sustain you" (NASB). What I'm going to tell you may sound simplistic, but I know it works because it points you toward God Himself. Here's what you should do:

Think of the particular burden that is weighing you down. Now, in a few words, write your burden on a small piece of paper. (If you have more than one burden, write each one down on separate pieces of paper.)

Seal each burden in its own separate envelope. Then go to a place where you can be alone to pray. Get on your knees and, with both hands, lift up each envelope. Tell God your burdens as well as your fears and your doubts. Tell Him EVERYTHING about this burden because this is the last time you will be speaking of it in such detail.

As you do this, you may notice that you are crying and your arms may hurt as you lift up your burden. But hold that envelope up there until the pain in your arms is equal to the pain in your heart. Then drop your arms and say, "Lord, take it."

Now look at your watch or clock, and, on the outside of the envelope, write down the date and time that you gave your burden up, for example, "On June 10 at 4:00 P.M., I gave this burden to my heavenly Father and He took it."

Finally, put that envelope some place where you keep your treasured things. Perhaps that would be your Joy Box.*

---

* I've described how to make a Joy Box in other books, including *Splashes of Joy in the Cesspools of Life,* and *Stick a Geranium in Your Hat and Be Happy,* and I touch on it again in chapter 7.

Now you are ready to walk by faith because you know everything is okay. Of course, Satan will be quick to tell you everything is NOT okay, but hold on to Romans 1:17, which says, "The just shall live by faith" (KJV), not by listening to Satan or anyone else who wants to fill your mind with doubts and fears.

As you walk through each day, rely on the knowledge that God has your burden; you gave that burden to Him on such-and-such a date. And because you gave Him your burden, now you have hope. I see that hope every day in my mailbox. Not all of the letters I get are sad or full of pain. I get a bunch of letters from folks who are upbeat and full of hope because, in one way or another, they have cast their burdens on God. One woman wrote to say:

> I have been in a "parenthesis" for five years and cannot see the end, but I am focusing on Jesus Christ.

Another mother reminded me that I had published an earlier letter (in the *Love Line*) she had written about her daughter, who is an alcoholic. Now she was writing back to say:

> Well, I wanted to let you know some good news. With the help of our blessed Lord and lots of prayers, she is doing a turn-around. She has stopped drinking (I believe) and has entered school to be a medical assistant. She is doing most excellent in her studies, and seems to be getting along much better with her husband and four small children. She seems to be finding herself at last and I am confident that this will last. But even if it does not last, it has been quite exciting to see her change, gain a little weight and get more control of her life—at this time at least.
>
> So there is hope. Prayers do work. The Lord is Good.

While Spatula reaches out to people in every conceivable kind of mess, a large portion of our ministry deals with parents who have discovered that one—and sometimes more than one—of their children is gay. When one mother went through this kind of shock she got in touch with us and we sent her literature, prayed with her on the phone, and helped "peel her off the ceiling" with our spatula of love. Eventually, she wrote to tell us:

> Because of what I learned from you, I am able to not only love but also enjoy my son's company. What you shared made sense and I found it to be true. My husband and I have a good relationship with our son. When I first found out, I was in shock. Then depression came, followed by a suicide attempt and six weeks of psychiatric hospitalization.
>
> That was three and a half years ago. I chose to adopt your attitude, which I now know is God's attitude, and now I believe . . . God has used all of this for good as He promised in Romans 8:28.

So many parents who contact Spatula are estranged from their children in one way or another. It's a special joy for all of us when a mom can write something like this letter we received:

> I praise God that both of my children are strong Christians, though it hasn't always been so. There was a time when just the mention of God made my daughter angry and now she and I have long discussions about the love of God and how we want to grow more like Him, along with many other God-centered topics.
>
> My daughter knew I prayed continually for her. I made sure she had her tapes of Amy Grant that she had loved before she left the Lord. She loved Amy's voice and listened to the tapes "just for the music"—but, oh, how I prayed those words would hit their mark. They did and I praise God.
>
> For about five years my daughter was a big part of the world. She could drink the guys under the table and I prayed, "Lord, make her sick." It didn't happen at once, but it did happen. To this day even a sip of wine makes her sick.
>
> She told me after she was back with the Lord how much she loved us and was thankful for our prayers, but mostly that we never condemned her and that she knew she was always welcome and loved no matter what she did. Those words were the greatest gift she could have given me.

Hope Helps Us Live—and Die

The counselor who helped me when my life was so bleak once wrote to me to say that my ministry encourages people to survive their losses. And then he added:

EVEN DYING PEOPLE DIE MORE GRACIOUSLY
WHEN THEY HAVE HOPE,
EITHER FOR RECOVERY OR FOR HEAVEN.

That's a good thought! In fact, it's burned into my memory, and I see its wisdom confirmed when I receive letters such as the following:

In the first week of October, my twenty-year-old daughter and seven-and-a-half-month-old granddaughter were killed in an auto accident. They were victims of a drunk driver. My daughter was an unwed mother who dropped out of high school at seventeen and a half and left home. She had been living on government assistance for two and a half years.

It was very difficult for my husband, son, and me, but we did maintain contact with her and included her in family activities.

Until she became pregnant, she had been in church with us at least every other week. During the last year of her life, she had not attended church. Three months before she died I explained my concerns to our pastor. The pastor, after several attempts, did get our daughter to come to his office and talk to him. She talked with him in late September, repented of her sins, asked for forgiveness, and vowed to try to change her life. Ten days later, she and her daughter died. We look at the last few months of her life as a miracle!

I treasure this mother's letter because it reminds me of the power of hope. When the daughter turned to God in faith, it not only gave her hope, it also provided hope for her mother who, in just a few short days, would be left behind to struggle with the deaths of a child and a grandchild.

Hope means the most, perhaps, when we face the stark reality of death. Many people who telephone or write to me are coping with the death of loved ones. A precious child, wife, or husband is gone—totally GONE. Death is so FINAL. There are no instant replays or second chances. What can we do when we face death? How can we find strength to go on? How can we find closure for grief and pain?

In chapter 2 we will talk about these questions and how to find the kind of strength that can make all the difference.

Gloomee Busters

GOD SAID IT, I BELIEVE IT, AND THAT SETTLES IT.
(Then why doesn't it make sense?)

☐ ☐ ☐

I'D UNSCRAMBLE THE EGGS
IF YOU'D READ ME THE RECIPE BACKWARDS.

☐ ☐ ☐

PRACTICAL GUIDE FOR SUCCESSFUL LIVING:
PUT YOUR HEAD UNDER THE PILLOW AND SCREAM.

☐ ☐ ☐

CHOICE, NOT CHANCE, DETERMINES DESTINY.

☐ ☐ ☐

JUST FOR TODAY

JUST FOR TODAY I will try to live through this day only and not tackle my whole life problem at once. I can do something for twelve hours that would appall me if I felt that I had to keep it up for a lifetime.

JUST FOR TODAY I will be happy. This assumes to be true what Abraham Lincoln said, that, "Most folks are as happy as they make up their minds to be."

JUST FOR TODAY I will adjust myself to what is, and not try to adjust everything to my own desires. I will take my "luck" as it comes, and fit myself to it.

JUST FOR TODAY I will try to strengthen my mind. I will study. I will learn something useful. I will not be a mental loafer. I will read something that requires effort, thought and concentration.

JUST FOR TODAY I will exercise my soul in three ways: I will do somebody a good turn, and not get found out; if anybody knows of it, it will not count. I will do at least two things I don't want to do—just for exercise; I will not show anyone that my feelings are hurt; they may be hurt, but today I will not show it.

JUST FOR TODAY I will be agreeable. I will look as well as I can, dress becomingly, talk low, act courteously, criticize not one bit, not find fault with anything and not try to improve or regulate anybody except myself.

JUST FOR TODAY I will have a program. I may not follow it exactly, but I will have it. I will save myself from two pests: hurry and indecision.

JUST FOR TODAY I will have a quiet half hour all by myself, and relax. During this half hour, sometime, I will try to get a better perspective of my life.

JUST FOR TODAY I will be unafraid. Especially I will not be afraid to enjoy what is beautiful, and to believe that as I give to the world, so the world will give to me.

—Source unknown

□   □   □

Though no one can go back
and make a new start,
anyone can start from now
and make a brand new end.
—Carl Bard

□   □   □

☐ ☐ ☐

I wish I had a box so big
That every grouch I'd pack,
And when I'd shut the lid I'd see
That none of them came back.

I'd lock it so securely
And I'd cast away the key
And then I'd throw the box into
The deepest, deepest sea.

And in its place I'd get a box,
The biggest I could find,
And fill it right up to the brim
With everything that's kind.

A box without a lock, of course,
And never any key;
For everything inside that box
Would then be offered free.

Smiles there'd be in plenty,
And twinkles for the eyes.
A face adorned with these would surely
Give a glad surprise.

And grateful words for joys received
I'd freely give away,
Thanksgiving songs to pass around
To cheer the dullest day.

The children would come running up
To share the good things found,
For the joys are so infectious
And there's enough to go around.

Oh, let us each begin to pack
Our grouches right away,
And open wide a box of praise
To brighten every day.
                    —Source unknown

☐ ☐ ☐

GOD DOES NOT SEND US ANSWERS TO OUR SUFFERING.
INSTEAD, HE TAKES IT UPON HIMSELF.

☐   ☐   ☐

But those who hope in the LORD
    will renew their strength.
They will soar on wings like eagles;
    they will run and not grow weary,
    they will walk and not be faint.

(Isa. 40:31 NIV)

2

If You Can't Go Around It, Over It, or Through It, You Had Better Negotiate with It

Death is God's way of saying,"Your table is ready."[1]

The first time I saw the Ashleigh Brilliant quote that titles this chapter,[2] I couldn't help but think of how true his cryptic words are of the last great enemy—DEATH. As my good friend Marilyn Meberg says, "We're all marching relentlessly to the grave."

To stave off that "happy" thought, we try to use face-lifts, tummy tucks, hair coloring—anything to avoid the fact that age is taking its toll on us. We spend millions trying to deny what is happening to our bodies as we acquire various physical limitations. When our eyesight fails, we wear glasses. When our hearing goes, we adapt to hearing aids. And when our minds go . . . then we're REALLY in trouble!

Perhaps you know why women over fifty
don't have babies?
They would put them down somewhere
and forget where they left them.

Death stalks all of us, so we have to adapt the best ways we can to the new challenges that come with aging. But in many ways, dealing with the prospect of your own death is easier than facing the death of a loved one, particularly if the person you lose is young and has much of life yet to live.

There is a finality to death that is inescapable. You can't go around it, over it, or through it. All you can do is negotiate—not for a reversal that could bring your loved one back, because there is none. Instead, you plead for some kind of understanding, some way to make sense of it all as you try to get through it, allowing your grief to take its course and let the pain eventually drain away.

Death comes in many ways, but when you think about it, all those ways can be grouped into two categories—expected and unexpected. Terminal illness is probably the most common cause of expected death, but it's not the only one. In a way, we half anticipated the death of our son, Steven, from the moment he marched off to fight in Vietnam. We lived in fear from that day until four months later, when the Marine staff car drove up and two young men in full-dress uniforms came to our door. While the news that Steven had been killed in an ambush near Da Nang was a shock, it was not as total as the one that would come later.

Five years after we buried Steven, death visited our home again. During the winter and spring of 1973 our oldest son, Tim, who was twenty-three, went through training to become a Los Angeles County deputy sheriff. He also took an accelerated training course at the Los Angeles Police Academy. Although he completed all the training successfully, Tim chose not to enter law enforcement and decided he would go back to college that fall. For a change of pace, he and his friend, Ron, decided to spend the summer in Alaska, where they hoped to find work while they enjoyed seeing some new horizons.

Because he knew I loved to celebrate the first of every month, Tim called me (collect, of course) on August 1, 1973. He asked me what I was doing to celebrate the new month and, of course, I told him I was just WAITING for a collect call from him! As we talked, Tim sounded excited about what had been happening at the church he and Ron had been attending throughout the summer. He said he would be home in just five days to tell us all about his experiences—especially what God had been doing "to put a sparkle in my eye and a spring in my step!" That didn't sound like my conservative, sedate son who had never showed much emotion or excitement about anything! I spent the rest of the afternoon thinking about how thrilling it would be to have him home in five days to share how God had become so real in his life.

At dinner a few hours later, I was telling Bill and our two younger boys, Larry and Barney, about Tim's phone call and we were all marveling at what he had said. Suddenly the phone rang again. Was it Tim wanting to tell me something else that couldn't wait until he got back? No, it was the Royal Canadian Mounted Police calling from Whitehorse, Yukon, to inform us that our son had been killed in a head-on collision with a drunk driver. That was a TOTAL SHOCK and I'll describe it in more detail later in this chapter as I deal with letters sent to me by folks who are coping with the same kind of unexpected blow that only death can deliver.

Grief Has Different Stages

One mother wrote to me and said, "I am reaching out to you because of your expertise in pain." Perhaps losing two sons in violent deaths should have made me an expert on this kind of pain. But I don't think anyone can really become an expert; you merely settle for being a survivor. There were plenty of times when I was ready to fold up and be admitted to the local Home for the Bewildered, but somehow God kept me going, always trying to find something positive, and even something humorous, to get me through the day.

Humor helps to combat my own grief and helps me accelerate the grief process for others. I love little quips and quotes and
have collected hundreds of them over the years. Humor is not
something to be used to make fun of a situation, only to make
fun out of what seems to be a hopeless catastrophe. Folks need
something that will help get them through the times when
nothing seems to calm them, not even reminders of comfort
from the Bible given by well-meaning Christian friends. It's not
that these Scriptures aren't true; it's just that the pain is so intense you can't appreciate what the words are saying right at
that moment. Later these Scripture verses can become very
meaningful, but, ironically, there were times during my own
sieges of grief that the following observation made a kind of
crazy sense to me:

MAN CANNOT LIVE BY BREAD ALONE;
HE NEEDS PEANUT BUTTER, TOO.

I guess I try to be the eternal optimist. And you know the
difference between an optimist and a pessimist, don't you?

An optimist is a person
who thinks he knows a friend
from whom he can borrow.
A pessimist is one who has tried.[3]

Of course I'm well aware that in those first hours and days
after death strikes, you aren't ready to hear much of ANY-
THING, whether it's inspiration from the Bible or somebody's
attempt to make you smile. You can only struggle through these
fresh stages of grief and hope that someday you may get to a
place where you can smile and even laugh again. Many letters
come from people who say, "I hadn't laughed in a number of
years, but then I read your book. . . . "
There is nothing magical about my books. It's just that FI-
NALLY these people have reached a stage in their grief where
they can find something to smile about, where they can feel the

first glimmer of joy after going through that long, dark tunnel they plunged into when death struck their family.

Through personal experience and dealing with grieving families, I've learned there are at least three stages to grief:

First, there is SHOCK, often accompanied by PANIC.

Second, there is SUFFERING, when you grieve and feel as if you want to die, yourself.

Finally, there is RECOVERY, when you wake up one morning without that overwhelming urge to go back to bed and just forget about living.

When death comes, there is no escaping this three-part process. Because we have families or close friends we truly care about, there is no way to avoid suffering; sooner or later, death pays a visit to every door. That's the bad news. But there is good news as well.

Grief doesn't have to be all bad; it can be something good. Grief is the healing mechanism God uses, particularly when we allow Him to enter into the process. One of the most valuable little books I've ever found on grief and the grief process is *Good Grief* written by Granger Westberg more than thirty years ago.[4]

Westberg points out that when the Bible says "Grieve not," it doesn't mean we're supposed to be like the Stoics, those Greek philosophers who never showed any emotion. Westberg believes the Bible sees grief as a normal and potentially creative process. He refers to the part of 1 Thessalonians 4:13 that says, "that you may not grieve as others do who have no hope" (RSV). Then he suggests this paraphrase: "Grieve, not as those who have no hope, but for goodness' sake, grieve when you have something worth grieving about!"[5]

In his little book, Westberg describes ten stages of grief. His first stage is like mine—SHOCK—which serves as a temporary anesthetic in response to hearing about some horrible tragedy, such as losing a twenty-year-old son in a blazing car crash. When we go into shock, we're making a temporary escape from reality. Sometimes shock lasts through the funeral of the loved one so that a surviving wife or mother, for example, might be praised for her "serene faith" because she seems almost radiant as she greets those who come by to pay their respects. In truth, she needs to be watched carefully and should be visited soon after the funeral when the serene exterior breaks down and she has to face what has really happened.

If we're to pass through the pain and suffering that come from a terrible tragedy, we must move on through the temporary escape mechanism of shock and into reality. Granger Westberg subscribes to the idea that, as soon as possible, we should help those people who are facing a heavy loss by letting them do as much for themselves as they can. We want to help them "get on with their grief work." Sometimes well-meaning relatives and friends try to do everything for the widow or the surviving parents. There are things that we can and should do, of course, but the sooner we let a person deal with immediate problems and make some decisions again, the better off that person will be.[6]

Many of the additional stages of grief in Westberg's outline fall under the stage I call SUFFERING. This is when our "grief work" starts in earnest—because grief definitely is hard work. When death takes our loved one, we need to express the strong emotions that well up inside. Bottling up our grief is the worst thing we can do. Looking "serene" at the funeral is not necessarily a sign that all is well. We may have a temporary period of "serenity," but then we realize how dreadful our loss is and there is an uncontrollable urge to "let it all out." According to the experts, nothing causes more stress than losing a loved one, particularly a spouse or a child. Crying it out makes all the sense in the world because, in addition to venting the emotional flood, it actually removes harmful chemicals that build up in the body due to the tremendous stress!

Men usually have a harder time showing grief than women because they are taught from boyhood that "big boys (and certainly men) don't cry." They are culturally conditioned to be "invulnerable," so they shut off feelings such as hurt, disappointment, sadness, and fear. When men face grief, they may explode in rage, run from their feelings, or simply bottle them up.

In one study of separated and divorced men and women, researchers found that men responded to emotional pain by "denying it, drinking, immersing themselves in work or dating, taking up risky pursuits such as sky diving, going completely and sometimes criminally out of control, or developing stress-related illnesses such as ulcers, colitis, and frequent vomiting."[7]

Women, on the other hand, cry much more easily and as a rule are less vulnerable to stress-produced diseases like ulcers and heart disease. In other books I've discussed my technique for shedding tears: Lying across a pillow, face down, takes away restrictions of the chest and throat and you can really sob your heart out and drain away the poison of the pain.

But while tears bring a lot of relief, they are no guarantee that you will be immune to another common stage of suffering—depression. I wasn't, and I know how it feels when God seems to be unreachable and uncaring. When tragedy strikes, we are sure no one has ever faced the same kind of grief we are facing. No one could possibly understand. These are some of the feelings I'll deal with in chapter 6; I know how devastating depression can be.

Physical symptoms of distress are also typical during periods of grief. We seem to feel ill or we sense that we have a "pain" somewhere, but it is more psychosomatic than real. This feeling of being ill or in pain means we haven't worked through some of the real problems related to our loss. Unless we can deal with these emotional problems we may remain ill, and going to the doctor to get prescriptions, shots, or other therapy won't help much.

These are just a few of the levels of grief and suffering we may go through when we face the sudden and unexpected death of a loved one. In the remainder of this chapter I'll share letters from folks who have struggled with this kind of loss. I have grouped their letters to try to deal with some of the more important questions that are bound to come up in the wake of the news that "Your son has just died in a car wreck," or "Your husband's body was found hanging in the garage—it looks like suicide."

The Hardest Death to Handle

Perhaps the hardest situation occurs when a loved one takes his or her own life. Added to the shock felt by those left behind are their questions—and often their guilt. Why? Was it my fault? Should I have seen it coming? Could I have helped in some way? Where is this loved one now? One mother wrote:

> My son completed suicide in October and I know that he believed in Jesus Christ as the Son of God. And I believe he is with the Lord, but a shadow of a doubt is always creeping in. . . . You know that Tim and Steven are with our Father in heaven. If only I had that 100 percent assurance. . . .

This mom wants to believe that her son is with the Lord, but she can't be 100 percent sure because the tiniest doubt keeps creeping in. Stated directly, her question is this:

Does a Christian who commits suicide lose his or her salvation?

This question comes in many forms. I'm writing this chapter in early spring, and since Christmas I've gotten letters from more than fifteen families who have experienced a loved one's suicide. They are looking for answers, comfort, and, above all, assurance that their loved one is "okay." Does God forgive even something like THIS?

After all, the Bible tells us that our bodies are God's temples and His Spirit dwells within us. We read the words that warn that God will destroy anyone who destroys His temple (see 1 Cor. 3:16–17). And there is also the issue of the suicide taking into his or her own hands something that is only God's prerogative. Moses quotes God as saying, "I put to death and I bring to life" (Deut. 32:39 NIV). And there is also that familiar reminder by the psalmist, "My times are in your hands" (Ps. 31:15 NIV). Other verses from the Scriptures could be quoted that seem to say it is possible to lose your salvation. (See, for example, 1 Cor. 10:12 or Heb. 6:4–6.)

On the other side of the argument, you can quote the words of Jesus from John 10:27–30 (NIV):

> My sheep listen to my voice; I know them, and they follow me. I give them eternal life, and they shall never perish; no one can snatch them out of my hand. My Father, who has given them to me, is greater than all; no one can snatch them out of my Father's hand. I and the Father are one.

I am not a theologian, so I can escape debates about eternal security. The scholars have argued that issue for hundreds of years and they aren't even close to unanimous agreement.

But when talking to the grieving survivors of suicide, I prefer to believe that even suicide doesn't negate a person's salvation. Salvation is a very individual matter and many factors enter in. Paul R. Van Gorder, a teacher with the Radio Bible Class program that originates in Grand Rapids, Michigan, has this to say about suicide and the possible loss of salvation:

> No, a Christian who is a suicide does not lose his salvation. . . . We must remind ourselves that salvation depends entirely upon the grace of God. No amount of human effort or self-worth can bring redemption. Once we have received it as a gift, we are not in danger of losing it for some unconfessed sin. . . . If that were the case, then it seems logical to assume that no one would reach heaven. All of us have sins we have forgotten about or never confessed. . . .
> We do not know what happens in a human mind that causes a person to take his own life. But we do know this: if that person was genuinely saved, he will "never perish." Though he may succeed in his suicide attempt, he will continue to have the gift of eternal life.[8]

After Mr. Van Gorder's thoughts were included in an issue of the *Love Line* newsletter a dear woman telephoned and said, "Do you know you just killed a lot of people in your newsletter because you said it's all right to commit suicide?"

Of course I told her I had no such intention and was only trying to comfort people who were left behind to struggle with the question of Why? From my knowledge of suicidal people, they don't decide to do it based on thinking God will forgive them. They are much too desperate to think that through to its conclusion.

I know about that desperation because I came dangerously close to that very state of mind, myself. When depression over my son Larry's homosexuality (see chapter 6) became unbearable, I drove to the top of a viaduct where I intended to go over the edge and end it all. But I was still thinking clearly enough to have two things hold me back:

First, the training I had received while growing up caused doubts in my mind about my eternal security if I killed myself. I had been taught that you don't enter God's throne room UNINVITED.

Second, I feared the attempt wouldn't kill me, only maim me, and I'd be crippled, making baskets for the rest of my life in the Home for the Bewildered.

Suicide is always a poor choice. It is like walking out of the opera during the overture just because the conductor drops his baton. Suicide is a permanent solution to a temporary problem. The only trouble is, suicidal people don't see their misery as temporary. They see their problem as overwhelming and believe suicide is the only way to end the pain.

But what about our original question? Does God send all suicides to hell? Or, to put it the other way, do all suicides go to heaven? As I said before, God only knows.

One mother's letter began:

> This is another one of those difficult letters, but I felt you would want to know. My son took his own life last week. He was still living in a homosexual relationship but having difficulties with it. I have no peace at this point, not knowing if he repented before his death, and not knowing where he is now. Except for this area of his life, he was such a fine, loving son. I find it hard to believe that with all the promises in the Bible and all the prayers offered for my son, a loving Father would not hear and answer. . . .

You cannot tell this darling mother who is grieving with such a loss that if she had prayed more or if she had only trusted God more her prayers would have been answered. You cannot glibly tell her she can move this mountain in her life "if only she has enough faith."

What you CAN tell her is that there are no pat answers for how God works in our lives. Many things have to be completely left to Him alone. Perhaps this is another of those secret things that will never be revealed to us (see Deut. 29:29).

So many parents write us with stories that have no happy endings . . . their child has taken his or her life, and it's over, final! In other cases the pain tortuously repeats itself. One mother wrote:

> My mother committed suicide when I was four. An uncle I was living with committed suicide when I was eleven. My son, at the age of twenty-three, kept up the family tradition by also committing suicide.

In another tragic case, a mother called and said that just a few days before, their teenage son had told them he was a homosexual. His father had ordered the boy from the house, and the very next day they found him hanging in the garage.

I also hear from many parents whose children are far from home and dying with AIDS. The parents don't know how to help, what to say, or what to do. This is happening more and more as the worldwide AIDS epidemic accelerates. We will address some of these concerns when we focus on homosexuality and AIDS in chapters 4 and 5.

For the hurting parents whose children have died through suicide or in other violent ways, we must all hold tight to the promise that God loves our children and He has provided a loving sacrifice for them. HIS BLOOD IS A COVERING FOR OUR CHILDREN . . . and the bottom line is that when you completely relinquish them to HIM, God is in charge and in complete control. Our loving Father loves them more than we do.

Remember that those who take their lives go to meet a just and loving God. Your loved one is in His hands. None of us live lives totally free from sin. We all make some very bad mistakes, but I still like the German proverb that says:

THOSE WHO LIVE IN THE LORD
NEVER SEE EACH OTHER FOR THE LAST TIME.[9]

In the face of suicide or any other unexplainable tragedy, I want to hold on to the comfort in that promise. But to do so FULLY there can be no grudges, no unfinished business, no lack of forgiveness when forgiveness is needed.

Suicide Must Be Forgiven

Those who are left behind after a suicide may feel angry with the one who has done this to himself or herself—and to them. Temporarily at least, they resent the loved one who has died by his or her own hand. Sometimes they feel ready to die, too. Considering this, they may think:

If I die, too, I'll forgive you.
If I live, we'll see!

There is a lot of truth in that little quip. The question we often ask ourselves is:

How can I forgive the one who committed suicide?

One dear mom wrote to tell me about the hundreds who attended her son's funeral following his suicide. Many of them were his teenage friends who were challenged by the youth minister to think about their purpose in life. This mom gets very lonely for her son because he had been so much fun—life with him had never been dull. He had won blue ribbons for his artwork and he also was an excellent musician.

Perhaps what she remembers most—scenes that are frozen in her mind—are memories of when her son was just a little fellow with a sweet smile and a certain way of tilting his head and making observations that only a mom could really appreciate. But this same mom also admitted a lot of ambivalent feelings:

> In January, my world was turned upside down and started spinning out of control when I was told that my beautiful talented son had committed suicide (one month before his sixteenth birthday). I remember saying over and over, NO, this can't be, I was going to pick him up from school in two hours. I was so numb I couldn't feel anything. When I was able to feel, it was guilt, anger, and being alone because no one knew the hurt that I was feeling.
>
> I couldn't find anyone to be mad at, so I got mad at myself and God. There were times I was mad at my son. He had so much to live for, how could he do this? But when I was mad at him, I would also feel guilty. I could never stay mad at him when he was alive. He knew just how to work dear ole Mom, so I never stayed mad for a long period of time.
>
> I miss him and still find myself wondering why, but I thank God for allowing me to be his mother for fifteen years. I know I wasn't a bad mother, only that God could take better care of him. My son may have the answers, but I don't think they will be important when I see him again.

We forgive a loved one for committing suicide in the same way we forgive anyone for doing anything wrong to us. This mom solved the forgiveness problem with her mother's heart. She couldn't stay mad at her son for very long, even after he had dealt her such a terrible blow. She still loved him so much, unconditionally, that she was able to make peace with it.

Moms Always Feel the Most Guilt

The same mother mentioned earlier in the chapter who was left with the shadow of a doubt concerning her son's salvation also admitted she struggles with guilt:

My son was an alcoholic and had been in treatment twice. This is always very hard for me to talk about. I attend another group called Survivors of Suicide. In those meetings, gradually in many cases it comes out that the loved one was addicted to drugs and/or alcohol. I believe this makes the death that much harder, as our relationship before their death was generally not a very good one. In addition to the usual guilt over the death, and especially suicide, those of us left have added guilt over not being able to control the alcohol and drug use. Especially when you are a mother. As you say, God and mothers are supposed to fix anything.

Who is more susceptible to feeling guilt than a mother? A mom is sure she is the one who should have fixed things or said something or done something that would have made all the difference. The mother quoted above feels guilty for not being able to control her son's use of alcohol and drugs.

One thing we moms need to understand is that we cannot control everything—particularly our children when they want to use drugs or alcohol. Those are choices they make, and we parents are not to blame.

In *Good Grief*, Granger Westberg says one stage of our grieving is feeling a sense of guilt about our loss. He doesn't mean normal guilt, which people often feel when they violate standards and values they know are right. What Westberg is talking about is "neurotic guilt" that is felt for no reason or that is completely out of proportion compared with how responsible you might be.

Neurotic guilt often grips us when we think about things we should have said to or done for the one who has died. Parents write about failing to talk with children the night before they died in an accident. Perhaps there was an argument and they weren't speaking. Perhaps the child got home late from a date and the parents had already gone to bed.

Other parents tell me they feel guilty about thoughts they had before a child was taken suddenly. Sometimes they weren't good thoughts, and they know the Lord isn't pleased with them. They know they "ought to feel guilty" for having those thoughts—and so they do.

It also helps to understand that everyone has neurotic feelings to some degree. I had my share when Steven and Tim died, but in each case the guilt washed over me for different reasons.

After Steve was killed in Vietnam, I kept thinking, *If only I hadn't gone down and signed those papers that allowed him to go into the Marines two months before his eighteenth birthday.* Yes, I could argue with myself and point out that he could have gone in anyway in two months and all I tried to do was keep him from grouching around the house because we wouldn't let him join the Marines with his friends.

And then, of course, I could argue the other way and tell myself if I had made him wait those two months until he was eighteen he probably wouldn't have been in that particular place and been caught in that particular ambush. Neurotic guilt causes lots of regrets, lots of "if onlys," and all we can do is look back and say that at the time, we did what we thought was best.

In Tim's case my memories would flash back to that last phone call. Part of what we had talked about was my offer to pay to have Tim's car shipped home from the Yukon rather than have him drive the Alaska Highway and spend five days on the road. Perhaps I made the offer because I had some kind of motherly premonition of disaster, but Tim just laughed and said, "Mom, there are no places to ship cars from up here. This is the Yukon!"

A week after that phone call I had to go to the same mortuary where I had identified the body of our son, Steve, five years before TO THE DAY. Steven had been shipped home by the government in a hermetically sealed casket. This time I went to the SAME viewing room to identify my son, Tim, whose body had been shipped home by the Canadian government in a pine box. As I looked at what was left of Tim, I went through all the "if onlys." If only I had INSISTED that he ship the car and fly home. If only I had been more positive about it. If only I had squashed the idea of that long drive home.

But then I had to return to reality and accept some facts. Tim was twenty-three when he died, old enough to know how to ship a car if he wanted to. The truth was that Tim had wanted the adventure of driving home. When his camera was found, we had his film developed and the last picture he had taken of himself was one on the bank of the Yukon River. He had wanted to make that trip.

One reason guilt feelings are so hard to sort out is that real guilt and neurotic guilt are often interwoven. Perhaps we did say things we shouldn't have said. Perhaps we did think thoughts we shouldn't have thought. Aren't those sins in God's eyes? Yes, but they can be confessed and forgiven, just like other sins. The point is, to carry a load of guilt around with you after a loved one is gone is wasted energy.

We have to let go of the loved ones who are taken from us, and we have to be free from our guilt at the same time. We must trust them to God because, no matter how much we may second-guess ourselves, we did all we could do at that time, and what was done (or not done) is a done deal—finished. If we feel we have in any way wronged the one who died, we confess it, accept God's cleansing forgiveness, and go on. It doesn't mean we stop our grief work, but it does free us to work on areas that need our attention.

To constantly carry a burden of guilt after we lose someone through death is to limit God's forgiving power when, in fact, God's forgiveness is unlimited. We must seize this truth and hang on to it. After all, when Jesus told Peter that he should forgive "seventy times seven" (Matt. 18:22 KJV), what Jesus was really saying was that we should forgive indefinitely. If God teaches us this standard, surely He holds the same standard for Himself.

Fear and Doubt Often Ask "Why?"

Fear and doubt are commonly mixed in with feelings of guilt after a loved one's death. Perhaps the first question many people ask when death strikes down a loved one is:

WHY did God let this happen?

I'm perfectly willing to compromise, but God wants to have everything His own way.

A mother wrote to me about losing her manic-depressive middle son to suicide when he was thirty-two. He left behind a wife and two children who undoubtedly asked many questions beginning with "Why?" The mom's letter went on to say:

I feel like a failure, yet I know I did my very best. I sure would like to talk with you. Your attitude is so great. I keep praying and have tried to put the children in His hands, but when my son committed suicide, I really became scared of God.

Why did He let this happen? We all loved Mark so much
and his children miss and need him so much.

All this mother really wants to know is, "Why is there evil in
the world?" I sure don't know, but God does. I do know that
when Adam and Eve ate that piece of fruit in the garden, it had
tremendous repercussions for all of us. We live in a fallen, broken world and NOTHING IS IDEAL. There are no guarantees
that people won't get drunk, cross center lines, and kill us or
our loved ones.

Yes, it's true that God could intervene. He could reach down
and turn steering wheels, He could cause bullets to miss their
mark, and He could foil suicide in any number of ways. Not
only could He do these things, but in some cases He has done
them. The question that is so hard to grapple with is: Why does
God seem to intervene in one case but not in another? We don't
know the answer to that question. We can only trust that God
knows what is best and within His permissive will (not necessarily His directive or intentional will), what has happened has
happened. Along with Job, all we can say is, "Though he slay
me, yet will I hope in him" (Job 13:15 NIV).

Anger Is Always Part of Grief

When death takes someone we love, sooner or later we are
bound to feel anger. In *Good Grief*, Granger Westberg points out
that this anger often includes hostility and resentment. He admits that this doesn't sound very much like "good grief" because resentment and hostility are unhealthy emotions and
they can do tremendous damage if we allow them to take over
our thoughts.

At the same time, I've talked to many Christians who are
angry over the death of a loved one but just can't admit it.
They've been taught that anger is a sin, and instead of admitting their anger they speak of being "hurt," "shocked," and
"devastated." Actually, though, they are very angry and wish

they could lash out in all directions. When you're in the resentment/hostility stage, you're angry with the whole world.

. . . You're angry with the loved one who has committed suicide. As one widow wrote to me, "My husband had the nerve to hang himself on Christmas Eve."

. . . You're angry with doctors who either didn't do enough to save your loved one or who tried to help but your loved one died anyway.

. . . If a car crash has killed your loved one, you're angry with the other driver or you're angry with the police for letting drivers like this run around loose.

When Tim was killed, we learned that his little VW had been smashed to bits by a three-ton truck driven by a drunken sixteen-year-old. In those first days after the accident, I felt such WRATH that some drunk could cross over the center line and send two boys into eternity. Yes, I knew that, while their crushed bodies were left in that VW their spirits had been ushered immediately into God's presence, NEVERTHELESS, anger boiled up within me. How UNFAIR! How WRONG! Anger seethed within me and boiled up again and again like a volcano repeatedly erupting into clouds of ash and rivers of molten lava.

And a lot of my anger was directed straight toward God. For at least two weeks I drove to a nearby dump late at night where I could sob and sometimes scream out my rage. How could God do this to us AGAIN? Hadn't we had enough pain with Bill's accident and Steve's death in Vietnam? But NOW THIS! I had one deposit in heaven; I didn't NEED another one. Sure, I had two children left, but I wanted THIS ONE! How unfair could God be to make us bear another loss like this?

Fortunately, God doesn't reciprocate when we get angry with Him. Instead, He works quietly to bring about His will and whatever will ultimately glorify Him. The night of the accident the parents of Ron, the boy who died with Tim in the wreck, came to our house to learn what had happened and before they left they had placed their faith in Christ.

A day or so later, Tim's picture appeared in the local paper with a headline that said, " TWO LOCAL BOYS KILLED ON THE ALASKA

HIGHWAY." In no time, several darling college girls began coming to our home to show me letters Tim had written to them the day before he started home. (I guess Tim wasn't as conservative as I had thought he was!) Tim's letters told the girls about his experiences that summer and how God had become real to him. These girls were eager to know more about the kind of God that could turn Tim on like that, and at least two of them accepted Christ right there in our home.

It was then that I began to see through my pain and grief and realize that the death of my son and his friend might be an end to their lives here on earth, but it was just the beginning of their work here. The next week we held a memorial service that was attended by nearly a thousand people, and later we heard still more reports of how others who had attended the service had been touched by the Savior. Many more people were brought to salvation when articles about the boys, with titles such as "Their Death Was Only a Beginning," appeared in various magazines and their story was told in a special segment of "The Unshackled" radio program.

Though my grief was still very real, I began to understand that, in God's economy, the timing of my son's death was right. My anger dissolved as I saw others accepting Christ because of Tim's testimony. You see, anger cannot reside with joy. The joy of seeing others come to the Lord because of Tim's death helped FLATTEN OUT that anger and allow a measure of JOY to replace it.

The Trip to Whitehorse Wasn't Easy

A month or so after Tim's memorial service, Bill and I traveled to the town of Whitehorse in the Yukon Territory to settle an insurance claim concerning the accident, and also to collect Tim's personal effects. When we arrived at the site where the crash had happened, the oil spill from Tim's little VW was still visible on the south-bound side of the road.

I thought of how Tim had trained with the sheriff's department and the Los Angeles Police Academy, how he had driven police vehicles and learned all about law enforcement and traffic. Yet here, out on an open stretch of the lonely Alaska Highway outside of Whitehorse, all that training hadn't helped when a three-ton truck had crossed the line and ended his life. I wondered what Tim's last thought had been. Had he suffered? Had he called for help? We talked with the Mounties and they assured us that Tim's death had been immediate, which was at least a measure of relief. It helped to know that Tim had gone immediately into the presence of God with no time to hurt after he had been smashed by the truck.

To claim Tim's personal effects, we had to go with the Royal Canadian Mounted Police officer to an area where vehicles were impounded until final disposition was made of the case. After being hit by the truck, the little VW was a mass of crumpled metal. A yellow barrier tape fluttered around the car and a fierce guard dog was on duty (to protect the evidence, the officer told us). He helped us get past the dog and under the barrier tape. Then I reached into what was left of the backseat for Tim's camping gear and his Bible. I could see the blood splattered on the car seats and the windows, and all I could think was how grateful I was that Tim's death had been QUICK and he hadn't suffered.

Later I had a picture of the smashed VW enlarged, and I attached it to the back of a large picture of a happy, smiling Tim. Often, when I go out to share my story, I use these photos to demonstrate to my listeners what REALITY is. I show the pictures as a reminder of how quickly lives can be changed forever by a loved one's sudden death in faroff places like a rice paddy in Vietnam or a smashed little VW on a lonely highway in the Yukon.

Bill and I had to stay in Whitehorse for a few more days to wait for the train that would take us back to Skagway, where we would finally catch a boat back to the United States. Whitehorse is a small community, and we were treated very kindly by the local townspeople; they all knew about the tragic accident. The teenager who had driven the truck that had killed Tim and Ron was in the local jail. He had been so intoxicated it was two days before he knew what he had done.

But what about the boy's parents? The accident wasn't THEIR fault. We located them and asked if they would come to our hotel. We wanted to share with them our feelings about God's redemptive love for all of us, regardless of our choices. The boy's parents came, and they were lovely people, grief-stricken over what their son had done. Actually, I believe they were overwhelmed that we even wanted to talk with them. They were quiet and reserved at first; then we played a tape recording of Tim's memorial service for them and showed them letters we had received about how God had used Tim's story. As we talked, we saw their reserve melt into openness, and we were able to honestly love them and feel a rapport with them.

Our son was dead and now their son was in jail, facing the consequences of what he had done. WHOSE PAIN WAS WORSE? Can we measure such pain? A broken heart is a broken heart, whether it's caused by death in a fiery crash or by having a son who has to live all his life with the knowledge that his bad choices killed two young men. My heart hurt with compassion for those parents. In fact, as God filled us with compassion for them, it squeezed out any anger we may have still felt toward their son. Somehow we knew God was still in control of it all, and being angry over the Why? of it wasn't so important anymore.

Traveling to Whitehorse wasn't easy, but meeting those hurting parents and letting God's love flow through us to them in their dark hour of suffering made it all worthwhile.

Does the Pain Last Forever?

One of the most frequent questions I get is stated in many different forms, but essentially what people want to know is:

How long will my pain and grieving last?

I heard from one mother who had purchased *Stick a Geranium in Your Hat and Be Happy* to read strictly for enjoyment and inspiration. She had no pain or tragedy in her life when she bought the book. But that changed a few months later:

> My 19-year-old daughter was killed in an automobile accident. Because the police were unable to find any positive identification, my husband and I, like you, were forced to look at our child and say, "Yes, that's our daughter." So, I can honestly say I know how you feel.
>
> I'm reading your book again, but for a different reason. I know Terri is in a better place. I know she's free from pain and heartbreak and I know God will see us through this, but how long before the ache in my heart eases, or, as her brother Tim (he's 20) says, "How long before the empty feeling in my gut goes away?"
>
> I'm not really asking for answers. It just feels better to say this to someone who really knows how I feel.

Another mother wrote to say that reading *Geranium* made her laugh and cry at the same time. She had lost a son in his thirties when he died in an auto accident, and she had been trying to get her life back. But it had been "so very difficult," she said.

I understand those "How long?" questions. How long does the empty feeling stay in one's gut? How long does the void remain after a bright, happy, caring child is struck down by a disease in a twinkling? The only answer I have is that, for each of us:

THE PAIN LASTS AS LONG AS IT HAS TO.

We are all different, and we all grieve at our own rate.

This past year has been one of real loss for my friend, Delores, who lost a son to AIDS. Recently, on the one-year anniversary of his death, flowers were put on the church platform in Brent's memory and a tribute was given to him. After twelve months of grieving, those flowers and the tribute read by the pastor represented closure for Delores. The day after the church service she called me and said she had mourned enough; somehow the passing of the one-year mark was what she had needed. Now she was going to clean out her son's room and get rid of things she had previously been unable to part with.

Some people may find closure a few months after the loved one's death. Others need a year, and some take longer. For Delores, the flowers on the platform and the tribute from the pastor signified the turning point; she sensed it was time to zip up her grieving and get on with her life. No longer could she make her son's room a shrine where she kept his collections and other personal effects. She decided to clean it out, paint the walls, install new carpet, and add some new decorations. Closure had begun.

Recovery Begins with Hope and Joy

As we are able to let go of a loved one who has died, we move into the last part of our "grief work," the step Granger Westberg calls "struggling to affirm reality." This doesn't mean we become our old selves again. We will never be our old selves again. We come out of any kind of deep grief as different persons than we were before. We can come out stronger, kinder, and more understanding of the problems of others, or we can come out bitter and self-pitying, uninterested in others' problems because we have too many of our own.

One good definition of the word *affirm* is "to bear witness to." Bearing witness is an important part of our faith. In his work with hundreds of people who went through deep grief, Granger Westberg saw that the ones who coped best were those who had a deep faith; God and His love were very real to them. The person with real faith takes that faith seriously and practices it diligently, staying in training, so to speak, so he or she can be in shape to wrestle with whatever comes.

I read somewhere that the future has two handles. We can take hold of tomorrow by the handle of anxiety or by the handle of faith, and . . .

IF YOU GRASP TOMORROW WITH FAITH, YOU KNOW THE HANDLE WON'T FALL OFF.

Scripture tells us that God will never test us beyond what we can bear (see 1 Cor. 10:13). I know Jesus talked about having faith that could move a mountain, but I doubt He asks for that kind of faith in a flippant or easy manner, especially when we are facing terrible agonies of grief and suffering caused by the death of loved ones. And keep in mind that Jesus also said even a mustard seed of faith can do a great deal. Think of it this way:

IF YOUR FAITH CANNOT MOVE MOUNTAINS IT OUGHT TO AT LEAST BE ABLE TO CLIMB THEM.

And as we climb the very real mountains of pain, we can start looking for splashes of joy, even when joy seems impossible. A question many people ask me is:

Will I ever know joy and laughter again?

The fact is, joy will return if you are willing to look for it. One woman who had lost her husband wrote, "In the last couple of months I am truly experiencing that GOD REALLY DOES LOVE ME!" Then her letter continued:

My husband died instantly with a massive heart attack four years ago at Christmas time when we were in Virginia visiting his mother. He was fifty-two and we had absolutely no warning. . . . it just happened and he was gone.

Like you, I have been in the tunnel (for me it was a deep, dark, cold well that I couldn't get out of and it seemed that no one would help me) and I just wanted to die for a long time.

The recovery road is very hard and takes a long time and a lot of hard work, work that I really didn't want to do. I never thought I would experience joy again BUT I AM! I even feel giddy at times with this wonderful feeling of love and joy that can only come from God. . . . I didn't think I would ever feel like this again and it is JUST WONDERFUL!

Philippians 4:13 Really Does Work

Personal experience has taught me that you can find joy in reality. Terrible things can happen. Loved ones can be plucked away in any number of tragic situations. Nonetheless, as we affirm our faith within reality, the Lord does help us. I have never received a more powerful example of how we can have joy despite the pain and grief than the following letter that came to me recently:

> Seven years ago my husband and two-year-old son were killed in a house fire. It was not an accident. It was a homicide and suicide due to an illness my husband had.
>
> I am left with two teenage daughters to raise by myself and need all the help and encouragement I can get. My girls are fourteen and fifteen years old. The last seven years have been difficult just trying to put our lives back together—we could not have done it without the Lord's help! All we are and all we have are from HIM!
>
> The verse I claim is Philippians 4:13: "I can do all things through Christ who strengthens me." This was the Scripture passage that hung in our living room and the only thing in that room that survived the fire. I know God left it there to remind me that no matter what happens to me or around me, God's Word will always remain firm.

This mother knows what hope is all about. A major part of coming out of the black tunnel of grief is hope. When we have done our grief work, hope gradually starts to dawn. The dark clouds start to break ever so slightly and the rays of the sunshine through in slender glimmers of light. What seems to be an endless time of grieving begins to run its course and recovery actually seems possible.

Granger Westberg believes that a true sign of hope is wanting to get back into things that we couldn't manage to do when we were still in the tunnel. Not only do we want to participate in old activities, but we want to try new things. As Westberg puts it, "Hope is finding out that life can become meaningful again."[10]

Hope Always Expects the Best

When biblical writers used the word "hope," they usually did not mean "wishing something were so." The biblical concept was more of a settled anticipation, a favorable and constant expectation. The Greek verb form for *hope* used in the New Testament frequently is related to the concept of trust. For example, in Titus 2:13, Christ is called "that blessed hope" (KJV).

When death strikes a family, it usually seems as if hope is exhausted. But hope can be rekindled. After the Babylonians sacked Jerusalem, the prophet Jeremiah wrote his book of Lamentations. In the early chapters he mourned the devastation of the once mighty city of God and the Lord's anger with His rebellious people. Jeremiah called himself a man who had seen affliction by the rod of God's wrath. He had been trampled in the dust and deprived of peace, become a laughingstock among his own people, and had "forgotten what prosperity is" (see Lamentations 3, especially vv. 1, 14, 16–18). But as Jeremiah remembered his bitter and galling afflictions and how his soul was so downcast, he went on to say, "Yet THIS I call to mind and therefore I have hope" (Lam. 3:21 NIV, emphasis added).

What was the "THIS" Jeremiah had in mind? You may recognize his next words, which inspired one of the great old hymns of the church, called "Great Is Thy Faithfulness":

> Because of the LORD's great love we are not consumed,
> for his compassions never fail.
> They are new every morning;
> great is your faithfulness. . . .
> The LORD is good to those whose hope is in him,
> to the one who seeks him;
> it is good to wait quietly
> for the salvation of the LORD. (Lam. 3:22–23, 25–26 NIV)

Even when we've landed with our faces in the dust, even when we are caught in a wringer, we can always have hope. And even when hope is lost, it can be regained; we can refocus our perspective. As we wait on the Lord, our strength will be renewed and so will our joy. In the Scriptures, hope and joy always go together. I like to say hope and joy are sisters.

Hope is God's holding power that gives a consistent flow of joy deep beneath the waves of trouble in the winds of sorrow. Hope invades the mind and heart with joy and gives us the deep confidence that we are God's forgiven children and that He will never let us go.

THE SUREST MARK OF A CHRISTIAN
IS NOT FAITH OR LOVE, BUT JOY.

We Found Hope in a Duffel Bag

About three months after Steve died in Vietnam, a large, dark green duffel bag arrived at our door. The return address was simply "U.S. Marines." Bill and I took it to a back bedroom and carefully opened it. Inside was Steve's gear—big Marine boots with the dried muck and mud still on them, mildewed fatigues, some books, and a Bible. Everything smelled of rot and mold. We almost choked as we went through it, partly from the stench but also from the emotions that swept over us.

There was also a camera and some trinkets. Then Bill opened Steve's wallet, all dry and crusty from the effects of heat and moisture. Steve had lain in that rice paddy three days before they had found him. And inside the wallet, all tattered and torn, was my last letter to him. The final page of that letter said, in part:

> I came to work early today to get this letter off to you and hope you can make it out as I am typing fast to get the message across. Usually I write letters to you with jokes or news about the kids and happenings around home . . . but today I felt a special need to reaffirm our faith in eternal life and being prepared to meet God. I particularly wanted to assure you that whether you are at home here in West Covina or over there in Vietnam, you are still SAFE in God's hands, and even if your life would be sacrificed for us in Vietnam, even THEN, Steve, you are safe in the arms of Jesus.

We all love you and miss you in a thousand ways. I think of you pouring ice water from the fridge, and cutting watermelon and spitting the seeds all over the sink, and scraping the trash barrels on the driveway as you dragged them out each week for pick up. I keep hearing you out by the pool with the kids, and enjoying the tube. Our thoughts are with you daily and our prayers.

Somehow today, I wanted to get all this on paper to you to think about, and to let you know we are proud and thankful for you, especially for your faith in what we believe also, because it seems to be so important now.

Even death, should it come to us, EITHER of us, or any of us, that is, brings us just a step closer to God and to eternity, because we have placed our faith in Jesus Christ. . . .

Somehow I think you understand me, just as I understand you. I love you, just as your dad does, and so do the kids. We miss you every day, hope you got the box OK, the one with the Silly Putty especially. That was from Barney. He misses you particularly, and remember you told him to hit a homer for you. About the only homers he hits are in the front window of the house, I am sorry to say.

Take care, love always,
Mom and Tribe

As usual, I had kissed my signature at the close of the letter, and now the lipstick was all smeared and blurry, but that didn't matter. Steve had read the letter and had kept it with him as he went into battle, even though his instructions had been to burn all his mail in case he was captured. Instead, Steve had stuck the letter in his wallet, probably intending to burn it later. Or perhaps he deliberately kept it with him as a symbol of the hope he had in Christ and of the family back home who loved him and shared that hope with him. (Steve's buddy, Tom, who had escaped death because he was held back from patrol for other duties, later paid us a visit and explained that my letter had arrived the VERY MORNING of the ambush in which Steve had been killed.)

Sitting there in that bedroom surrounded by Steve's smelly Marine gear, I was reminded of Jeremiah's words in Lamentations. We, too, had been afflicted and filled with bitter herbs.

Our teeth had been broken on the gravel of grief. We had been
trampled in the dust. Prosperity seemed like a forgotten word,
and our souls were downcast.

But as I re-read the letter Steve had taken with him into his
final battle, I realized that, despite all the pain, we still had an
ENDLESS HOPE and with it ENDLESS JOY. The Lord's great
love and compassion fail not. Truly, they are new every morning. Great is His faithfulness. Steve was our deposit in heaven.
We could pick up the pieces of our lives and move on.

Gloomee Busters

HOPE MAKES A DIFFERENCE

Hope opens doors where despair closes them.
Hope draws its power from deeply trusting God and what He
    does to change people's lives.
Hope lights a candle instead of "cursing the darkness."
Hope regards problems, small or large, as opportunities.
Hope cherishes no illusions, but it does not yield to cynicism or
    despair.

—Adapted. Source unknown

□ □ □

It is a great comfort to know
that God has His hands
on the steering wheel of the universe.

□ □ □

FAITH CAN MOVE MOUNTAINS,
BUT ONLY HARD WORK CAN PUT A TUNNEL
THROUGH.

□ □ □

WHEN YOUR DREAMS TURN TO DUST—VACUUM!

☐ ☐ ☐

A farmer was taking his little boy to a distant place. While walking they came to a rickety bridge over a turbulent stream. The little boy became apprehensive. "Father, do you think it is safe to cross the stream?" he asked.

The father answered, "Son, I'll hold your hand." So the boy put his hand in his father's. With careful steps he walked by his father's side across the bridge. They made their way to their destination. That was in the daylight.

The night shadows were falling by the time they returned. As they walked, the lad said, "Father, what about that stream? What about that rickety old bridge? I'm frightened."

The big, powerful farmer reached down, took the little fellow in his arms, and said, "Now you just stay in my arms. You'll feel safe." As the farmer walked down the road with his precious burden, the little boy fell sound asleep.

The next morning the boy woke up, safe at home in his own bed. The sun was streaming through the window. He never even knew that he had been taken safely across the bridge and over the turbulent waters.

That is the death of a Christian.

—Source unknown

☐ ☐ ☐

God saw that you were getting tired and a cure was not to be.

So he wrapped His arms around you and whispered, "Come with Me."

Golden heart stopped beating . . . hard-working hands at rest.

God broke our hearts to prove to us, He only takes the best.

—from a letter written to Spatula
by a mother who had lost her son

☐ ☐ ☐

GOD
has not taken
them
from us;
He has hidden
them
in His heart
that they
may be closer
to ours.
—from a bookmark. Source unknown

☐ ☐ ☐

I will . . . transform her Valley of Troubles into a Door of Hope. (Hos. 2:15 TLB)

3

*There's One Place
You Can Always Find Me . . .
At the Corner of Here and Now**

What's down in the well comes up in the bucket.

This poem caught my eye the other day when I was reading Dear Abby. It sums up life for a lot of us:

Dear Abigail Van Buren: Please give me your advice:
My job is gone, my shoes are worn, I live on beans and rice.
The government won't help me; my state is going broke;
My boy has been arrested (they caught him sniffing coke.)
My wife has up and left me; my son resides in jail;
The bank in which I own some stock will be the next to fail.
My pants are getting shabby, and bagging at the knees;
I can't afford a bar of soap to wash my BVD's.

---

* For the title of this chapter I am indebted to Ashleigh Brilliant for Pot-Shot No. 778, © 778 Ashleigh Brilliant Enterprises, 1975. Used by permission.

My daughter says she's pregnant, but doesn't know the guy;
My cotton's full of weevils and my cow is going dry.
My hens have all stopped laying—I can't afford their mash;
My checks are quickly bouncing, and the stores insist on cash.
I've lost my only savings on horses at the track;
The Klan is out to get me because my friends are black.
I asked the priest to help me, while making my confession;
He blamed it on the Protestants for causing this recession.
And so I turn to you, my friend, before I go to ruin;
My only source of good advice is Abigail Van Buren!
                                        —George

Not to be outdone, Abby succinctly replied:

Dear George:
Please do not appeal to me
To heal our sick economy.
It's plain to see we've lost our pants;
Now give the other guys a chance.[1]

Many of the things that happened to "George" have happened to people out there in Spatula Land—and a LOT more. Many of them write to me or call me to pour out their hearts, and some can even see a little humor in their situations. For example, I talked with one lady who later wrote back:

After I last spoke with you, everything was going along fine. I had a CAT scan and ultrasound prior to starting chemotherapy after my mastectomy and it has been discovered I have probably cancer of my right kidney, which is being removed next Monday. I would appreciate your prayers that it will be found to be benign! The good Lord delivered me to this world with two of most things. I seem to be going out with only one of everything! Fortunately, I had a CAT scan (actually an MRI) of my head and I don't need a transplant there. Any eccentricity is due to my English heritage and/or raising four children!

After reading *Geranium*, a woman, who sounds very much like a pleaser who's almost fed up, wrote to share her frustrations.

While she doesn't face cancer or surgery, she has remarried and now has several adult stepdaughters who make each day seem like a giant drip of Chinese water torture.

The stepdaughters always want her to baby-sit, and if she tries to say no, she is roundly criticized. They also come over quite often for dinner, but no one ever lifts a finger to help. This frustrated mother sums up her life by trying to see at least a glimmer of humor:

> I was almost ready to kill myself a couple of weeks ago and the Lord helped me. I tried talking to my husband but he can't see it . . . so I'll just keep praying for his eyes to be opened and for a holy boldness for him and myself. I do love these kids in spite of all this, though—most of the time. Ha! Ha!

Both of these women are trying to smile through their grief, but they are both facing long, hard roads that have different kinds of bumps. It reminds me of Francis Thompson, the English poet, who said:

> Grief is a matter of relativity:
>> The sorrow should be estimated by its proportion
>>> to the sorrower;
> A gash is as painful to one as an amputation to
>> another.

Five Steps Through the Pain

Many—almost all—of the letters I receive share the pain, but then they go on to say things like: "We're trusting God . . ." "We've learned to give this over to the Lord . . ." "God is giving us strength for this . . ." I'm encouraged when I read these words about trusting God because, after all, *God only knows!*

In another book,[2] I've talked about traveling near Palm Springs, California, and coming upon a roadside stand with a sign that advertised "Desert-Sweetened Grapefruit." I've often shared the analogy that those of us who go through pain are like that. The bitter desert of grief sweetens us as we learn to give our problems completely to God. The grapefruit story includes my description of several steps that we go through when ongoing pain plasters us flat to the ceiling.

I'm repeating those steps here without apology. I guess I feel a bit like Robert Fulghum, who says he often repeats himself in the hope that sooner or later he just might say something right. Like Fulghum, I'm still wrestling with dilemmas that are "not easily resolved or easily dismissed. . . . Work-in-progress on a life-in-progress is what my writing is about. And some progress in the work is enough to keep it going."[3] So, here once again are my steps for dealing with pain:

FIRST, WE CHURN, a process I often liken to having your insides ground up in a meat grinder, or having a knife plunged into your chest.

SECOND, WE BURN as the shock wears away and the anger takes its place. We may want to kill someone—a child who has caused us unbelievable pain, a drunk driver who has killed a loved one, a spouse who has deserted us for another. Whether we're screaming in anger at the top of our lungs or silently gnashing our teeth, the burning within is a CONSUMING FIRE.

THIRD, WE YEARN for things to change. We look to the happy past, the good old days when life was good and God seemed close and our family gave us nothing but blessings. But now the good old days are gone, and while we know dwelling on the past is futile, we still do it anyway. The yearning stage can last longer than any other.

FOURTH, WE LEARN—a lot of things. We learn what we are really made of. We may learn from others, perhaps in a support group. We discover that we are in a process of long, slow growth. The spiritual values we've always taken for granted ("Oh, of course, I believe that . . .") have now become much more than nice theories. As pain makes us more compassionate and more loving, we find that our values are a real part of who we are, not something we'd like to be.

LAST, WE TURN our problems completely over to God. We finally see that we can do a lot of thinking, feeling, and talking, but only two words really help: "WHATEVER, LORD!" Whatever God allows in our lives, He will get us through it some how, some way. No matter how ridiculous life may be, we can hand it all to the One who is STILL in control. This is honest relinquishment, and because this learning to let go is so important, much of chapter 6 will be devoted to that subject.

One thing to understand about these five stages is that you don't go through them once and then say, "Whew! I'm glad THAT'S over!" No, you may go through many of these stages again and again. You can reach the fifth stage and believe you've turned it over to God and the very next day you can be back churning or burning or yearning. It happened to me. It still happens from time to time. But I find that I'm in those painful stages less often and for shorter times.

To Learn and Turn—ADAPT

The best stages to be in are LEARN and TURN. I want to learn what God has for me, and then I want to keep turning it all over to the One who cares for me far more than I could ever imagine.

For anyone with ongoing pain, my best advice falls somewhere between LEARNING and TURNING. The word I want to key in on in this chapter is ADAPT. I often hear the advice that we must "accept whatever life brings." We must accept our pain, our sorrow, our grief. Accepting others is always a good idea, but I resist the idea of resigning myself to accepting pain. Instead, I'd much rather ADAPT to the challenges that pain may bring.

Adaptability is one of the most important qualities for having a healthy life, even in the face of chronic disease and continual problems. Circumstances of our lives are constantly changing. Either we adapt to fit these new challenges or our well-being deteriorates.

Some years ago researchers did a study of infants who were laid next to a cold metal sheet that had been placed in their

bassinets. Some of the babies turned away from the cold as soon
as they felt it while others simply lay there touching the cold
metal and crying. The adaptability and spirit of the first group—
the ones who turned away from the cold metal—is similar to
the spirit found in a group called Candlelighters that is made
up of parents whose children have cancer. They support each
other in adapting to the terrible circumstances surrounding
their families. They have chosen to light a candle instead of
cursing the darkness of ongoing pain and suffering.

One reason I am against mere acceptance of one's problems
or limitations is that it leads to becoming "resigned to your
fate"—just plain giving up hope. You become trapped in "if-
only" thinking that prevents you from doing what you want to
do and need to do.

Recently I saw a picture of an Indiana license plate bearing
the "two forbidden words":

IF ONLY

Saying, "IF ONLY I had done this," "IF ONLY I had gone
there," or "IF ONLY I had done that," can lead to all kinds of
situations, most of them bad.

IF ONLY can fill your stomach with ulcers.

IF ONLY can give you high blood pressure.

IF ONLY can deprive you of fun in your profession.

IF ONLY can take the zing out of your marriage.

IF ONLY can depress you to the point of suicide.

You see, yesterday is gone forever and tomorrow may never
come. TODAY IS IT! So give it your best shot, and at the end of
the road you will be at the place of your choice instead of being
haunted by IF ONLY, IF ONLY, IF ONLY. . . .

Wayward Children Can Drive You Up the Wall

My mail tells me that painful, ongoing situations, problems,
diseases, and challenges are bad enough. Muttering "IF
ONLY' will only make them worse. A million and one things

can happen, and they often do. By far the greatest number of letters I get about ongoing pain come from parents of children who have caused them tremendous disappointment. In many cases children simply choose to rebel against all the values they've been taught. In other cases, they make poor choices that affect the whole family.

Strangely enough, adult children often blame their problems on their parents. So parents might as well grin and bear it. Someone sent me a little placard that sums up a BASIC AS-SUMPTION held by many (most?) adult children:

> I KNOW I AM RESPONSIBLE FOR MY LIFE
> AND MY DECISIONS.
> I KNOW IT IS IRRESPONSIBLE TO BLAME
> OTHERS FOR MY PROBLEMS.
> I ALSO KNOW THAT EVERYTHING WRONG
> IN MY LIFE
> IS MY PARENTS' FAULT.[4]

In the rest of this chapter, I'd like to share letters from folks whose children have caused them ongoing pain. Some are struggling, groping for answers. Others are learning how to take action and adapt to their situation.

What do you do when you raise a child to have Christian values and pour your life into teaching him or her the difference between right and wrong, and then have that same kid throw it all back in your face by growing up to follow a lifestyle totally different from what you have taught? In other words:

HOW DO YOU COPE WHEN THE APPLE OF YOUR EYE
BECOMES A BONE IN YOUR THROAT?

To watch helplessly as a darling child you have nurtured and loved goes off on a detour is one of the most frustrating emotional vacuums a parent can endure. Discouraged parents go through a kaleidoscope of emotions—anger, shame, hurt, feeling unappreciated and resentful—I know because I've been there.

These feelings can be caused by a runaway child or an adult child who drops into the gay lifestyle or a thousand other situations. Children can go astray of the law and be arrested or even jailed. Perhaps they are chronically dishonest, or heavy into the use of alcohol or drugs. They may be dabbling in satanism or another cult. Perhaps they have "disconnected" from the family or they may be still living at home at the age of twenty-nine, still expecting you to support them. They may have married into agnosticism or some kind of abusive situation. Or perhaps they are not married and just have a live-in partner.

When a child has gone morally or spiritually astray, it becomes a deep emotional injury to the parents. It is like having a knife thrust into your chest and having no way to remove it. You have to learn to live with that knife, to move carefully so it won't dig deeper and cause more pain than you already have.

Frequently I get letters from parents whose grown children have chosen to live in sexual immorality of some kind. Their questions could be summed up as follows:

How do I deal with their "shacking up," living together arrangements, pornography, etc.?

One mom has four sons who are "good boys," but her fifth—the oldest—is a "heartache and an embarrassment to our family." The real trouble started when he was in junior high and got in with the wrong crowd. She writes:

He began secretly listening to hard-rock tapes that he borrowed. He used headphones and was up in his room and we didn't know. He also began smoking marijuana. We were so dumb we didn't recognize the odor. He was always spraying Lysol in his room.

Throughout his teenage years he skipped school and got in minor trouble with the police (speeding, etc.). We sent him to a Christian school for grades eleven and twelve. Then we sent him to a Christian college. He was there three months and got expelled for drinking.

He now quits jobs (is unemployed at the moment) and has moved out of our home and into a trailer a few miles away.

He has recently moved a girl of about 19 or 20 into the trailer to live with him. He says she is pregnant and he has to "do the right thing" and let her live there. Her parents and other family members are all for this arrangement. When we ask him when the child is due, he keeps moving the due date up. We have not seen her so we do not know for sure. . . .

Our son doesn't think he is doing anything wrong. He says he asked God to forgive him, but he continues to live in sin. We have some communication with him, but not much.

How do we handle this? He wasn't raised like this. Even with all his trouble he went to church each Sunday until the last year. We prayed for God to help him for years and to send him a good Christian friend—but He never did. We are so confused. PLEASE help us in any way you can! I'm so depressed that this is affecting my entire life. I can't live like this. I don't know anyone else with this problem. I feel so guilty.

Wayward sons are hard enough, but wayward daughters can *really* tug at a mother's heart. One mom wrote to tell her daughter's story:

In high school we had a good relationship, if that means she told me nearly everything. But following my advice was another thing. I went through the worries of knowing she felt sex was a normal thing for two who are "in love"—and she has been in love many times. I did discuss birth control since my talk about abstinence was not being accepted. It was a relief when she graduated never having become pregnant!

But then I learned that while out with friends she had tried alcoholic beverages—becoming drunk a few times. So naturally, I was afraid every time she was with friends, especially when she was driving.

Speaking of driving—she bought a used car—it has been well used during the past two years: (1) Going too fast and skidded on gravel road, landed on its side in ditch, car roughed up—daughter OK. (2) Not paying attention, hit van in front who stopped suddenly—property damage only. (3) Pulled out in front of car—didn't see it—was hit on passenger side, car worse, daughter OK. Plus several more

minor accidents. The Lord has sure had His hands full pro-
tecting this daughter—but He has continued to do so.

This mother's letter continued and mentioned that her
daughter started staying out all night with friends, causing the
mother to be unable to sleep. Confrontation led to the
daughter's moving out and trying to live first with an ex-
employer (male), and when that didn't work moving into a
girlfriend's apartment. Currently the daughter is on good
terms with her mother but causes her all kinds of grief by
going from one boyfriend to another. The mother closed her
letter by saying:

> Barbara, it seems it will never end. I thank God for giving
> me strength to make it through all this so far—and you've just
> heard a little of it.
> I love my daughter. We have so much fun together—but
> when she calls on the phone my heart is back up in my throat
> until I learn it isn't an emergency or crisis this time—she just
> called to say Hi!
> Thanks for being my sounding board. This has been
> therapeutic. It's the first time I've put it in writing!

This mom's letter is a good example of how emotional pain
knits itself together in various degrees of intensity as we feel
anger, disgust, fear, grief, embarrassment, shame, guilt, and
hurt all at once. We all experience grief when there is a loss,
such as a runaway child or a wayward child. The child may still
stay in touch, as the daughter described in the letter above has
done, but in some ways her communications are more disturbing than not bothering to call at all.

What this mom is really grieving for is the "loss" of her
daughter in the sense that she has lost her daughter's personality and her spirit, and she just doesn't know her daughter any
more. The little girl she brought up to know better has disappeared into an adult who seems bent on her own destruction.

The biggest perk for me in this mom's letter is that she
thanks me for being her sounding board and speaks of how

therapeutic putting it in writing has been. Lots of folks find relief in sharing their emotions by writing to me or talking with
me on the phone. As they share, parents finally realize that
when a child is off doing his or her own thing, they can't help
by being distraught themselves. They realize they have to get
their emotions under control by refusing to play the blame
game.

Especially when dealing with wayward children, playing
the blame game (blaming yourself for what they have decided
to do) only leads to wallowing in guilt and self-pity. Guilt im-
mobilizes you and makes you unable to be the kind of sup-
porting parent your kids need. As for self-pity, you go in
circles, centering more and more on yourself, which only in-
creases your misery.

For parents who are feeling guilt and self-pity about what
a child may be doing or has done, I have one important reminder:

WHERE THERE IS NO CONTROL
THERE IS NO RESPONSIBILITY.

Face it, your adult child is out of your control. That means
your child is no longer your responsibility. When an adult child
goes off the deep end of rebellion, a mother has to remember
that she has had eighteen years to build in her values. If her
child has gone against those values, it doesn't mean she has
failed. She did her job, and what her son does with what she
did is really his or her choice. Children are going to do their
own things. But along with that, remember that God can pull
their tails whenever He wants to. They may think they are in
control, but their times are in HIS hands.

As for feeling guilty because she doesn't know anyone else
with the problem, this Mom should realize that in today's society premarital sex and sleeping together before marriage are
more the rule than the exception. So-called "living-together"
arrangements are especially hard for parents who grew up in
my generation. There were people who "slept around" and

"shacked up" back when I was young, but today it is a completely different ball of wax. If a young man or woman can't see what's wrong with fornication, it's doubtful that the mother is going to convince him or her otherwise.

For this mom to accept guilt over her son's immoral conduct is only to play the futile blame game. When our kids stray from what they've been taught, we don't have to accept their way-wardness. Instead we can ADAPT, and the best way to adapt is to realize that we can't handle the situation for them. Our children must decide for themselves the kind of life they will live. We must realize that we have loved them, trained them, and taught them. Now it is time to let them go. (For more on letting go, see chapter 6.)

I often hear from parents who feel uncomfortable because Proverbs 22:6 hasn't seemed to work in their family. This verse says, "Train up a child in the way he should go, And when he is old he will not depart from it" (NKJV). Parents want to know, "If this verse is a promise to Christian parents, why has it failed in our case?" Or maybe the real point is that they believe they have failed, and that only makes them feel all the more guilty.

I used to ask the same question until I learned a little more about what the original Hebrew means. In my copy of the New American Standard Version a marginal note on Proverbs 22:6 says, "According to his way." Best-selling author and master Bible teacher Chuck Swindoll believes this means:

> God is not saying, "Bring up a child as *you* see him." But instead, he says, "If you want your child to be godly and wise, observe your child, be sensitive and alert so as to discover *his* way, and adapt your training accordingly."[5]

Right along with this interpretation is the way the Amplified Bible expands on Proverbs 22:6:

> Train up a child in the way he should go [and in keeping with his individual gift or bent], and when he is old he will not depart from it.

The "his own way" interpretation of Proverbs 22:6 isn't suggesting that you let your kid run amuck as he or she grows up. The overall teaching of Scripture clearly tells parents to give their children the best training and nurture they can (see, for example, Eph. 6:4). At the same time, if your kid goes off on a detour, it does not mean you have failed or that God's Word is null and void. It simply means that after you have done your best to train your children by respecting the kind of persons they are, they make their own choices and they are responsible for those choices.

I like the way one mother put it. She believes Proverbs 22:6 means, "Train up a child according to his own temperament, learning the best way he responds to you, to life and to God."[6] The principles in Proverbs 22:6 are sound, but they do not guarantee a charmed life for your kids.

You want to do your best to fill your children's reservoir with the right values, to give your children a built-in system for right and wrong. Then, when they make their own choices in life, it is your hope that their good, solid training will surface often, particularly if they get into deep water and find themselves floundering. It is then that they often remember what they have been taught. It's true that God's Word never returns void. Whatever we write on the hearts of our children is not erased by time and there is no question that early training is vital.

And there can be payoffs—wonderful payoffs. This past Mother's Day my youngest son, Barney, sent me a lovely plaque. I doubt that Barney was thinking about how this plaque beautifully sums up Proverbs 22:6, but I'd like to believe he was just trying to tell me something very special:

MOTHERS HOLD THEIR CHILDREN'S HANDS
FOR A WHILE . . .
THEIR HEARTS FOREVER.

How Can You Love When Your Heart Is Breaking?

Loving our kids through the tough times is always our goal, but that doesn't make the pain any easier to bear. In fact, the pain can INCREASE. Parents write and ask me in one way or another:

How do I cope when my kids break my heart?

For example, I got a letter from a mother of "four wonderful sons" who told how she had lived the "best mother, best cook, best grandma" life for quite a while—and then it "all fell apart." One son ran them into bankruptcy but they forgave him and the many lies he had told. Three years later, however, he still won't talk to his parents. Two other sons married girls from families with totally different values from the Christian ones they'd been taught at home. Now the wives have forbidden their husbands to see the parents and have also refused to let the grandparents see their grandchildren. This brokenhearted mom and grandma writes:

> I just can't seem to find my life. . . . How do you block out memories of love, caring, up all night taking care of them when they were little? Den mother, Scout leader, birthdays, seeing their eyes light up on Christmas . . . I feel I'm in prison and I've done nothing. I can't get dressed. It's not fair. I keep asking, Why? The one son who stuck by us is so upset with his brothers and their wives that it has destroyed his feelings for them. So my family is nothing any more. I used to laugh, but I can't find <u>me</u> anymore. My life was my family. I feel like my life was for nothing.
>
> How can you repair a broken heart? . . . I don't know what tomorrow will bring. I pray a lot to God. How in God's name do I cope? Time, is that the answer? I'm running out . . . I don't want to hear one more person say, "It could be worse," or "You had no shoes, that man had no feet!" Your pain is "your pain." I just want it to go away. I knew an older woman once who, years ago, had electric shock treatments, and she couldn't remember her childhood and some of her family at the time. I thought, How terrible! But now I think I'd go for it.

It's obvious this mom can't accept what has happened, and I don't blame her. I wouldn't accept it either, but I would try in every way I could to ADAPT. After all, no matter what happens to us:

BROKEN HEARTS KEEP ON BEATING[7]

As this mother says, her pain is her pain. That's absolutely right. So often when we are in pain we want it to go away. We want God or somebody to fix things and take away our discomfort, but in many cases there is no way to escape it, and that is why we must learn to adapt, to live with that knife in our chest and keep it from twisting around too much.

Drugs and Alcohol Equal Lots of Pain

It's hard enough raising children and hoping they absorb the right values, but when drugs and alcohol are added to the equation, stress multiplies quickly. When kids go off the deep end with chemicals, it's hard to remain very positive. At a time like that, it's easy to define an optimist as "a person who hasn't been given all the facts yet." In fact, I've talked to parents who could easily find some dark humor in the quip:

WE SHOULD HAVE HAD RABBITS
INSTEAD OF KIDS . . .
AT LEAST WE WOULD HAVE GOTTEN
ONE GOOD MEAL OUT OF THE DEAL!

One dad wrote me twice to share the frustrations of having a son in drug rehabilitation; his letters said in part:

I don't suppose you've had the opportunity to "guide" a child through a drug rehab program. . . . Our son has been going up and down . . . like a roller coaster. I recently was asked by staff (in the rehab center) to witness one of his rebellious states—carrying around a chair like he was going to defend against lions (or swing it at somebody).

When I grabbed him by the sweatshirt and told him to drop it, all he could do was scream at me, "Let go of my shirt, man!" He then proceeded to rip off both pockets of my new shirt. Sure I was angry, but it was as though I was face to face with the demon inside him.

Later, he had to be restrained because he just "wants to be left alone." He seems destined to destroy himself—and only the intervention of God will prevent it.

Surely I ask, "When?" and I hear the answer, "In My time." I resign myself to accept that voice, hoping it is not a mirage. . . .

The family support group keeps encouraging us, things will get better. Sometimes I believe all the positive feedback for an entire 24-hour period, but the next day dawns and I've got to turn the pepper grinder again. Then I slide into the valley and find I'm believing only half of all the positive stuff only half the time. That means I'm only 25 percent positive that he'll get better or I'll feel less of a failure. . . .

P.S. I'm sorry for the mood swings, but what do you expect from a guy who just turned 40, reading a book written by a woman?

I admire this dad for reading my book to find some answers and for admitting he needs to find some direction in life. And I really enjoyed his "P.S." because in recent years a little book has come out entitled *Everything Men Know About Women.*[8] Inside, the pages are *completely blank!* So, for this dad to glean some insight from a woman's perspective is truly a compliment.

Putting kidding aside, however, I want him to know that, yes, things WILL get better, but perhaps they will get worse FIRST. He has to be prepared for the long haul with his son, and it *will* be like a roller coaster, not a smooth escalator. He can't glide effortlessly to euphoria. It will be up and down, and down and up, and sometimes he will be knocked off his pins trying to make sense out of what is happening. One thing is for sure:

THERE IS NO PLACE
FOR A MOTHER TO GO TO RESIGN!*

I want this dad to know there are no ex-parents. Once you have a child, it's like getting a life sentence in prison with no hope of parole! So here's how I would answer that dad:

Search out the positive. Cling to the hope that time will be your greatest ally, and be thankful you are a man and not a woman with more than just mood swings to complain about. You don't have to worry about PMS or hot flashes, which often afflict moms as they go through problems with a wayward child.

One day you'll look back at all this and laugh. Believe me, *trust* me; I see it happen all the time. Folks who think they will never get beyond the pits find out that one day they are back on top. They are back in balance and life goes on. I love your honesty and openness. Most men cannot show the transparency you have. But hang on to the fact that you *will* get through this and you *will* feel better!

When Your Kids Hurt, You Hurt

Sometimes parents endure ongoing pain, not because their kids have rebelled or rejected them, but because life has dealt their children a severe blow. For example, one of the most painful things parents can endure is to give a child in marriage and see that marriage disintegrate for any number of reasons.

In some cases, I get letters from mothers who have had three or four children wind up in divorce! Here's what one pastor's wife went through in an eighteen-month period:

November: I had a segmented mastectomy, chemotherapy for six months, 25 radiation treatments.
March: Youngest daughter divorced.
June: Oldest daughter divorced.

---

*Believe me, I know! (See Barbara Johnson, *Where Does a Mother Go to Resign?* [Minneapolis: Bethany House, 1979].)

July: Broken ankle—therapy for two months.
October: Third daughter divorced.
February: Next-to-oldest girl divorced after 15 years—
husband walked out for a 21-year-old.

This mom said she is coping, and that God has made the family stronger through all of this. Then she added:

We know now more than ever that His grace is sufficient for any and all situations. (I think I could write a book sometimes. Ha!)

Another mother of three children, all in their thirties (six grandchildren), thought everyone was happily married, and then "things happened." Her letter continued:

Our second daughter's husband went bankrupt in his construction company and became a drinker and a woman chaser, and they were divorced. At the same time our first daughter and her husband were having their second child and, three weeks after the son was born, he left her for her best friend. They were divorced three months after the second daughter's divorce. Both girls had been married twelve to sixteen years.

It has been seven years of struggle both financially and mentally. We all live in the same small town. Two months ago our son and his wife (married sixteen years) separated. No divorce yet, but who knows. They have two children.

Throughout all of this we have had the love and support of our church family and friends and the love of God and His promises that there is a way through our struggles, one day at a time.

Both of these moms are adapting to the devastation of multiple divorce as best they can. Like many other parents, they are looking for the best possible answers to questions like these:

How do we help our children through a divorce?
What part should we play?

Both of these mothers appear to be nonjudgmental. They are accepting their kids and adapting to the situation as best they can. In most cases, these are the first steps parents can take.

When a grown child's marriage ends in divorce, parents can be supportive but not patronizing. The same principle about every child making his or her own choices applies. Perhaps your son or daughter chose an individual you really didn't approve of. It will do no good now to criticize and say, "I told you so . . ."

The best thing to do is back off and let your children live their own lives. You may be tempted to step in, take over, and start parenting again, but avoid that at all costs. Instead, try to give them lots of emotional support because their self-esteem is probably at an all-time low.

Of course, you may need to help financially, and if the divorce has left your daughter a single mom, she may be looking to you for help with child care. Always keep in mind that you walk a very fine line. You are needed—sometimes desperately—but you must wait to be invited. When your kids ask for your help or advice, you can give it. Always keep in mind however:

ADVICE IS LIKE SNOW,
THE SOFTER IT FALLS, THE DEEPER IT SINKS.

The Pain Goes On and On and On . . .

Every day letters come from parents who are learning to cope with situations that once seemed overwhelming. One mother wrote to thank me for the message in *Geranium*, commenting that all her life she had been the serious member of the family and she appreciated the wit and humor in the book. Then she said:

Although my situation is different (whose isn't?), I could definitely relate to your story. I am the mother of two sons, both alcohol-drug addicted for over 20 years. Recovery

Sometimes I get so frustrated that I don't know whether to cry, scream or wet my pants!

©PAULA

entered my family a little over three years ago. I say recovery "entered" the family, as today the entire family is in recovery, including my husband and I from our co-dependency issues.

Another mom shared her deep concerns about her daughter, who has had problems with alcohol—and automobiles. The mother explained:

This week she was caught driving while her license was suspended. She wasn't drinking—the brake light on the car wasn't working so she was stopped. She isn't gay and definitely likes the opposite sex as she has a seven-year-old son and is divorced from her alcoholic ex-husband. But at one time she drank, being in this unlovely situation. (That was the reason for the suspended license in the first place.)

So tears are often near the surface. And along comes your *Love Line* and I read and cry and laugh—and like the poem says, "I find some work to do!"

The stories of ongoing pain I've shared in this chapter are truly only the tip of the proverbial iceberg. Just a sampling from my weekly mail reveals:

. . . a precious red-headed granddaughter born with only a third of her brain because of her mother's drug abuse.

. . . a mother struggling to help her oldest daughter, who has been psychologically ill for twenty years. Her daughter-in-law is a recovering manic depressive, another daughter is slowly conquering panic attacks, and still another daughter combats marriage problems but won't share any of her feelings with the family.

. . . a mentally retarded daughter who has had open heart surgery and part of her stomach removed. Her sister may have to have brain surgery, and the father in the family has been out of work most of the time recently.

. . . a fourteen-year-old boy who flipped his four-wheeler and spent thirty-three days in ICU only to be moved to a private room where he remained in a coma.

The Real World Is One Rough Place

Do you see why I believe "God only knows"? So often I would like to fix everything for these dear folks who write to tell me how life has welcomed them to the real world. I do my best to send them whatever help I can—tapes of messages I've given, suggested reading that might help them with their particular problem, or suggestions of organizations that might be able to give them experienced or professional help. But the bottom line is this:

TAKE YOUR BROKEN DREAMS TO JESUS . . .
ONLY HE KNOWS THE ANSWERS TO YOUR PROBLEMS.

Only as we turn to Him in faith will we feel His comforting hand on our lives. In most of these same letters that recount disasters great and small, folks often add their thoughts about faith and trust in God.

A neighbor was telling me recently how difficult it was to
leave her daughter at college and how depressed she has
been. She does not know any of the problems we are having
with our son (you can share with so few people) but I was
thinking of how wonderful it would be to be able to bring a
child to college—to know where the child was and that her
life had purpose and direction. There are some situations we
cannot change—but we can change our attitudes about them.
As long as there is life, there is hope and it is this which really
keeps us going, especially in the midst of the trial. Like Daniel
in the Old Testament, we have experienced the fire, but it has
not consumed us. . . .

□ □ □

In these . . . I held the family together and supported
my dear husband and children but *I* began coming totally
"un-glued"! . . . the strain on my marriage, children, and
my sanity multiplied. I hadn't taken care of ME! It never
even crossed by mind! I couldn't function at home or work.
My emotional strain turned into physical problems: chest
pains, choking, insomnia. . . . Don't ask me why I picked
up the phone and called you (someone I've never met) for
advice. And over a distance of thousands of miles, God
used you to guide me to the information I needed in my
life!

□ □ □

We learned that we couldn't answer the questions and life
went on anyway. God has been our only solid ground and at
times I was angry at Him for the mess our lives were in. We
are learning to cope and get on with life. Thank God for
people who are willing to share their stories. I hope that by
sharing our "endless hope" we can help others know that God
can handle any problem. . . .

□ □ □

Knowing today that recovery is a process, I feel a newness
of my spiritual faith in God and His Son Jesus. Only God can

perform miracles; both my sons' sobriety is proof of that. The road back has been very rocky, but with God's help the rocks can become stepping stones. . . .

☐   ☐   ☐

I read your book from cover to cover all night and in my diary copied down many of your quips. I cannot tell you how many times over the next few months God continued to use you in my life. You had been through phases I had not yet entered, but you gave me light along the way. I have now passed through some of these phases and have not only by God's grace been forgiven but have also forgiven my now-ex-husband and his fiancée, and the "others" who chose to be involved in our divorce. God had restored me into His joy, despite my circumstances. . . .

All of the above comments remind me of the old saying:

WHAT'S DOWN IN THE WELL
COMES UP IN THE BUCKET.

In other words, whatever reservoirs of strength and hope you have deep inside will come up when pain inevitably invades your life. One of the most dramatic examples I have ever heard of drawing on inner strength is this story that ran in *People Weekly* concerning a teenager who slipped and fell into a piece of spinning farm machinery that amputated both of his arms in just a few seconds:

He Tried to Keep His Blood Off Mom's Carpet

John Thompson, eighteen, was alone, doing chores on his family's sixteen-hundred-acre North Dakota farm when the accident happened. Realizing his arms were gone, he struggled to his feet and staggered back to the house where he used a stub of bone hanging out of what was left of one arm to open a screen door. Then he used his mouth to turn the doorknob and get into the house.

Somehow he got the phone off the hook and managed to dial his uncle's home a few miles away by holding a pen in his mouth. His seventeen-year-old cousin answered and he told her he needed an ambulance because "I'm bleeding very bad and I don't have any arms."

Then John hung up, went into the bathroom and crouched in the bathtub because he didn't want to stain his mother's carpet with his blood! Family members arrived a few minutes later and tried to help John keep his spirits up as they waited for the ambulance to arrive.

Through it all, John Thompson never lost consciousness or his sense of humor. When his aunt told him the ambulance would be there in a second, he quipped, "One thousand and one . . . well, it's not here."

When the ambulance crew hurried in to take John to the hospital, they were stunned by what they saw. They were also amazed when John reminded them to retrieve his arms, which were still lying near the power take-off mechanism that had ripped them off. He even directed them to garbage bags in the kitchen so they could pack the limbs in ice!

Miraculously, John's arteries had closed off as if a natural tourniquet had been applied; he was rushed to a medical facility twenty minutes away. A little later he was air-lifted to a trauma center where six microsurgery experts waited to reattach his limbs, one of which had been severed above the elbow and the other one torn off at the shoulder. The operation went well, but doctors were not sure about how much use John would regain of either arm. Afterward he faced at least five years of grueling physical therapy.

With his usual positive attitude, John was already trying to figure out what he'd be able to do with his hands and how he would finish high school. In talking about the accident, he said, "I'm grateful for everyone's prayers and everything, but anyone would have done what I did. You do what you have to do."[9]

Few people will ever have to face the incredible trauma John Thompson went through, but many of us face our own particular traumas, and what John says is as true for us as it was for him: "You do what you have to do." And as you do it, what's down in the well comes up in the bucket. That's why it's so crucial to be able to draw on reservoirs of inner strength that only God can provide. As the psalmist puts it:

> HE TURNS A DESERT INTO POOLS OF WATER,
> A PARCHED LAND INTO SPRINGS. . . .[10]

How much pain can we take? God only knows, but Jesus promises: "If anyone thirsts, let him come to Me and drink" (John 7:37 NKJV). He will provide the living water that will make all the difference.

> A little love, a little trust
> A soft impulse, a sudden dream,
> And life as dry as desert dust
> Is fresher than a mountain stream.[11]

In this chapter, we have touched on several "ordinary" ways kids can cause ongoing pain for their parents. Obviously, there are many others, but in chapter 4 I want to focus on one painful problem I used to think was extraordinary.

The day I discovered my own son was a homosexual, my world was shattered. Anger, rage, and homophobia were all part of my initial reaction. I felt I was the only one in all the world who had a homosexual child. I learned a great deal in the next few years, as Spatula Ministries was born. Now I know homosexuality is not as unheard-of as I thought it was back in 1975. It is our RESPONSE that makes it so unreal to deal with; that's what we will look at in the next chapter.

Gloomee Busters

> Life is like an ice cream cone:
> Just when you think you've got it licked—
> IT DRIPS ALL OVER YOU!

□   □   □

IF AT FIRST YOU DON'T SUCCEED,
SEE IF THE LOSER GETS ANYTHING.

□　□　□

When life drops a pooper
That's unkind to our noses,
Use it for fertilizer;
It's your chance
To grow roses![12]

□　□　□

I DON'T MIND THE RAT RACE
BUT I COULD DO WITH A LITTLE MORE CHEESE.

□　□　□

The secret of dealing successfully with a child
is not to be its parent.

□　□　□

CAN YOU THANK ME FOR TRUSTING YOU
WITH THIS EXPERIENCE
EVEN IF I NEVER TELL YOU WHY?

□　□　□

Parents: People who bear infants,
bore teen-agers, and board newlyweds.

□　□　□

MONEY ISN'T EVERYTHING,
BUT IT SURE KEEPS THE KIDS IN TOUCH.

□　□　□

Climbing the Musical Scale

DO—Do not worry over things that may never happen, and even if they happen, worry will not help. Do count your blessings before you count cares.

RE—Radiate good will and a spirit of benevolence. Like laughter, it is infectious and makes yourself, as well as others, feel better.

ME—Mete kindness, understanding, tolerance, and forgiveness generously. You reap as you mete.

FA—Far-reaching are the therapeutic benefits of spiritual thinking. You become as you habitually think. Resentment, hatred, spite, envy, and vengeance pack radioactive fall-out that gnaws at your vitals. They are self-consuming.

SO—Sow the seeds of love, friendship, empathy, and helpfulness. These hardy seeds take root in the crustiest ground.

LA—Laugh at yourself now and then. He who can laugh at himself is less apt to be at war with himself. Laugh at yourself, even if you don't feel like laughing.

TI—Teach yourself awareness and appreciation of all the wonders of nature. Thank God daily for the precious gift of life. Genuine gratitude and discontent are never found together.

DO—Do not expect someone else to open the door to happiness for you. You must do it yourself. You alone have the key. Turn it.

—Source unknown

□ □ □

There are times, regardless of the score,
just to be ALIVE is to be winning.

□ □ □

SOME DAYS YOU'RE THE BUG . . .
SOME DAYS, THE WINDSHIELD!

□ □ □

Blessed are the flexible
for they shall not be bent out of shape.

☐   ☐   ☐

My grace is sufficient for you, for my power is made
perfect in weakness. (2 Cor. 12:9 NIV)

You're a WHAT?!?

What to Do When Your Favorite "Who" Becomes a "What"

With everything that is going on today, some sins look almost "acceptable" compared with other alternatives. I got a letter from one mother who received a disturbing call from her son. He told her he and his wife had separated, that it was all his fault, and that he had a "terrible problem."

The son asked his mother to call his wife, and when she did so, her daughter-in-law said, yes, it was true that her husband had had an affair and that it was possible that he might have given her a "terrible disease."

Because the daughter-in-law was so distraught, the phone conversation ended rather quickly and when the mother-in-law hung up she feared the worst. Could it be that her son was gay and he had given his wife AIDS? She had to wait three days before she was able to fly to the city where her son and his wife lived to get more details about the crisis. Her letter continued:

I let him talk without interrupting him until he came to the telling of his affair. I insisted he tell me who and when he told me, I said, "You mean with a GIRL?" He said, "Yes, of course!" My first words to come out were "Oh, I'm so GLAD!" He thought I had really flipped because he knew of my deep Christian beliefs about marriage and adultery. When I was able to explain about my terrible misunderstanding, he was horrified, but as we talked he finally said, "Well, Mother, now I know how to tell you bad news . . . just tell you something worse first, then you will be so relieved you won't be overcome by the bad news!"

As terrible as those three days of waiting and wondering were, this mom learned some lasting lessons. She grew in her faith as God helped her cope with the most difficult testing of her life. And through living in stark fear of AIDS for three days she now has tremendous compassion for all families who face this deadly situation. She said, "I'll never be the same person I was before this three-day trial."

I never learned the last chapter of this story. I'm not sure if the couple got back together, but I know this mom kept loving her son through it all. While her views on adultery didn't change one bit, she was able to see that, as bad as an affair can be, there could be things that are even more devastating.

She was waiting to hear the awful words, "I'm gay and I've tested HIV-positive," and when they didn't come, she heaved a great sigh of relief. But what happens when you do hear your son or daughter (or spouse) announce, "I'm homosexual . . . I have a lover . . . I'm moving out"? What *do* you do when your favorite "who" becomes a "what"?

When the Bomb Drops Out of the Closet

I've talked to many parents who say, "If only he had run off with some woman. I could handle *that*! But THIS?"

I don't judge these parents at all for giving one trauma more weight than another because I understand. I did it too. When I discovered that my son, Larry, was a homosexual, the emotional effect was like the explosion of a hundred-kiloton bomb. And since starting Spatula Ministries more than fourteen years ago, I have talked to thousands of parents who have heard those same fateful words and their reaction has been just like mine was. It may not be rational or even Christian, but for most parents, on a scale of one to ten, hearing that their child is gay is a thirteen!

That's why we named our ministry "Spatula." As bad as so many things can be—losing a child through death, hearing the fateful word *cancer*, learning that your daughter's marriage is breaking up due to adultery, and on and on—there is something about the word *homosexual* that literally makes people hit the ceiling, and only a spatula of love can peel them off and help get them back down on their feet! Here are just a few samples of how parents reacted when they got the news:

> Our 34-year-old son, who has a wife and two children, told us in June that he was gay and he and his wife would be getting a divorce. We were both devastated. I am just now beginning to care if I live or die.

□ □ □

> I spoke with you for a few minutes when we heard of our lovely son Peter's lifestyle choice. Oh, how it hurts! One day I'm up, the other I'm down. Today is **BLACK** and I couldn't even go for my walk.

□ □ □

> My husband became so distraught that he wanted to kill our son, his friend, our younger son, me, and himself. He thought that would be the only "way out."

□ □ □

> This past Monday my husband's and my world was destroyed. Our 19-year-old son told us he is a homosexual. What else do I need to say? We are Christians, have worked in the church, taught Sunday school for young people for 20 years. We're highly respected in the community. . . . What do we do now? I begin to rest in Jesus and then panic sweeps over me to drown me. The suffering of his father overwhelms me! The devil has struck at our most vulnerable point.

□ □ □

If you think I sound composed—I am today. I've waited two weeks after reading your book to find a day I could write instead of wanting to color or cut out paper dolls. My friend gave me pre-cut paper dolls, says she doesn't trust me with even the round-tip scissors! Good friends are hard to find!

☐   ☐   ☐

My daughter came home for spring break and told me she is a lesbian. I lost it. I grabbed my Bible and begged and cried and screamed (something I have never done), threatened suicide, but nothing changed except that she turned completely away from me.

I can identify with all of these parental emotions—and more! After losing Steve and then Tim, I thought I had had my fill of the cup of suffering, but I was wrong. As bad as dealing with the deaths of two sons was, there were many things about those deaths that were easier than dealing with learning the truth about Larry.

Larry and I Had a "Perfect" Relationship

As my mind goes back to that incredible day in June 1975, I clearly remember the kaleidoscope of emotions that seemingly struck me all at once. Larry didn't come to me and admit he was a homosexual; instead I discovered it accidentally by finding homosexual material in a dresser drawer where I had gone innocently looking for a BIBLE STUDY BOOK for a friend of his. Accompanying the initial shock was total disbelief and even denial. How could this be? He had shared so much with us, particularly enjoying music with me and so many other fun things we had done together.

During high school, Larry had worked the night shift in a local In 'n' Out hamburger place, and after getting off work he would bring home hamburgers for both of us. He'd always come home smelling of onions and french fries and sometimes find me watching the Johnny Carson Show. He'd flop down on the big puffy chair next to the TV; then we'd eat the burgers and he'd share with me the funny things that had happened at work.

One night he described a really fat lady who rolled up to the drive-through and ordered fifteen hamburgers, fifteen orders of fries, and fifteen chocolate shakes! She was alone in her car and when she drove up to the window to pick up her order, Larry automatically asked the routine question, "Is this to eat HERE or to go?"

We had a good laugh about that story and many others. He'd tell me about his friends who came by to see him and other conversations about people we knew and enjoyed. It was our time to share, watching Johnny Carson, eating hamburgers, drinking Cokes, and laughing—always laughing.

Larry has a rippling laugh that is infectious—absolutely contagious—and VERY AUDIBLE. I was always afraid we would wake up Bill or Barney with our raucous laughter, but we did have FUN.

All through those years there wasn't even a hint from Larry about his struggle with homosexuality nor any kind of indication that this was part of his life. He had many opportunities to tell me when we sat there alone at night in the quiet of our darkened house, but he never said a word about his personal struggle.

As I thought back over some of our conversations, I remembered once that he wanted to know what I thought about eternal security. I have always been persuaded that the believer is secure in God's love, and out of my own reservoir of Scriptures I told Larry why and how I knew this was true and how it applied to my own life, as well as his. After discovering that Larry was gay, his questions about eternal security made a lot more sense to me.

Another puzzle in June 1975 was the Mother of the Year plaque Larry had given me only a month before on Mother's Day. It told me what a wonderful mom I was and added some other flowery phrases that come to mothers on special days. But now, where had the darling son I thought I knew so well gone?

What had happened to the laughing, happy-spirited boy who suddenly had a DARK SIDE I never knew before?

When I made my devastating discovery in Larry's dresser drawer, there was no time to get answers to my frantic questions. Larry wasn't there and I was due at the airport in forty-five minutes to pick up my sister, Janet, and her husband, who were flying home from a vacation in Hawaii. We had all planned to go to Disneyland that evening and then celebrate Father's Day together before they continued their flight home to Minnesota.

I'm not sure why, but I picked up all of the "stuff" I had discovered and threw it in the trunk of my car. I'm also not sure why I wrote Larry a note that said:

> Larry, I found the magazines and stuff in the drawer and I
> have it all with me. I love you and God loves you, but this is
> so wrong. Can we just get through tonight and, after the
> relatives leave tomorrow, talk about it? Please meet us at the
> flagpole at Disneyland at 8:00 so we can enjoy the big bicen-
> tennial parade and fireworks with them anyway.

If I had wanted to keep things quiet until after my sister and husband had left, it would have been better to have left the stuff undisturbed in his dresser drawer. It would have been better to just smile through it all, have a wonderful time at Disneyland that evening, enjoy a great Father's Day, put them on the plane with smiles, and THEN go back home to confront my son and tell him what I knew.

Nothing Made Sense—NOTHING

What I did instead made no sense, but then life wasn't making much sense right about then. As I drove at what seemed to me to be pell-mell speed to the airport, I felt all the symptoms of a panic attack: shortness of breath and a strong suspicion that an invisible elephant was sitting on my chest and a shag rug had somehow been stuffed down my throat. And for some crazy reason, my teeth itched!

Deep inside I felt pain, as if I were being gored by a bull. I had never been *gored* by a bull, but I was sure THIS is what it had to be like. Strange groaning sounds were coming out of my mouth, and I wondered if this was "only" a panic attack—or the beginnings of a heart attack.

What was going on? After all, I was no stranger to crises and shocking news. Nine years before I had picked up my half-dead husband on a dark mountain road with his head smashed open from an accident, and I'd held together as I went to call for help and then got him down that mountain road to the local hospital.

And just two years after that, death had come to our door for the first time when Steven had died—and I coped with that. Then five years later, death had paid a second visit with the phone call from the Yukon telling me Tim was dead. I hadn't felt any rugs in my throat or elephants on my chest THEN, so what was going on THIS time?

Was I having all these symptoms because I had a stack of homosexual magazines and letters written to my son in the trunk of my car? Should I dump them somewhere before meeting Janet and Mel at the airport? But how could I dump them without being seen? I had no sack to put them in. Besides, maybe it was illegal to have such material—maybe they were like drugs or something.

I knew nothing about homosexuality and I certainly had no way to cope with learning that my darling son was one. But worst of all, I felt so BETRAYED. How could Larry have kept this part of his life from us so completely? Why didn't he say something to me, especially since we had shared so much together?

My Son Had Always Been So Thoughtful

Thinking back to the night of Bill's accident, I recalled how Larry was only eleven at the time, yet he had been so mature and so steady. After I had called an ambulance for Bill, I left Larry up at the retreat center in the care of other people from our church. Then I hurried back to where I had found my husband and got there just in time to join him in the ambulance for the ride down the mountain to the hospital. Without any help or prompting from the adults present, Larry got on the phone and called our family doctor, our pastor, and his teacher at the Christian school he attended and told all of them what had happened. By the time the ambulance arrived at the hospital, all three of them were there waiting for us!

Larry had the presence of mind to do this telephoning while everyone else was praying and trying to figure out what to do. He was only eleven years old, but I really believe he had the gift of mercy even at that young age, and he knew how to use it.

And during the next two years, Larry was so caring and thoughtful as we battled with doctors' diagnoses that said my husband would be blind and a vegetable for the remainder of his life, which they estimated at only five years at best. More than anyone else, Larry had made it possible for me to get through that incredible time of adjustment. As I learned to be the nurse and total support for Bill, Larry helped me iron out life's wrinkles; he'd cheer me up when the stress hit me hard.

When I found out Larry was gay I asked, How could he BE-TRAY us like this? How could he have been living ANOTHER LIFE that we knew nothing about? Had I been so busy with Bill's recovery that I had not looked for any signs? But then, why would I look for signs when everything appeared so normal?

Now I know that part of the reason for Larry's secrecy was that he was, as always, trying to be kind. In great pain himself, he wanted to spare us the pain of knowing what neither he nor we could understand.

All the time only feelings of anguish and betrayal flashed through my mind during that drive to the airport. But I also distinctly remember planning that I would somehow get through the weekend and then on Monday I would go about getting Larry's problem FIXED. After all, I thought, God and mothers can fix anything, and surely there was some kind of pill, injection, medication, or therapy that would FIX MY KID. Nothing was impossible for God and mothers!

Already I was anticipating my confrontation with Larry. I would tell him that he must either "turn or burn." Then he would recite 1 John 1:9 and it would all be over. He would STOP whatever he was doing and he would be cleansed. This terrible thing would be out of our lives and we could fit the pieces back together.

No, there was nothing that could not be FIXED, and certainly my confrontation with Larry would do just that, fix it, and this horrible nightmare would be over with, ONCE AND FOR ALL!

But while I tried to reassure myself about being able to fix Larry, I also thought about Scripture verses that talk about a "reprobate mind." Was a reprobate mind something you could have and then lose later? Did Larry have a reprobate mind because of the materials I had found in his room? What exactly WAS a reprobate mind?

Surely all the filth in my trunk could not be a part of the boy I loved so much. Who was this person who had this dark side in his life that had never surfaced before? Did God love him and forgive him? Could I love him and forgive him? Could things ever be the SAME again?

Parents of Gay Kids Can Get a Bit Confused

My questions piled up, one upon another. As I look back on that incredible day in 1975, I can see that panic, pain, and anxiety were mixed with ignorance, misunderstanding, and naiveté.

In 1975 I didn't know anyone who had a homosexual in the family, much less a homosexual child. It was such an UN-NATURAL thing! To run off with a girl would have been sinful, but at least that was a natural type of sin. This was abnormal—because it was something I knew nothing about.

That was 1975. Today I hardly know anyone who DOESN'T have a homosexual somewhere in the family. Since starting

Spatula Ministries, I have gotten letters that show I'm not the first mother who thought her child could "just be fixed" somewhere. For example, one parent wrote:

> My daughter has just become a lesbian and she is in college. She has three weeks' vacation at Christmas and we wondered if she came to California during her school break if you could fix her up before school starts so she won't have to miss any school over this?

Since Spatula Ministries was begun more than fourteen years ago, I've been asked just about every kind of question by parents of gay children. Often they write or call while they are still coping with the initial shock of learning about their child. My own experience helps me sympathize when they sound a little confused and upset, and when they get words wrong and concepts twisted. Following are some excerpts from ACTUAL letters that have come in the mail, including one letter that began: "Dear Spatula MISERIES."

☐ ☐ ☐

> I found out my son is a homosexual. He keeps asking why we are treating him like a leopard. What does he mean? We have not even seen him for several weeks. What does he think we are doing . . . operating a zoo?

☐ ☐ ☐

> Ever since we learned our daughter was a homosexual my husband has been impudent. What should I do for his impudence?

☐ ☐ ☐

> My daughter wrote some letters to a friend and talks about being a lesbian. Isn't Lebanese what Danny Thomas is? What does that have to do with girls writing love letters to each other?

☐   ☐   ☐

My husband told me that he is a homosectional. Where can he get help for sectionals?

☐   ☐   ☐

I have tried for many months to know why my son could possibly be a homosexual. I finally realized that out of the five children he was the one I didn't breast feed. I am glad I have the answer now because this has disturbed me so much trying to figure out the cause of his problem.

Parents Ask the Hard Questions

Recently a lady wrote to tell me: "I read that sweating will keep boys from getting involved in homosexuality!" If only her information were correct, but I'm afraid sweat glands don't have a whole lot to do with it! Not only does my mail show me there is a lot of confusion about homosexuality, there is also a lot of real agony among parents who desperately want to know the answers to very real and tough questions. In the rest of this chapter, I want to deal with some of their most frequent queries:

My husband and I were actively involved with our son when he was young and spent much time with him. He has always seemed so happy and well-adjusted. He was involved in Boy Scouts and 4-H (all masculine activities). How can he be gay?

This is quite possibly the most frequent question I receive. I often hear from parents who say their children accepted Christ when they were young and that they regularly attended a Bible-believing church as they grew up. They even went to a Bible college, yet these children turn out to be homosexuals. In fact, they often have their first homosexual experience at a Bible college! Parents ask this question in dozens of ways: "We tried to do everything right. We tried to bring our children up in the nurture and admonition of the Lord. So what went wrong and what can we do for our child now?"

As for "what went wrong?" no one is totally sure. Some say homosexuality is all the result of choice, but in all of my counseling experiences, I have never met a homosexual who *chose* his orientation (nor, for that matter, do I know any heterosexuals who have chosen their orientation). Recent studies indicate that sexual orientation probably has a genetic component. But even among those who believe that environmental factors are involved, most are quick to point out that such influences occur long before a child is old enough to "choose" such a thing.

I have talked with and read the opinions of a dozen or more Christian psychologists, psychotherapists, and counselors, and *none* of them agree on the cause of homosexuality. At this point, it is safe to say that no one can explain it completely. It may be that a multiplicity of reasons contribute to being homosexual. I've been learning about this for fifteen years and I still have more questions than answers. But I do know this: We are all living in a fallen world. *Nothing is ideal or perfect.*

GOD CALLS US TO BE FAITHFUL;
HE DID NOT PROMISE WE WOULD BE SUCCESSFUL.

I tell parents: You tried your best to be the parents God wanted you to be. Keep in mind that God was Adam's parent, and look what a mess he turned out to be! So who are you to expect you can do better than God? Just love your children, and believe that the reservoirs of Scripture and training they have will prompt them to get their hearts right with God. Pray that their decisions and choices of behavior will eventually be regulated by their commitment to the Lord, and trust that the Lord knows more than you do about the hard places in their lives.

As parents, our prayers should be that our kids will stand clean before the Lord. If they have a good biblical marriage, that is fine. If they remain unmarried, that is fine also. To be celibate is a lonely life, but there is a gift of celibacy. No one seems to want it, but it is a gift. The main point, however, is that parents cannot blame themselves for the actions of their children. Whatever choices your kids make, they must answer to God, not you.

□ □ □

How should we react to our son's announcement that he is gay? Doesn't the Bible teach that we should withdraw ourselves from anyone who is deliberately sinning?

There are verses that say we should not keep company with brethren who are indulging in sinful behavior (see 1 Cor. 5:11 and 2 Thess. 3:6) and I appreciate what those verses have to say in a corporate church-body setting, but I don't think they necessarily apply to family relationships. More to the point, I don't think we can pull a verse out here and there and hang all of our theology on that. The flow of God's message is God's redemptive love for all of us.

As for how these parents should respond to their son, I would suggest they consider some important factors. First, if the son is under eighteen, I do not ever advise turning him out on his own. Sending a teenager out on his own only throws him into the arms of the promiscuous lifestyle. I draw the line, though, at eighteen. If the son is older than eighteen and is practicing a promiscuous lifestyle rebelliously and with no concern for parents' feelings, then my advice about the best way to respond is this: Do what will be the MOST COMFORTABLE FOR YOU. Perhaps this would not be total "unconditional" love, but you cannot let the behavior of one person destroy your entire family. Tell your son you love him and will pray for him, but that to preserve your own sanity, you prefer not to be faced with this in your home.

Then help your son get settled in another place and show thoughtfulness by helping him stock the refrigerator with food and get other necessary items such as facial tissue, soap, bathroom tissue—*anything that reminds him of your unconditional love for him.* Many parents may feel their child is not worthy of their love, but then who *is* worthy of unconditional love?

Be aware that condemnation will not bring about any change in your son's lifestyle. It is only conviction from God that can cause a shift of behavior in ANY of us. Only God can take a heart of stone and make it a heart of flesh (see Ezek. 11:19).

□ □ □

Our homosexual son says he is the happiest he has ever been. How can he be so happy when he has been taught that this lifestyle is so wrong?

It seems that many children, boys in particular, go through a great deal of anguish as they grow up having emotions they feel are not right. They are so afraid someone will find out, and many of them struggle for years trying to live two sides of the coin. Then, when they are discovered or when they reveal that they have a homosexual orientation, they are RELIEVED because now they can be out in the open and not have to hide their struggle any more.

As for their being happy, that is hard to say. All I know is I have never met a Christian homosexual, man or woman, who told me he or she would *choose* to be gay. The complicated array of factors that contribute to homosexual feelings are so complex and interwoven that they cannot be explained in a few paragraphs. Many whole books try to explain them and fail to come up with conclusive answers.

As I was finishing this book, I noticed that for two days Ann Landers had devoted her column to the question, "Are you glad you are gay, or would you rather be straight?" According to Ann, responses came in thirty-to-one saying, "Yes, I'm glad I'm gay." But I repeat, in more than fifteen years of working with homosexuals of all ages, I have never met a homosexual Christian who said, "I'm glad I'm gay."

Ann Landers ran several letters from gays, some of which said they were glad about their orientation; but others said things like this: "Am I glad I'm gay? You've got to be crazy. I've been beaten up, spat on and discriminated against in the job market. Who would choose THIS?"

Another homosexual wrote Ann to say, "Am I glad I'm gay? My response is an unqualified *yes*. It's thrilling to know that there are people out there who would happily kill me because of my sexual orientation. I am delighted that the government discriminates against me at tax time when I can't file jointly. I'm ecstatic that I'm barred from serving my country in time of war. I'm overjoyed that all major religions reject my lifestyle. I love it that I could lose my job if the truth were known. Best of all, it's great to be viewed as an outcast by one's own family. This is what it means to be gay."[1]

Unfortunately, this gay person's letter, filled with bitter sarcasm, is all too true. Sometimes the persecution can be even worse for a Christian homosexual. A gay son may tell his parents he is "happy," but deep inside he is usually lonely and afraid. It is our job to love our children and to provide all the comfort we can as we assure them God still loves them. Christ's loving sacrifice has provided a way for all of us to be forgiven and accepted by the Lord.

□ □ □

Should I tell any of my friends that my child is gay?

Each family's situation is different, but a key principle is not to let your child muzzle you so you have to bear all the pain yourself while the child goes off blissfully to pursue his lifestyle. In a sense, when this happens the child has dumped all his pain on you. He has come OUT of the closet and put you IN!

In most cases, it is wise to tell the rest of the IMMEDIATE FAMILY what is happening. Tell them why you are hurting and what you are going through at this time. Otherwise, people may think you have cancer or you're getting a divorce because your emotions are in such obvious upheaval.

In referring to the "immediate family," I do not usually include grandparents. Telling grandparents is not always helpful because they may be much too old for this kind of shock. A lot would depend on their emotional strength and resiliency.

But the immediate family can bind together to pray for the loved one who has gone into this lifestyle and, above all, to show unconditional love toward him. If they are together in this, they will be more united and caring for each other than ever before.

If your homosexual child has instructed you not to tell anyone, tell your child that you need support too. After all, he has his own support system out there in the gay community and you need one also.

Obviously, you shouldn't advertise for support. It isn't wise to put an item in the church bulletin for prayer, for example. But you can select a few close friends you can trust. Most parents are usually able to find one or two other couples with whom they can open up and be honest about their feelings.

Also, it is best to tell your boss at work so that he understands why you may not be acting like your old self. Let the boss know you are going through a grief process that is every bit as real as the grief you would feel if your child had died.

The overall principle is to BE SELECTIVE and tell only those who you think will be supportive. Keep Ecclesiastes 4:10 in mind: "If one falls down, his friend can help him up. But pity the man who falls and has no one to help him up!" (NIV).

You are in for a long haul and you need to share your problem with a few who can encourage you spiritually. They may not know a lot about homosexuality. They may not have ever experienced this kind of thing themselves, but if they are compassionate people, they can give you a great deal of emotional nurturing.

The bottom line is this: *Do whatever it takes to make yourself more comfortable. Think of yourself, not specifically of what will help your child.* This may sound selfish, but I emphasize it for a good reason. You need all the support you can get right now. Your child will do his thing and leave you to pick up the pieces. Just be sure you don't fall apart as well. Do whatever will help you get your priorities in order to keep your home together.

PAMPER yourself during this time. There's a big knife stuck in your heart and you must do what you can to keep it from twisting and causing even more pain. Be selfish because you are the wounded one now. Anything you can do to help yourself, any way you can bring some comfort to yourself, is okay. You can reach out to help your child later, but right now you need warm support around you, SOME SUPPORT WITH SKIN ON. When you're going through a difficult time, you need a little pampering. But most of all, you need HOPE.

I treasure the following letter I received from Dr. Wells, the psychologist who counseled me through my first year of agony after learning about Larry. Several years after I got Spatula Ministries going, I sent Dr. Wells one of my books and some of the other materials I had developed for parents, and he wrote back and said:

> Your ministry seems clearly for parents of homosexuals. It encourages them to survive their losses. . . . For your parents of homosexuals, their hope is for recovery from their pain, even though their chief hope may be healing for their loved ones. Keep instilling hope. They are motivated. They will benefit from your service.
>
> Don't expect the unmotivated to receive help. . . . Where there is no control there is no responsibility.

In these few words from Dr. Wells is a great deal of wisdom, but not all of his advice is easy to hear. Letting go of your gay child is the hardest part. When you see your child taking a detour in life that is leading him toward what you see as a cliff, it is so difficult not to want to intervene and stop him. But here is where you have to depend on the values that you have built into your child. You love your kid enough to put him in God's hands while you get on with your own life.

Whatever you do, don't let your child's behavior put you in the Home for the Bewildered, wringing your hands and saying, "What have I done?" Realize that you have done your best and then move on with your life. Have faith that you WILL GET THROUGH THIS. He or she is your child whom you love unconditionally, whatever he or she is doing. This child is in need of your love right now—and always.

☐   ☐   ☐

The parents of our son's "friend" are very accepting of the gay lifestyle. Our son resents the fact that we cannot condone how he is living. We want him to continue to visit us, so what should we do?

What the parents of your son's friend do is their decision; they will live according to their values. The first thing to understand is that there is a big difference between accepting your gay son and his friend as persons who need your love, and accepting the gay lifestyle. Your son probably is involved with a young person similar to himself. Your best approach is to show God's love to both of them.

Perhaps you will be more comfortable at first if you meet with your son and his friend at a neutral place for lunch. But it will be even better when he can bring his friend to your home. The warm memories of home can help in the healing of your relationship with your son—much more so than the impersonal atmosphere in a restaurant.

Sometimes you have to weigh which alternative is most painful and try to do the less devastating thing. The estrangement of not seeing your son can be far more painful than accepting him *no matter what his situation is.* Neither choice offers a smooth road; we just have to decide for ourselves which one we can live with the easiest.

From fifteen years' experience, I have learned that parents who do have their child come home, even with his friend, get through all this the best. Your son's friend is probably a very nice person, just as your son is. What would Jesus do? I believe He would show unconditional love in this situation.

My friend, Anita, tells of having her gay son call and ask if he could drop by for the weekend. When she said, "Yes, of course," he dropped his little bombshell and let her know "WE'LL be by around six for dinner." Her son had never brought his friend home for dinner and at first Anita was not prepared for their first face-to-face meeting. Thoughts of her son in bed with this man kept popping into her mind, but then she somehow found the strength to see this young man in a different light. She writes:

Some of my anger faded away; afterward, as I reviewed our conversation, I realized that I had handled it well, something I could not have done without the Lord's healing in my life. As years have passed, I have been able to leave my son in the hands of God. This gives me the peace that I need. I still have difficult times, but I am learning and growing.[2]

☐ ☐ ☐

My gay daughter wants to come home for a few days this Christmas and bring her girlfriend with her. I can't stand to see them together. Should I allow them to share the same room? Should I make them sleep in separate rooms, or should I simply forbid them to come at all?

First, I believe you should open your home to your daughter and, yes, to her girlfriend as well. Do all you can to keep the communication channels OPEN. Reassure your daughter of your love and care. God is in charge of her and has not negated her because of her actions. Think of your daughter as needing love and direction. Your love is imperative to her right now while she is struggling with her identity crisis.

While I have never had to face the issue of having a child bring home a homosexual friend for the holidays, my own policy would be "Sleep in separate rooms." Tell your daughter that, while you love her with all your heart, you simply cannot accept the idea of her and her friend sleeping together under your roof. Tell her that while you love her very much, you do not condone her lifestyle and that you hope she understands how you feel. If she brought home a boyfriend you would still not put them in the same room either!

If your daughter decides to bring her friend for the holidays and stay in your home according to your conditions, trust God for strength when they walk in together. I believe He will give you the strength to love them both as people who need care, not condemnation.

☐ ☐ ☐

What can I say when I am face to face with my son's "friend"?

Make friendly conversation, just as you would with any other person in your home. Reach out in Christian love to the friend as well as to your own son. Make your home a loving place and they will be comfortable with you. What would you have to gain by making them feel uncomfortable? This would change nothing.

Most parents tell me they like their son's (or daughter's) friend and have no difficulty showing hospitality once they get to know this person.

□ □ □

Our daughter wanted to have a party for her friends on the women's volleyball team at her college. We let her go ahead but then we were horrified to discover that the whole group is lesbian. My husband nearly had a heart attack when he was told that his daughter was one of them. Where can I get help for my daughter? Is it right that this is allowed in a state college?

First, get help for yourself and do not worry about your daughter right now. Remember what my counselor, Dr. Wells, advised in the letter quoted earlier: Don't expect the unmotivated to want help. The kind of help that's needed right now is for your husband and yourself. You cannot take your daughter someplace and get her FIXED. It is you who are bleeding inside, so get the help you need. Your daughter will do her thing and, until she wants some counsel, you are helpless to provide it for her.

As for what happens in a state college, there is nothing you can do about that. There are even Christian colleges where these kinds of relationships go on. For years we Christians have tried to sweep all of this under the rug, but now the rug has become so lumpy we have to deal with it. Be aware that you are going through a shock experience, *but you will get through it.*

□ □ □

*We have learned that our son is homosexual and we are just
sick. We have other, younger, children in the home. How can
we keep this from them, or should we tell them?*

In our experience we have found that it is best if the whole
family is involved in getting through this. If children are very
small they will not be able to understand, but any child older
than seven or eight can comprehend when something is definitely wrong at home and they wonder what it could be.

If possible, get the whole family together to share what is
happening. Let the younger children know you are going
through a difficult time and that their older brother or sister is
hurting just as much as the family is hurting. Nonetheless, *you
will all still love him.* He is still part of the family. This is a time
when the family must bind together because the healing process will be a long haul.

□ □ □

*I know the Bible has many verses that can comfort hurting
people, but what does it have to say to the parents of a homosexual? Please give me something I can cling to right now.*

The Bible is RICH with verses to encourage hurting people,
whether they have a homosexual child, a dead child, or a wan-
dering mate. There aren't any "special" verses for parents of
homosexuals. The best approach I know of is to get out your
Bible and go through it to find verses that have a personal
meaning for you, verses you can adapt to your own situation.

Look up subjects such as pain, disappointment, anxiety, and
comfort in a concordance. You will find dozens of verses that
you can cling to and, best of all, finding them yourself will be
like finding buried treasure. The Word of God is rich with treasure, but it all lies in the eyes of the beholder. You need verses
that are meaningful to you and that fit your problem. Finding
them yourself will bring you through your despair faster than
having to just absorb what someone else has already mined
from the rich veins of God's Word.

For example, just to give you a start, here are references of verses on comfort from the Thompson Chain Reference Bible:

Psalm 35:5; 42:5; 103:13; 119:50; 138:7

Isaiah 46:4; 61:3; 63:9

Matthew 5:5

John 14:1

Romans 8:28

1 Thessalonians 3:7; 4:13

So get busy and make this a real project for yourself. When you find verses that are real treasures for you, memorize them. Or write them out on small cards and carry them with you. Also, try sticking verses on your bathroom mirror, or paste them on household products that you use often—such as your bottle of Joy or box of Cheer. In countless ways, you can make these verses a part of yourself. Soon you will begin to feel your anxiety lifting and God's peace descending on your heart.

Let God's Word speak to you. Write His Word on your heart, remembering that it not only helps you not to sin against Him, but it also brings light, and light is what *you* need right now. Get going and find that light! Then you can start to dispense it to others who are groping in the darkness.

□ □ □

I read in one of your books that I should show unconditional love toward my homosexual child. How can I do that when the Bible itself puts conditions on what we do with our lives?

The Bible does put conditions on our actions, but God never puts conditions on His love for us. There is a BIG difference. While I talk a lot about unconditional love, I'm well aware that for human beings to achieve TOTALLY unconditional love is impossible. But isn't that what being a parent is all about— attempting the impossible? Herbert Vander Lugt puts it this way:

I know it's hard to show unconditional love when a son or daughter keeps hurting you and making you feel ashamed. But if you are a Christian, you have the responsibility to keep on loving them. And you can, through the power of the indwelling Holy Spirit. It will help to keep these two facts in mind: (1) We human beings are highly complex creatures—so complicated that we cannot understand everything about ourselves, let alone others. (2) All of us, the respectable as well as the wayward, are in continual need of God's grace and mercy.

When dealing with a person who is rebelling against you and God, remember this: We are all alike in that we are complex creatures. We aren't just animals; we're moral beings in God's image. We possess a conscience, but we have been flawed by sin. We live in a universe that is both beautiful and ugly. The beauty reflects God's goodness, and the ugly demonstrates the reality of sin and the curse.

Moreover, we often have ambivalent attitudes. Sometimes we want to fulfill our lower desires, and at other times we long to be better. We often do things we hadn't intended to do. Time and time again we regret something we did or said—even after we become Christians! How true in our experience are the words of Paul, "I have the desire to do what is good, but I cannot carry it out. For what I do is not the good I want to do; no, the evil I do not want to do— this I keep on doing. . . . What a wretched man I am!" (Rom. 7:18, 19, 24 NIV)[3]

Over the years, we have talked with hundreds of parents who are devastated by homosexuality in their families. Each situation varies, depending on background, economics, and family relationships. But there is always one common denominator: *Showing unconditional love toward the gay child accelerates healing of the relationship.*

Unconditional love is the anchor that every gay child needs for the stormy journey. When he knows his parents love him, it tells him God has not negated him either, but that God loves him wherever he is on the path. It is a long journey to wholeness, for both the parents and the child, so remember:

UNCONDITIONAL LOVE IS LOVING
WITHOUT CONDITIONS.

Behind the question about the "conditions" the Bible puts on our lives is another question that desperately needs clarifying, particularly in the Christian community:

Is homosexuality a sin?

At first glance, many Christians would say, "Of course it is." But others would say, "Homosexual behavior is a sin, but not homosexual orientation." Stephen Arterburn, founder and director of New Life Treatment Centers, puts it this way:

> When you're talking about this, please never use the word "homosexuality" as sin, use the word "homosexual behavior." It's a very small thing, but if you want to have any kind of hope of dealing with people, I think you have to make that distinction between the two. . . .
> Homosexuality is a definite preferential attraction, it's an erotic attraction to members of the same sex. Whether a person acts on that attraction is the key issue, I believe, in the eyes of God. . . .
> I believe that a person who is experiencing the homosexual lifestyle, if they want to, can establish a life and a lifestyle outside of homosexuality that is very satisfying and enriching. In fact, many, although not all, can go on and have heterosexual relationships that are quite satisfying and get married.[4]

I'm just glad that I don't have to be the judge when it comes to understanding homosexuality. I don't think condemnation solves this problem. Only conviction from God can change any of our hearts. We can't just pull a few verses out here and quote them to that person; it has to be redemptive love that rescues any of us from the choices we make.

Choosing Your Response to "I'm Gay"

When your favorite "who" becomes a "what" you must choose how you will respond. There are two basic approaches:

1. The *wrong* approach is to banish your child from the family. Have nothing to do with him at all. Forbid him to ever visit your home, and let him know he's certainly not free to bring along any friends if he ever is allowed to come.

2. The *right* approach is to love your child unconditionally. Let him know he and his friend are welcome in your home under certain conditions and that, while you do not approve of his lifestyle, your love for him will never change or fade.

Over the years I have received many letters from parents at every stage of their journey through the nightmare of learning their child is homosexual. Some are ready to commit suicide, and others are full of hate, homophobia, and righteous wrath, quoting biblical proof texts about not having anything to do with sinners.

Other letters plead for help, wanting to know what to do and how to do it. And then there are letters from parents who have struggled with the shock, shame, and guilt but now understand. They have adapted to the situation and they have HOPE.

As one father described this hope he said "it's not hope that my son will change, but hope that grows from a confidence in what we've always experienced in our lives when we thought we knew what was best for us . . . the knowledge that God has a better idea."

This father's letter went on to tell how he and his wife had survived, not with a magic cure-all, but with several key means of support. At Spatula support group meetings they had the opportunity to pour out their hearts in a nonthreatening, nonjudgmental atmosphere. They learned they would survive, and they did!

In addition to their support group, they found many members of their immediate family who were comforting and understanding of the situation, so they didn't have to live a secret life. One of their biggest milestones came when they stopped focusing on straightening out their child and acknowledged that that was God's business. The father's letter continued:

This is not to say we exulted in his circumstances. Rather, we reminded ourselves that God loved us unconditionally and He would have that be a model of our love toward our children.

This was a major factor in the restoration of our relationship to our son. When he recognized that we were not preoccupied with straightening him out, he was able to let down his defenses and freely express his love toward us. Also it allowed him to freely share his hurts and fears with us . . . and for us to be a comfort to him. (It's funny how our stereotypes imagine a person totally given to sexual expression. The reality is that the fears and hurts of the homosexual are generally those that we ourselves experience. The burden of their homosexuality does, however, I believe, heighten their pain in relationship to what others might experience.)

Another insight came to us as we weighed the advice of well-meaning friends that we should distance ourselves from our child; that was the importance of a healthy parent-child relationship in the restoration of the child and the parent (yes, both need to be restored!). Never does a child need the love and security of his parents more than when in the throes of dealing with his homosexuality. Even a casual knowledge of the homosexual issue shows the vulnerability of the homosexual to the drug scene and suicide. What a terrible time to abandon your child, right at the time when he needs you most!

We still hurt, but less often than before. We are still afraid, but rarely. We are not naive. We know there will be pain down the road. But the good news is that God is in control (wasn't He always?). We have a deeper, more loving relationship with our child than before. We have new friends that we never had before, friends who love us with the full knowledge of our circumstances. We know the fulfillment that comes from reaching out to others with empathy and helping them get through a tough time. We look forward with anticipation to what God's plan is in our lives . . . ahead to how He will take this low point in our lives and turn it to blessings. We've moved from "Why me, Lord?" to "Thank You, Lord!"

"I Didn't Choose to Be This Way!"

The wife of a pastor who had served his denomination for well over a quarter of a century wrote an anonymous article in her denominational paper, telling of the shock she and her husband felt when they received a letter from their son saying he had struggled with homosexual feelings since the age of twelve. The letter came just two months before his graduation from a Christian college. There were long telephone calls, crying, and angry shouting, but not many answers. During one of their talks with their son, the mother asked him if he knew how much he had hurt them. His answer cut deep into her heart: "Do you know how much I've hurt all these years? I didn't choose to be this way."

From that moment, this mother—and dad—devoted themselves to unconditionally loving their son. They joined our Spatula support group and shared their story to let fellow Christians know how badly homosexuals need the right kind of love. In her article, this mother wrote:

> The homosexually oriented person needs more of the very thing we too often go out of our way to deny them. We must love as Jesus loves—unconditionally. This does not mean we endorse the homosexual lifestyle. . . .
>
> The second reason for opening my heart is to let other parents know that you can survive and find support in other Christian parents who hurt because of a child who is convinced he is gay.
>
> Were it not for us finding other parents who were willing to share their own journey, we would have died. They helped us to get beyond the searching for a reason for this happening to us (blaming ourselves proved to be a dead-end street) to asking how we could now become a part of a solution. We found that there is something we can do for our adult child— we can love him. In fact, that is really all we can do—but we must not fail to do it. Our motto has become: "FROM THIS MOMENT ON . . . LOVE!"[5]

From these parents, who both write of a journey that has brought them from despair to new levels of understanding, come two key pieces of advice for what to do when your favorite "who" has become a "what."

As the father quoted above said, acknowledge that God is in control. Pray that He will help you stop asking, "Why me, Lord?" and help you become able to start saying, "Thank You, Lord!"

And as the mom says, when it's all said and done, when all the opinions have been uttered, preached, shouted, and shared, there is only one thing we can do:

FROM THIS MOMENT ON . . . LOVE!

I think in closing this chapter the most helpful sentence I could share is what my son Larry said when he was interviewed recently on "Focus on the Family." It blankets the whole, wide area of how we can seek wisdom on this:

> If we as Christians can purpose in our hearts to be kind and loving in all that we do, put away a condemning spirit, and learn the fear of the Lord, then surely the light of Christ will be able to shine in our disbelieving world and restoration and revival will take root in the lives of those we touch on a daily basis.

Gloomee Busters

DON'T WORRY ABOUT THE WORLD ENDING TODAY
IT'S ALREADY TOMORROW IN AUSTRALIA.

□ □ □

You can't go back
and unscramble the eggs.

□ □ □

I CAN NO LONGER FACE LIFE
SO I HAVE DECIDED
TO GO THROUGH THE REST OF IT BACKWARDS.[6]

□ □ □

If my life resembles a garbage dump
it is up to me to sort it through,
turn over the soil, and plant flowers
to make use of all the natural fertilizer.

☐ ☐ ☐

DON'T LET YOURSELF SUFFER NEEDLESSLY—
FIND A NEED TO SUFFER.[7]

☐ ☐ ☐

BE STILL AND KNOW THAT I AM GOD.
Be still, MY MUSCLES, and know God's RELAXATION.
Be still, MY NERVES, and know God's REST.
Be still, MY HEART, and know God's QUIETNESS.
Be still, MY BODY, and know God's RENEWAL.
Be still, MY MIND, and know God's PEACE.

—See Psalm 46:10

☐ ☐ ☐

Psalm 1

No matter where I am blown or pushed,
    I will flourish!
Those with less strength would wilt and die
    on the soil on which I now stand.
But because I DO love the Lord,
    I WILL SURVIVE AND IMPROVE!

Others might expect me to wither,
    But God expects me to bloom.
I will show them how tough I am—
    I will bloom—IN AND OUT OF SEASON.

—Source unknown

☐ ☐ ☐

SELF-CONTROL INCLUDES MOUTH CONTROL.

☐ ☐ ☐

Wayfarers

There is no permanent calamity
For any child of God;
Way stations all, at which we briefly stop
Upon our homeward road.

Our pain and grief are only travel stains
Which shall be wiped away,
Within the blessed warmth and light of home,
By God's own hand some day.
                    —Martha Snell Nicholson

☐ ☐ ☐

Earth has no sorrow that heaven cannot heal.
            —from the hymn "Come Ye Disconsolate"

☐ ☐ ☐

JESUS

Whatever the question, He is the Answer.
John 14:6
Whatever the problem, He is the Solution.
Matthew 11:28, 29
Whatever the hurt, He is the Healer.
Luke 4:18
Whatever the bondage, He is the Liberator.
John 8:32
Whatever the burden, He is the Overcomer.
John 16:33
Whatever the need, He is the Supplier.
Matthew 7:7, 8
Whatever the sin, He is the Forgiver.
Psalm 103:2, 3

5

Life Is a Sexually Transmitted, Terminal Disease

Someone Jesus loves has AIDS[1]

AIDS.

Its frightening toll grows steadily until it looms on all our horizons like the scriptural pale horse whose rider, DEATH, is given the power to kill a fourth of the earth's population (or more).[2]

To give you an idea of how fast the plague of AIDS is spreading, realize that the first cases of AIDS in the United States were identified in 1981. AIDS occurred only as a trickle at first, but the total number of cases soon became a steady stream, exceeding 100,000 by July 1989.

Then, by late 1991—*just twenty-eight months later*—the stream became a torrent as 100,000 more victims learned they, too, had the terminal virus. Every year the death toll rises. In 1991 it reached 32,430.[3] A mother of four children, who has many family problems of her own, wrote to tell me she is well acquainted with the AIDS death toll. To her, it is more than just a number in the newspaper:

> I am an apartment manager of forty-eight units, 75 percent of which are occupied by gay tenants. I get along with people very well, but it breaks my heart to see this lifestyle, especially since I lost five tenants in the last year to AIDS. All I can do is pray for them and share with them my testimony of the Lord and how He has gotten me through my "tunnels."

AIDS is a particularly dangerous disease for homosexuals, but as almost everyone knows by now, AIDS plays no favorites. During that same twenty-eight-month period when AIDS cases reported in the U.S. doubled from 100,000 to 200,000, the number of people who contracted AIDS *heterosexually* increased 153 percent.[4] Among these cases was Magic Johnson, NBA superstar, who announced in November 1991 that he was HIV positive. Through numerous sexual contacts with different women, he had contracted the first stages of AIDS and now, even for one of the greatest athletes the world has ever seen, it is simply a matter of time.

If anything has changed the face of Spatula Ministries, it has been AIDS. I dealt with my first cases of AIDS in the early 1980s. There were just a few then, but now, like the national figures, my Spatula cases have skyrocketed also. What can be said to the sufferers of AIDS or to their parents? In many situations, parents have been plunged so deep into shock or rejection of their child they refuse to talk to a dying son or daughter. So I go instead and may find myself at 2 A.M., following a Spatula support-group meeting, helping a gaunt, hollow-eyed young man plan his funeral.

You may be thinking *how morbid!* But that's not necessarily true. Some of the most thrilling examples of faith in Christ I've seen have come out of helping folks deal with this dreaded foe called AIDS—what some Christians believe is God's judgment on homosexuals.

The Letter from Andrew

One darling young man named Andrew contracted AIDS and started coming, along with his precious family, to several of our Spatula meetings at the Crystal Cathedral. There's a piano in the room where we meet, and Andrew's mom and dad are gospel singers, as are Andrew and his sister. On several occasions, we asked the whole family to sing, and what a blessing they have been to everyone. One of their most encouraging songs was, "He Giveth More Grace When the Burdens Grow Greater." This special family was going through its own parentheses of grief, yet they ministered to all of us.

Later, a letter came from Andrew. My heart was touched by it and I knew it would touch the hearts of others, so I included it in an issue of the *Love Line*. For a young man in his twenties to write such an inspirational letter while facing certain death was unusual, and I know his letter will touch your life as it did mine:

Dear Barbara,

Next to the love I have for my beautiful Savior, my family comes first in my life. I read your "Love Line" tonight and couldn't sleep. All of the encouragement in those pages seems to come straight from the heart of God.

As I read, I began to think like a parent (is that possible?) and about how much this ministry has done for my family. I thought the open wound caused by my venture into the homosexual lifestyle (ten years ago) would never heal.

I'm sure you have heard before that "God answers prayer, but not always how we expect Him to." My family can say "Amen" to that.

That open wound has been sewn with the glorious thread of God's love for His children. I can now sing—Jesus loves even me, and I know that He does! I am His child. I am not perfect; I still stumble; but . . . I am His, and He is mine!

With AIDS in the picture I know that a difficult time may still be before us. But I can't help think . . . I could still be out there drowning. Just far enough from the lighthouse that I couldn't be helped. Praise Jesus! I am safe in His arms, and if He desires to take me home—I desire to go! And for my family—as the song says, "To multiplied trials, His multiplied peace!"

Barbara, please pray that if the Lord desires to use me to touch lives, as He has with you—that I would not be blind to that opening door. (The Lord must be so used to my blindness, He may have to get someone to kick me through it.)

I love you so much, Barbara. God bless you richly in His work. You are in my prayers, as are the lives you are ministering to.

Love in Christ,
Andrew

Folks often ask:

Do victims of AIDS die lonely, bitter deaths with no hope at all?

I have many more letters and memories of late-night conversations that prove there is ALWAYS hope, even for the person with AIDS. In fact, AIDS victims almost always have an advantage spiritually. They know they don't have long and they quickly come to grips with who they are and what is going to happen.

Andrew's letter is a good example. It reflects the inner strength the Lord has given him as he faces the unknown. He wants to be used to touch other lives in whatever way God chooses while he is himself going through the deep waters. What a wonderful truth it is for us that EITHER way we are winners! If we are taken to be with Him we are OUT of all this pain and spend eternity with Jesus! If He chooses for us to stay here, we are building up treasures in heaven where nothing can corrupt. Without Jesus, we face a hopeless end. But with Him, we have an ENDLESS HOPE!

In the rest of this chapter, I want to share letters from AIDS victims as well as their parents. These letters show that, from the Christian perspective there is faith, hope, and love, but the greatest of these is always love—or maybe a better word is "compassion." AIDS has changed our lives forever and we must reach out to each other. As never before, we all realize we are marching relentlessly toward the grave. Truly, life IS a sexually transmitted, terminal disease.

Should the Prodigal Be Allowed to Come Home?

One of the typical situations I often hear about is the AIDS victim who wants to come home to his family, but one or both parents want nothing to do with him. Their question always revolves around:

Do we accept a child whose deliberately sinful lifestyle has caused him to get AIDS?

At Spatula we talk with many young men and women who have been estranged from their families after leaving home and getting involved in the gay lifestyle. Then, when AIDS rears its ugly head, their normal approach, like the prodigal son's, is to go home to be with the family, to reestablish the broken relationships. Typical of the letters we receive from parents facing this problem is the following:

My son, after seven years, wants a reconciliation because now he has AIDS. I have seen and talked with him; however, his father does not want him to come home. There's been no change in his life, only now he wants us to accept him and be with him as his time comes. That makes it all the harder for those who have learned you have only two choices: (1) accept them and allow them to continue to be a part of your life when you feel so strongly about their sin, or (2) separate from them. Neither one offers a choice you are happy with, that's for sure.

I understand the pain involved in a choice like this. But what is more normal than to want to COME HOME? "Ye, who are

DENNIS THE MENACE

" I **HAD** TO COME HOME. 1 NEED
SOMEBODY TO BE ON **MY** SIDE !"

weary, come home," isn't that the song we sing at church?
Should the AIDS victim be allowed to come home? The best
answer to this question is to ask yourself the question I mentioned in chapter 4:

WHAT WOULD JESUS DO?

Wouldn't He care for the sick and injured and the dying?
Wouldn't He bring healing and comfort to those in distress for
WHATEVER reason? Surely we are to love our kids no matter
what. What better way could there be to show genuine Christian love than by opening our hearts to the AIDS victim, to

bring him home, to care for him, making his last months as comfortable as possible? When AIDS devastates the family circle, it is time for everyone to come together to share in the pain. Out of that can come blessings far above anything we could ask or think.

When you have a dying son, you don't weigh the question of how he got that way, whether he chose his orientation, whether it was inherited or learned. You only know you have a son with very limited time to be with you. How vital it is to be sure that at some time he has accepted Christ as his Savior. Perhaps there has been no spiritual growth to this point, but *now* you have the opportunity to promote some spiritual growth in his life.

You will be his caretaker and caregiver and be able to provide all the warm, loving influences of the home. Perhaps you can enjoy Christian music or some videos together ; there are many other ways parents can influence a child. You have it all, but time is short. You can make up for the years he was estranged by concentrating on unconditional love right now.

Trust God to bring healing to his spirit, if not to his body. Then you will get comfort from the fact that you made his last days as comfortable as possible. And, like many parents I know, you may be able to say that your family will be restored one day in heaven. As someone has said:

CHRISTIANS NEVER SAY GOOD-BYE
FOR THE LAST TIME.

No matter what your child has done, you love and accept him where he is and give him all the loving care he needs. The rest is up to God.

Another question that I often hear, especially among Christians, is:

Is AIDS a judgment of God on homosexuals?

Unfortunately, some Christians, even some pastors and Christian leaders, have said as much. There is more than one story like the one shared by Harold Ivan Smith in an article written for *Charisma* magazine. He described how a weeping woman called a minister and asked him if he conducted funerals for people who were not members of his church. The minister said, yes, he did, but he wanted to know if she was a member of any church and had she contacted her own pastor? The woman said, yes, she had, but that her son had died with AIDS. "And what did your pastor say?" the minister wanted to know.

The woman's voice broke, "Not only would he not conduct the funeral, he also did not want anything to do with us and said it would be a good time for me to move my membership."[5] In that same article, Smith mentioned a report on AIDS by then-Surgeon General C. Everett Koop, who made it clear that AIDS is not a homosexual disease. It is contracted by people of all races, male and female, homosexual and heterosexual. In short, AIDS plays no favorites.

Writing in *Christianity Today*, Philip Yancey weighs different views about the possibility that God has sent AIDS as a specifically targeted punishment against a certain group of people. He points out that many Christians doubt this is so:

> They see a grave danger in playing God or even interpreting history in His behalf. We can too easily come across as cranky or smug, not prophetic. "Vengeance is mine," God said, and whenever we mortals try to appropriate His vengeance, we tread on dangerous ground. Among the gays in my neighborhood, Christians' statements about the AIDS crisis have done little to encourage repentance. Judgment without love makes enemies, not converts.[6]

Yancey goes on to ask some obvious questions of those who see an apparent cause-and-effect link to behavior and sexual preference:

> What of victims who are not gay, such as a baby born to a mother infected through a blood transfusion? Are they tokens of God's judgment? And if a cure is suddenly found, will that signify an end to God's judgment? Theologians in Europe

expostulated for four centuries about God's message in the Great Plague: But it only took a little rat poison to silence all those anguished questions.[7]

Right along with the above question comes another that ponders the eternal destiny of people who may die of AIDS, particularly homosexuals:

Is it possible for someone who has died of AIDS to go to heaven?

My answer is, "You bet!" It's just as possible for someone to die of AIDS and go to heaven as it is for someone to die of cancer, alcoholism, heart disease, or any other ailment and go to heaven.

One young woman wrote concerning her uncle who died of AIDS, which he got as a result of his gay lifestyle. Her question was:

Is it possible for my uncle to have been saved? He lived somewhat of a double life: Christian to our family but also a fairly wild gay lifestyle. I'm having a difficult time reconciling this in my mind, along with the guilt of not making an effort to confront him with the issue and witness to him. As far as I know, he never turned from the gay lifestyle, but died believing he was okay and that God accepted him just as he was.

Was this young woman's uncle saved? Perhaps I am beating the same drum, but God only knows. Everything depends on what he decided to do about Jesus Christ in his life. As I said in chapter 4, homosexual orientation is not a sin, but practicing homosexuality is. When this woman's uncle stands before God, the first question will not be, "Were you a homosexual?" The first question will be, "What did you do with my offer of salvation?"

Dealing with AIDS victims or their families when they don't believe anything is wrong with the homosexual lifestyle is a difficult issue. The question here seems to boil down to:

How can I show compassion without agreeing with the AIDS victim's homosexual lifestyle?

One letter came in from a social worker who works across the desk from a dear Christian friend whose ex-husband is dying from AIDS. She said:

> I've tried to be understanding and loving, but at the same time let her know where I stand. She has been able to completely forgive her husband, but she also totally accepts his lifestyle choice. She feels that he is a happier person because he has finally owned up to "what or who he is." Her children accept their dad's lover as their "uncle" or "our dad's special friend." Susan and her ex want the children to have a loving (normal?) relationship with their dad up until the end—which isn't far away because he's very sick. Susan and I work together all day, every day, and I want to be a comfort to her. Any advice you have, I'd appreciate.

So often we worry about letting people know where we stand—giving our Christian testimony—that we forget the real issue. No, his lifestyle is not God's best, but if she has accepted and forgiven her husband and accepts his lifestyle, then that is her way of dealing with it, and it is not up to us to criticize her for this. We all have various mechanisms for dealing with stress and, at this time, this is her way of dealing with the horror of AIDS.

Her ex-husband has AIDS, his time will be short, and it will soon be over. We would hope that she will care for him as a man who was her husband and is still the father of her children so that there will be no regrets when he is gone. The family needs all the support they can muster and being a friend to her is the best way of being a comfort. Facing death, whether by AIDS or any other horrible disease, is always difficult. Let the family do it in their own way without being critical of their method. Just get in there and show Christian love to her, as well as to those she loves in order to help her through this.

Many letters come from parents who have watched their son or daughter die an agonizing death from AIDS. Even if the stricken child accepts Christ (or comes back to the Lord), there still may be gnawing questions that linger for these parents:

How do I live with the regrets? How do I cope with the guilt? And what about the biggest question of all: WHY?

A letter came from a mother who watched for forty-three days as her son suffered an agonizing death from AIDS. He had been checked into the hospital for exploratory surgery, which revealed lymphoma all through his body. Later blood tests revealed the cause. Two days later he had respiratory failure and just before doctors put him on a breathing machine he told his parents he had AIDS. They never heard him speak another word because for the next forty-three days the breathing machine never stopped.

Two months before her son died, this mother had decided to give him to God and try to go on with her life as best she could. She wrote:

I told the Lord, "I give up, Father. Mitch is Yours. Do whatever You have to so he will come back to You and live for You the rest of his life." I had prayed for him for years and years but never like that.

Well, you see what happened! Yes, Mitch came back to the Lord on his death bed (and I am eternally thankful) but he sure didn't have any chance to live for God. I think the thing that probably hurts worse than any of it is that he could never talk to me. He was able to write a few things that are very precious to me, but most of it was clouded by the drugs he was given for pain.

One minute I rejoice that God took him home out of all that misery as quickly as He did, and then I swing around and scream, "WHY? God, you could have healed him. You could have allowed him to at least talk to me!"

The hurt, the pain, and feeling of being in a void plus a feeling that part of me is gone is still there but not as severe. But the questions are always in the back of my mind. I keep telling myself I did the best I could. It was a choice he made as an adult. Then I try to go on.

This mom is not only battling her grief, but irrational guilt as well (see chapter 3). She is letting this false guilt rob her of the joy of knowing that her son is with the Lord.

The first responsibility for any of us is to place our faith in God through His Son, Jesus, and then leave the rest up to Him. How He wants us to live for Him or how long is strictly God's business. If this mom and I could chat, I would say:

I know how it hurts that you couldn't talk to your boy in those final days as he struggled for life and breath. But there are many ways to communicate. Just knowing you were there, feeling the squeeze of your hand, told him how much you loved him. I always say that as parents we love our children BE-CAUSE, not ALTHOUGH. Our love for them doesn't change when we find they are rebelling against us or caught up in a sinful lifestyle that we cannot approve. In fact, the bond between us can be strengthened when we pour out our love to them. As we minister to them, our love for the Lord and for others grows even stronger.

Love is always the healing balm for all of us. Love covers everything, even the "Why?" I, too, have often asked God "Why?" *Why* did Steven have to be in that particular ambush? *Why* did Tim have to be on the same road with the drunk driver of the three-ton truck? But asking why is pointless and debilitating.

A better question (which is not easy to ask) is "To what end?" You are already headed in the right direction, and now you must ask, "To what end?" You say your pain is already lessening and it will continue to be more bearable as the days go by. Keep telling yourself you did the best you could. You are not responsible for your son's choices. This is the way out of the tunnel.

Testing HIV Positive Puts Everyone in Limbo

I get many letters from parents of adult children who have tested HIV positive. Now the sword of Damocles dangles over the family in earnest. It is only a matter of time until the dreaded diagnosis of AIDS will come. Parents, usually moms, write to share their shock, bewilderment, and fear:

> My son finally tested positive for the AIDS virus after refusing to consider it for years (he was healthy for five and a half years despite being HIV positive), and now I think maybe it was better we hid our heads. He's not at a stage of sharing much with me as yet—in fact, I feel like I'm on the receiving end of his anger. With a house full of company, foremost my mother, I've been putting on my happy face and praying for strength—for all of us.

□   □   □

> We've been absolutely shattered in the last two weeks, and being in a small, rural community, have no one to share our grief and sadness with because of obvious reasons. Our 35-year-old single son has tested HIV positive, and he admitted to us two weeks ago he was gay. He is the eldest of our three sons. He also has a severe blood disorder and either of his diseases will surely kill him sooner or later. . . . My middle son called and talked to me this week about working on a "positive" attitude. . . . Later I relayed all this to my husband and he said, "Well, we are positive all right. We are positive we are in one hell of a mess here!" Then, we had a laugh over that.
> We need help from somewhere. We both are normally very strong, but this is horrible.

□   □   □

> A friend of mine at work is homosexual and has AIDS. When he was young he gave his life to the Lord, but as a young man he turned to the gay lifestyle. A few months ago when he was ill, he learned that he had AIDS. He knew he was HIV positive, but figured it would be years before his T-cell count would go down. He was wrong. His mother, who lives in another state, does not know he is gay, let alone that he has AIDS. . . . My friend with AIDS does not have a lot of

friends at the moment and I have been the support person in his life—the person he can talk to. The friend he lived with for many years is expected to die because of AIDS in a few months, if not weeks.

When the HIV-positive verdict comes in, it is devastating for everyone, the victim as well as parents and friends. Now we wonder *Who can we tell? What do we do?*

First, we must realize that eventually the fact will be known and it is up to the person who is HIV positive to determine how much he wants known about his illness. So many things hang in the fire, such as insurance, job security, and other ramifications. The person who is afflicted must be the one to determine how much and WHO to tell.

For parents, this is a time to help alleviate uncertainties their stricken child may feel. Now is the time for unconditional love. You, the parents, along with your child, will be living for many months, perhaps years, in a sort of twilight zone. You will not know from day to day if "this is it." You never know what's coming or when—suffering, blindness, loss of memory, complete deterioration. Because you love your child, you want to smooth away as much pain as possible, giving him total support to assure him of your care throughout the entire ordeal.

The Role of Forgiveness

It is important that parents go through this thing together with their child. This is the time to resolve conflicts and mend relationships, to make up for any breaks that may have happened in the past.

Forgiveness plays such a big role . . . in fact, it may be the only real answer to accepting what is almost too painful to bear. Without forgiveness, there will be hardness of heart, and hard, brittle hearts break more easily. But God can turn the heart of stone into a heart of flesh (see Ezek. 11:19).

By caring for a dying person, *no matter why this person is sick,* we can best demonstrate Christian love. Perhaps physical healing will not occur, but spiritual and emotional healing can happen. A young man who was gay came to our Spatula meeting; he had just lost his companion to AIDS and he, himself, had just tested positive for HIV. This young man had no church background and commented, "I don't go to church and don't know anything about Christians except that they HATE homosexuals."

What a sad commentary—that we Christians should be known for our dislike or hatred of others, rather than for our love. Parents who care for a child with AIDS have an unusual burden to carry. They are not only losing their child, but they have a stigma attached to the family because of AIDS. Often they withdraw from the church and from their friends and become isolated and lonely. After all, having AIDS isn't something you put in your church bulletin.

Christians must open their lives to the hurts of others, and if we have any questions about how to react to the victim of AIDS, we only need repeat the question, "WHAT WOULD JESUS DO?" We know the answer, and it provides the best possible advice.

Fortunately, attitudes in the church and among Christians have been changing in recent days. I keep getting calls from people who want to know how to help. I like what was said in an editorial in the *Wesleyan Advocate* about how God's people can act toward the victim of AIDS:

1. The loved one must be committed to God.
2. God's help and guidance in prayer must be sought daily.
3. We must believe that healing can and will come—to one's mind and emotions, if not for the loved one and the disease.
4. Forgiveness must be asked of God and given to the sinful.
5. We must refuse to condemn, for Jesus did not and does not.
6. We must communicate hope at all times.

In brief, AIDS stands for

Aches   and Alienation,
Isolation and Incapacity,
Despair   and Death,
Suffering and Sadness.

The church has not always been at its best in the face of these new challenges. But I hope that can change as more and more frequently the opportunity will come to reach out to parents and other loved ones who suffer from the shock of these social and spiritual lapses among family members. The Christian's attitude must be characterized by

Acceptance of,
Interest in,
Dedication to, and
Support for the person who has fallen prey to one of sin's latest curses.

Condemnation, judgment, fear, and rejection will only make the afflicted one's plight worse. Comfort, empathy, faith, hope, love, and understanding will be welcomed by anyone who is going through such a valley of despair.[8]

AIDS Puts Faith to Its Ultimate Test

As I said in the opening of this chapter, not all the reports on AIDS are grim. I have received many letters from parents who are rejoicing because they have an endless hope; they don't just see a hopeless end. Here are just a few samples:

You see, as I shared with you last year, our beloved son was homosexual and also HIV positive since April 1990. I can now report that he has a resurrected body because in September 1991 he went home to be with our Lord. . . . For 16 days he lived on life-support systems, and he had dialysis five times. Twice we were told death was imminent, but he rallied each time. The doctors had told us we would have to unplug him. Praise God, we didn't have to do that as he just closed his eyes and went home to be with Jesus. . . .

☐ ☐ ☐

It's been about six years now since we found out our son was gay. . . . I knew I had found a friend in you, Barbara, and you <u>called</u> me. That boggled my mind. We learned to love our son unconditionally, no matter what. So we have, and I'm glad. We have a wonderful relationship with him. It has really paid off—UNCONDITIONAL LOVE.

I eventually met his friend and Jesus helped me get through that. We became good friends, long distance, and now he is dying of AIDS. He has gotten quite bad and will have to be placed in an AIDS home. I can't explain my feelings. I have cried so much over the past couple of days. Today I called him and <u>he</u> (my son's friend) <u>comforted me.</u> He is a wonderful, sensitive young man who was brought up in a dysfunctional home by an alcoholic.

I just wanted you to know how helpful you have been over these past years. Thank you for reaching out to those of us who struggle with our feelings.

□   □   □

By absolute determination, many prayers, and God's grace, my son lasted until February. . . . Finally, one night my son asked to go to the hospital as he was having great difficulty breathing. For the first time, other than for an accident, he went in an ambulance. I rode with him and was quite aware that this would be our last trip to the hospital. . . . I stayed with him in his room, camping out, so to speak, until the fourth morning when he went to be with his Savior.

A very precious friend who was both an R.N. and a minister said he had rarely seen anyone go with such peace and grace. He assured me that my prayers had been answered. If it had not been for that death sentence, it is most unlikely my son would have heeded anyone who spoke to him of our Lord. Hallelujah! He waits for me in heaven and we will see each other once again.

Doctor Ralph Osborne, who formerly served on the staff of Hollywood Presbyterian Church with Dr. Lloyd Ogilvie, is a good friend and supporter of Spatula Ministries. Recently he shared with me (and Spatula Ministries) a letter from a highly respected professional friend who had been diagnosed with AIDS, but who had a burning heart much like that of the disciples who saw the risen Lord on the way to Emmaus in Luke 24.

It says so well what it means to have an endless hope in the face of a hopeless end, as far as this world is concerned.

Ralph asked if I might write something of my experience with God and His purpose in my life and the reality of my faith in Him.

I had been a Christian since the age of eight, but did not come into a vital relationship with Him until a year and a half ago. I entered into that relationship because I was tired of hating myself and being angry at God. What I discovered was that He was there all along but I had kept Him at arm's length because I never felt I was good or worthy enough to be accepted by Him. He took me as I was, and that fact allowed me to let God love me and I was able to love myself. That started me on an exciting journey. I can best describe it as an encounter with the Living Christ. I had an intellectual knowledge of Him and His attributes but had not come into a real relationship with Him.

Several months after my journey with God began, my faith was put to its ultimate test. I found out that I have AIDS. My worst fear in life was realized. Everything that I had ever hoped or worked for, all my dreams came screeching right to a halt in front of my eyes. I asked myself, "What do I do with this?" It didn't take me long to realize I was out of my league on this one! So, I put my life in God's hands again and said, "I am powerless over this. Your will is all that I have." Now, I listen to my doctors, do what they say, and give it all to God.

To me, this situation is a baptism of fire. It is going through the worst hell of your life but in the midst of that hell is an indescribable sweet joy, for you know that He is there with you in the midst of it all. It is the Divine Presence of the Living Christ.

I am learning many things about life and God in dealing with AIDS. One is that none of us has any guarantee for tomorrow in terms of physical life or death. I have quit living in the past or in the future. I try to embrace each day as a gift from God and discover what joy I might find in my work and those people around me. Having a disease like AIDS brings you face to face with your fear of death. As Christians, we should all have to face this fear. It is ultimately a very freeing experience.

I tell you all this, not that you will believe that everything in the Christian walk is rosy and easy, but that in the midst of great sorrow He is there. Whether it be the loss of a child, parent, or any loved one; the betrayal of a spouse, the loss of all possessions or a job, even in facing your physical death, He is there in full love and power. I would not have chosen AIDS for myself, but having this disease has been a very profound experience in that it has taken me to a depth with God that I might not have reached otherwise. I count the cost and it is sufficient.

God bless all of you.

Time Makes a Difference

I have often said:

EVERYTHING—EVEN AIDS—COMES TO PASS, NOT TO STAY.

New proof of that came when I received a series of letters from a mom who, when her son was dying of AIDS, wrote to let me know that something I said in one of my books hadn't been that much help at all. A few months later she wrote back to explain that during the past year her husband had died of an aneurysm and her son had finally succumbed to AIDS as well. She did not feel that my story and hers had much in common because her story "did not have a happy ending." But a few months later she wrote again and said:

After losing my son to AIDS last June, I have developed a philosophy about AIDS:

I've learned to accept without agonizing or arguing . . . it happened.

I've learned to forgive without forgetting . . . I can never approve.

We who are "touched" by this dreadful disease suffer GREAT AND GRAVE risks when confiding in another human being. . . . Don't take the risk unless you (as well as the other person) can live with it.

There will be many who need support and understanding
. . . It is hard to find. This disease will touch us all in some way
or another. Keep your sense of reality when dealing with it.

I salute this mom. She is right. AIDS is touching us all, but at
the same time it is helping many of us touch one another in
ways we had never dreamed possible. Today I was making Bill
a sandwich for lunch and I started thinking that if we give
someone a piece of bread with butter, that's KINDNESS, but if
we put jelly or peanut butter on it, that is *LOVING* KINDNESS.
It reminded me that I always want to give to others and add
that gracious touch. How true this is of those who have AIDS.
Loving kindness is just what these kids need—that EXTRA
touch.

In his powerful personal story, *How Will I Tell My Mother?*
Jerry Arterburn shares what that extra touch was like for him
in the final days of his life:

> In April 1987 I once again came down with pneumonia. No
> one thought I could survive it. I was determined to live
> through it, however, and once again I made a miraculous
> recovery. At that point I began to work on this book, and my
> life became somewhat more secluded. . . . For a while I lived
> with Steve and his wife, Sandy, in Laguna Beach, California.
> Then I went to stay with Terry, who has four kids and a saint
> for a wife, Janette. It was beautiful in both locations. What an
> inspiration to watch the whales in Laguna or the waterfalls
> and greenery of Tennessee. God's world is so beautiful, and I
> had never before fully taken the time to notice.
> The Bible says God never sends us a problem we cannot
> handle with His power. It also says He will provide comfort.
> In both cases, the Scriptures have held true for me. I have
> grown close to a sweet and loving Jesus and understand that
> sickness and disease do not come from Him. Our God is there
> to help us fight the evil forces. I have peace and comfort like I
> have never felt before, even though I know AIDS continues to
> ravage my immune system. I pray each night for all who have
> been afflicted. I pray that God will comfort all of us and all
> our families. God is a good God and a perfect God.

For me, during these difficult times of struggle, as each day grows darker, a new dawn draws closer. That closeness to the God I love gives me a superhuman peace and sensitivity that keeps me filled with hope for a new and better day.

> Sing, O heavens!
> Be joyful, O earth!
> And break out in singing, O mountains!
> For the Lord has comforted His people,
> And will have mercy on His afflicted.
> —Isaiah 49:13[9]

Gloomee Busters

> Have you ever felt
> that even though
> you're taking things
> "one day at a time" . . .
> it's about twenty-four hours
> more than you can take?

□ □ □

> Just when I was getting used to yesterday,
> along came today.[10]

□ □ □

> PEOPLE WITH TIME FOR OTHERS
> ARE HAPPY ALL AROUND THE CLOCK.

□ □ □

> Instead of giving someone the gate,
> try mending the fence.

□ □ □

MAKING WAVES ALMOST NEVER TURNS THE TIDE.

□   □   □

It doesn't take a dictionary
to learn the language of love.

□   □   □

The Bible teaches us the best way of living . . .
the noblest way of suffering . . .
the most comfortable way of dying.

□   □   □

The Harder Part

Inventing the artificial heart—
That was the easy part.

Who can splice a severed soul?
Who can invent a glue
    to mend a broken heart?
Can shattered minds
    be traded in for new,
Or egos rusted by despair
    be given body shop repair?

To find a cure for these
That are beyond prosthetic remedies
That is the harder part.

□   □   □

And God Said, "No"

I asked God to take away my pride and God said, "No." He
said it was not for Him to take away but for me to give up.

I asked God to make my handicapped child whole and God said, "No." He said the body is only temporary.

I asked God to grant me patience and God said, "No." He said patience is a by-product of tribulation. It isn't granted, it's earned.

I asked God to give me happiness and God said, "No." He said He gives His blessings. Happiness is up to me.

I asked God to spare me from pain and God said, "No." He said sufferings draw you apart from worldly cares and brings you closer to Him.

I asked God to make my spirit grow and God said, "No." He said I must grow on my own, but He will prune me to make me fruitful.

I asked God if He loved me and God said, "Yes." He gave His only Son who died for me and I will be in heaven someday because I believe.

I asked God to help me love others as much as He loves me and God said,

"Ah, finally you have the idea!"

—Source unknown

☐ ☐ ☐

For I am convinced that nothing can ever separate us from his love. Death can't, and life can't. The angels won't, and all the powers of hell itself cannot keep God's love away. . . . Nothing will ever be able to separate us from the love of God demonstrated by our Lord Jesus Christ when he died for us. (Rom. 8:38–39 TLB)

Where Do I Put My Hatred While I Say My Prayers?

This life is a test. It is only a test. If it had been
an actual life, you would have received further
instructions on where to go and what to do.[1]

As I waited to speak following a recent luncheon, a friend seated on my left began describing how she had learned her husband of seventeen years was a homosexual. He had divorced her to live in the gay lifestyle with a young man in one of California's beach towns. Our hostess, who was seated on my right and was getting ready to introduce me, overheard the story. She leaned over and said very distinctly through clenched teeth, "IF I FOUND OUT MY HUSBAND WAS A HOMOSEXUAL, I WOULD SHOOT HIM AND TELL GOD HE DIED!"

I understand why that lady was so vehement. We are taught from childhood that anger and hatred are BAD emotions no "genuine" Christian should have. Yet, when devastating pain hits, red-hot anger can well up from within us like lava spewing out of a volcano. We may refuse to admit we have these intense feelings but the more we try to deny them the more they can overwhelm us.

It's not easy to admit that hatred was ever a part of me, but it was. When I learned my son was gay my shock turned into boiling, raging anger that scalded both of us and left a scar that is still a visible reminder of how uncontrolled emotions can ruin a relationship.

My, What Lovely Purple Luggage

After discovering Larry's homosexual "stuff" in his dresser drawer, somehow I got through what I've come to call Black Saturday.* With the stuff in the trunk of my car, I managed to drive to the airport, pick up my sister, Janet, and her husband. I was in no condition to be with people, but I tried to keep from losing it. Unfortunately, the first thing I saw was Janet's two pieces of PURPLE luggage. Somewhere I had heard that lesbians love the color purple, and while I knew it was unreal, I couldn't stop thinking, *My own sister has purple luggage. She works for Billy Graham, her husband is a minister, and she's a lesbian!*

Trying to behave as if nothing was wrong, I muttered something about how pretty Janet's new luggage was, but then I realized I wouldn't dare open my car trunk because Larry's homosexual stuff was lying there, uncovered, ready to let the whole world know my secret. I hugged Janet and Mel and told them my trunk wouldn't open, so we shoved their luggage and a crate of pineapples they had brought from Hawaii into the backseat. Then I drove to a motel across from Disneyland, where we planned to spend the night after enjoying the special Disneyland bicentennial celebration being held that weekend.

---

* More complete accounts of "Black Saturday" may be found in *Stick a Geranium in Your Hat and Be Happy* (Dallas: Word, 1990), chapter 3, and in *Where Does a Mother Go to Resign?* (Minneapolis: Bethany Fellowship, 1979), chapter 1.

After we got settled in our rooms, we went over to the park to join fifty thousand other people in the bicentennial festivities. It was nearing 8 P.M., the time I had told Larry to meet us, so we waited at the flagpole on Main Street and in just a few minutes he walked up. Janet and Mel could tell something was really upsetting me, but they said nothing. They greeted Larry warmly, and we all talked for a few minutes. Then Janet and Mel excused themselves, saying they wanted to see the Mr. Lincoln exhibit.

Larry and I stood there by the flagpole looking into each other's eyes. Mine were full of panic; his were dark and full of apprehension. His first words were, "I'm a homosexual—or maybe I'm bisexual."

As fifty thousand people milled around us, I frantically tried to understand. *Bisexual? What was that? Sex twice a month? Why would he say that?* Bisexual was a foreign word to me, but I knew from the Bible what homosexual meant and when he used that word, it resounded in my ears like the crack of doom.

And it didn't help a bit when, at the very moment Larry expanded my vocabulary with his exotic new word, the Tinkerbell fairy came sailing through the sky above our heads, proclaiming loudly that the Main Street electrical parade was about to start! The thought flashed across my mind, *Now they're EVERYWHERE—even in the AIR!* Just then Janet and Mel came back and I tried to keep a stiff upper lip, but as somebody said, that only makes it very hard to smile.

Somehow I got through the entire evening without telling them about Larry. I finally had to the next morning, though, and they were as astounded as I was. Later, after having Father's Day dinner at Knott's Berry Farm, I took my sister and her husband to the plane. We didn't talk much—we just cried. What COULD we say? We hugged tearfully near the jetway and then they were gone. And there I was with my "problem."

Driving back from the airport, I tried to plan my next move. Bill had already talked to Larry alone early that morning and had returned to tell me, "It's just a phase." But I had an overwhelming feeling it was a lot more than that. Because Bill was going over to see his parents and drop off a Father's Day gift for his dad, I decided now would be a good time to have it out with Larry. We would get this whole thing settled once and for all. Surely he could be fixed. Surely God wouldn't allow this to happen to OUR family. There had to be some kind of medicine or pill that would fix Larry. I kept assuring myself that God and mothers can fix ANYTHING, even this.

How Could My Darling Son Betray Us?

No matter how hard I tried to block them, angry thoughts about how Larry had betrayed us kept flying into my mind. What had happened to the darling child who, at the age of three, would stand up before people and sing, "Hot-diggety-dog-diggety . . . oh, what you do to me . . . it's all so new to me . . . oh, what you do to me"? And as he sang, he would bounce to the words, making folks laugh at his antics. Was he gay THEN? Did all this happen suddenly? WHEN? What did I do to cause this? Surely it must have been my fault. Had I been too close to him? Did I enjoy him too much?

But, no, that couldn't be right. Larry had been full of life, with friends and activities of his own. It was just that he had made our home so ALIVE and FUN—he enhanced our family with his bubbly personality. And yet how could this be the same son who had collected all that pornography? Where did he get those letters from men in his drawer? Some of it was even addressed to our home! Had it come when I was gone? Had I just put it in his room without looking at what it was? And if I had looked, would I have known what it was anyhow?

That was probably it. There had been no reason to suspect. I didn't belong to any local chapters of the FBI (Family Bureau of Investigation). I had always honored Larry's privacy, as I did the other boys' concerning what they had in their rooms. But this must have been where I had been negligent—failing to check the mail he received, at least to look at the return address. Surely I had messed up somewhere to have this happen NOW!

After parking the car in the garage, I went in to face my son—the homosexual/bisexual who apparently had betrayed every bit of the Christian nurturing we had given him for twenty years. Larry was waiting for me, and at first neither one of us spoke. We each wanted the other one to start, and finally I did. I tried to be calm, but my anger quickly boiled up and soon I was lashing Larry with Bible verses, Christian self-righteousness, and a slap in the face. He retaliated with obscenities and a fierce stubbornness I had never seen before. Then came a shove that pushed me against the grandfather clock.

That day I heard words from my son that I had never heard before in my life, and he saw just how deeply homophobia can affect a frustrated mom who sees her whole world crumbling. I loved my son, but my hatred for what he was saying overshadowed that love. All that came through at the moment was disgust for him.

I'd Rather You Were Dead!

I realized Larry was sick—emotionally ill—and I knew I had to do all I could to get him some help. I was so upset that my desires to help him were blurred by my anger. At one point, I exploded, "I would rather have a son be DEAD than to be a homosexual!"

My words lashed Larry like a scourge, but all the time I thought I was doing the right Christian thing by reminding him that he was a believer and that he "knew what the Bible teaches." He had to know that "God can change anyone's life." And he was well aware that "God can cleanse us from any kind of sin and make us whole again."

But all my fervent pleas fell on deaf ears. Larry's facial expression was contorted and his eyes were dark and flashing. His look seemed to say, *It's no use, I can't talk to you. You don't understand.*

He was right. I didn't understand. I burst into tears again and fled to my own bedroom while Larry stormed into his room and slammed the door. Between my sobs, I could hear Larry crying as well. Even then my motherly instincts wanted to go and comfort him, but then my hatred flared up and I thought, *How can I comfort YOU when you're destroying our family?*

The next day Larry was gone. I found his room completely empty when I returned from a trip to a hot-line center in Anaheim, where I had gone to get some help. I wanted to find a mother who had been through my agony, but all they offered me was two ex-homosexuals. I told them forget it, I already HAD a homosexual, and if there wasn't a mother they could refer me to, I'd just go back home and try to cope by myself.

My Anger Turned into Depression

And that's what I did. A detailed account of how I tried to cope is found in *Where Does a Mother Go To Resign?* Finding Larry gone without leaving a note telling me where he was put me into a total funk. The anger that had raged the day before now turned inward to become depression.

Retreating into my bedroom, I spent most of my days and nights grieving. The wallpaper in the room had these wonderful pink and red roses that climbed up and over a trellis, and I lay in bed, counting the roses and imagining I was weaving them in and out of the trellis. When I got tired of this, I would look up at the ceiling at an air-conditioning vent and imagine myself threading roses through the grate.

I didn't spend all my time in the bedroom. On a couple of occasions I had to attend funerals of friends, where, strangely, I found some relief because at least there I could cry openly. No one thought I was weird because it was an "appropriate" time to shed tears.

And I'd also go out now and then to the grocery store, but even there this terrible curse that had descended on all of us followed me. Going through the dairy case I'd see the word "HOMOGENIZED" on a carton of milk and, irrational as it may sound, I'd think there was something HOMOSEXUAL inside.

But most of the time I was a recluse, staying in my bedroom where I could find comfort by sliding deep under my comfy quilt. I avoided contact with people, even my family. I didn't cook anything for an entire year. Bill lived on popcorn; Barney survived by working at Taco Bell.

But I didn't care. I just wanted to be alone and not have to accept any responsibility. I was wounded . . . the knife was shoved deep into my chest . . . and I just wanted to lie there quietly, so I wouldn't cause it to plunge in deeper.

My isolation was like a protective fog. I didn't have to see anyone or make sense of a conversation. No one confronted me and wanted to know what was wrong. Everyone who knew us felt I had still not recovered from the loss of two other sons. They had no idea of the REAL loss, because I couldn't and wouldn't tell anyone.

How to Know When You're Depressed

My homophobia kept me in a constant state of depression for almost a year. I've read quite a bit about depression and have learned that the word is used to describe everything from feeling blue to being seriously ill. Some experts believe depression is "more disabling than arthritis or heart disease—an illness [that,] in its severest form, drives 15 percent of its victims to commit suicide."[2]

In their excellent manual on the symptoms, causes, and cures of depression, *Happiness Is a Choice*, doctors Frank Minirth and Paul Meier list some 101 telltale traits and signs of the depressed person.[3] I doubt that I had all 101, but I had a lot of them!

Just a few of the signs of depression include feeling sad, bored, disappointed, lonely, lacking confidence, not liking yourself, afraid, angry, guilty. Those with depression have difficulty making decisions and they're frustrated with life. You feel desperate, as though you've lost your faith, and life is meaningless. You may think of suicide, and in some cases even make plans to do it.

While going through depression, you may get careless about how you look. You may move slowly and have drooping posture. Your face may sag. You may be easily irritated and want nothing to do with anyone, as communication with others becomes practically nonexistent.

Physical signs of depression include difficulty sleeping and, often, a major change in appetite or weight (I lost thirty pounds in less than three months). You also experience fatigue and total weariness. For the depressed person, life drains away all vitality, energy, and strength. Even breathing becomes a problem.

While spending almost a year in that bedroom counting all those roses, I experienced just about every symptom listed above. By the way, my final rose count was 1,597!

Dr. Wells Was Kind, But Candid

For a week or so after Larry left, I rode a roller coaster of emotions. Fortunately, however, I still had enough wherewithal to realize I had to get some help. But I didn't know where to go, and I didn't have anyone to talk to. Bill, sensing my desire to be totally alone, kept to himself. So I began writing things down to help myself keep in touch with some kind of reality. That helped me realize I was slipping into a box, actually an emotional coffin. I could see that no one else was going to peel me off the wall and put me back together.

Even though I was depressed, I never stopped praying. I decided to strike a deal with God: I would work as if everything depended on me, but I would realize that, in the long run, everything depended on Him.

And God honored the deal. He gave me the strength to get out of that coffin. It was my first small step toward getting well, but a long series of ups and downs lay ahead of me.

My depression drove me to see a Christian therapist named Dr. Wells. He was kind and professional, and he was also a personal friend for whom I had worked in the past as a secretary. But friend or not, he didn't pull any punches after I had talked and he had listened. Finally, when it was Dr. Wells's turn to talk, he told me what he thought about homosexuals from his years of experience.

According to Dr. Wells, I was no longer at the "mother level" with Larry. While I was still his parent, our relationship was really more on an adult-to-adult plane; therefore I should take no credit or responsibility for his choices.

"Well, I certainly don't want to take any of the credit," I said, "but I do feel responsibility to help him change."

Dr. Wells replied, "In my experience, I find that if they do make any change in lifestyle at all, it is their own decision and nobody else's."

I hated hearing that because the anger was still simmering inside me. With Bible verses for backup, I reminded Dr. Wells that all things can become new. Surely no Christian needed to be chained to a life that was so harmful. I wanted God to change Larry RIGHT NOW—yesterday, in fact.

What Was Larry DOING Out There?

All through that summer I continued my sessions with Dr. Wells, but my depression did not lift. I kept thinking about Larry being out there somewhere in what they called "the gay lifestyle." Was he hurt? Sick? Did he miss his family? How was he making a living?

My mind was a blender full of emotions that whirled around and around. I loved Larry. I hated Larry. I wanted to kill him. I wanted to kill myself. I wanted to bury him, and I wanted to bury myself.

I stayed on that roller coaster, sometimes feeling some improvement and then plunging back down again, mainly because I simply would not accept the idea that this thing had happened to our family and that Larry couldn't be fixed IMMEDIATELY.

As difficult as it was to have two sons die, neither tragedy put me in the deep depression that I experienced after learning about Larry. I continued to think it would be easier to have him dead than to be out there in the gay lifestyle, engaging in despicable acts with other men. In a very real sense, it is harder to let go of someone who is living a rebellious, destructive life than to let go of someone who has died. Somewhere I found the following observation that describes my feelings perfectly during those desolate months after Larry vanished:

THE BLACK TARPAULIN OF DEPRESSION HIDES
GOD'S SUNSHINE OF HOPE FROM OUR VIEW.

So I understand what people mean when they write to me and say, "I'm depressed," or "I've been in a depression for the last two years." My mail is full of pain, but it is also full of honesty:

> I'm presently battling intermittent depression and I know I can stick a geranium in my hat, dress up like a million dollars and smile until my face cracks, thereby fooling everyone around me, but happy I ain't. Pain I can handle. Misery I don't care for at all, but that's where I've been. We lost our daughter Cindy to ovarian cancer five months ago. We were with her throughout the L-O-N-G agonizing process until she died at her home. . . . I can handle death and loss, but the long agonizing process of dying hardly seems necessary and I admit to being angry at God for not intervening to either heal or take His child home sooner. Anyway, that's the basis for my depression.
>
> Let me tell you that your book really helped me and the strange thing is—you didn't tell me a single thing I don't already know and have used many times to counsel others.

☐　☐　☐

> Three days before our twenty-fourth wedding anniversary I came home from work to find a note on the desk that said he had moved out and intended to file for divorce. . . . Even though God was with me and gave me Scripture after Scripture to uphold me and embrace me and encourage me, the

pain was still more than I thought I could bear at times. . . .
In the last few weeks I have been really struggling with severe
depression and have been wondering what purpose my life
has. I'm very, very empty and dry; it's hard to even pray, and
when I do, I'm not sure what to pray for or even how to pray.
I am so very lonely. My oldest son is married and the youngest
one is away at college. There is no one to come home to at
night to share with, to be touched by. . . .

□   □   □

Thank you for the wonderful ministry. My husband has
been out of work for more than three years. I am at a point
where I don't know if I should murder him, make him move
out, or hang in there and keep praying. Of course, your book
has encouraged me to do the latter. . . . I realized there was
no light at the end of my tunnel, consequently I made an
appointment for my husband to begin treatment with a
psychologist and he has finally admitted to his depression.

□   □   □

Although my problem doesn't have anything to do with
homosexuality, the pain that I suffer because of my children is
very much the same. The guilt, the whys? the how-comes?
etc., etc., etc.
I feel as though I know you and wanted you to know how
much you have helped me already. I need to keep your book
handy and use it often to get myself back on the right track. I
know depression is an awful thing and a waste of time and
energy. I really want to live a productive life, as I know that
nothing I say or do at this point will change anything with my
kids.

The bad news in these letters is that all of these people are
depressed to some degree, but the good news is that they are
trying to tell somebody how they feel. One of the first things I
learned from Dr. Wells is that as long as you are talking and
ventilating, you are not in danger of "losing touch with reality."

One of the first positive steps you can take to conquer depression is to refuse to be isolated. Get help from somebody! The depressed person who doesn't get help can be in danger of slipping permanently into La-La Land and confined forever in the Home for the Bewildered.

Throughout that summer and into the fall, I continued to see Dr. Wells regularly, but my ride on the depression roller coaster continued. I did get a real lift around mid-October when I accidentally learned that Larry was still with his choral group and would be singing at the Los Angeles Music Center. With a friend accompanying me, I went to the program with high hopes, but the evening turned into a disaster. Just before the intermission, Larry spotted me in the audience, and when the group came back on for the second part of the program, his place was empty! He had fled and I never got to speak to him at all.

That put me into another sickening downward spiral and a deep depression that lasted well past Christmas. The calendar changed from 1975 to 1976 and I began seeing Dr. Wells a little less. By the following spring, I was telling myself I was improving. At least I was showing my normally cheerful self to the world; but inside there was still plenty of churning, burning, and yearning going on. I was still very angry, still in a chronic, low-grade depression, even though I was hiding it in the few contacts I had with others.

Maybe I'll Just Swallow a Razor Blade

According to doctors Frank Minirth and Paul Meier, one of the signs of depression is the belief that MORNING is the worst part of the day.[4] Right around Mother's Day, mornings began looking extremely bad to me. I guess the thought of Mother's Day without Larry was more than I wanted to handle. One day I muttered to Bill, "I wish you used double-edged razor blades. Then I could swallow one in a piece of bread and it might kill me."

THAT got Bill's attention! He insisted that I see Dr. Wells IMMEDIATELY. I did as Bill asked, but it didn't gain the results he hoped for. When Dr. Wells reviewed my case and saw that Larry had been gone almost a year, he dropped a bomb that shattered my cheerful exterior into a million pieces:

"Well, if Larry has been gone this long," he said, "very possibly he will never come home again. He may have found permanent emotional support in the gay lifestyle."

I went home in a total "downer" mood and retreated to the back bedroom where I slipped into a zombie-like trance. I didn't even bother to count roses. Later that same day Dr. Wells called Bill and told him I was extremely depressed when I left his office and he suggested having me put in Parkside West, a very fine institution in our area that specializes in twenty-four-hour care for people who are suicidal.

Bill told Dr. Wells he wasn't sure his health insurance would cover something like that but that he'd check on it and call him back. Meanwhile, he thought I could stay at home because I "wasn't vicious or anything."

The next day as Bill was about to leave for work, he told me that he would make some calls that morning to learn if his insurance covered me or not. After he drove off, I sat there considering my options: if Bill's insurance covered me, I was headed for Looney Tunes haven. If it didn't cover me, I was supposed to stay home and count more roses on the wallpaper. Then the thought hit me: *Why toy with suicidal thoughts any longer? Why not go ahead and get it OVER with?*

I got in my car, backed out of the driveway, and started down the street, not knowing for sure where I was going. All I knew was I couldn't go on like this. I wasn't functioning as a wife. I wasn't a mother. I had shut out my friends. I felt like a zero with the rim rubbed out—a NOTHING. How could God say He loved me and let all this happen?

One Sharp Turn Would End It All

As I headed up a high viaduct, I fully intended to get to the top, turn the wheel sharply to the right and plunge my car to the freeway below. All my troubles would be over—or would they? After all, it was only a drop of probably fifty feet; perhaps it wouldn't be enough to finish the job. Maybe I'd just wind up maimed and crippled for life, sitting in a wheelchair, making baskets—with lots of roses, of course.

As I neared the top of the viaduct, I already knew I couldn't kill myself. But I also knew I had to do SOMETHING to get rid of this horrible burden I had carried for almost a year. I had given Larry to God many times over the past months, but I'd always taken him back again. I knew the Bible's instructions to cast our cares on Him because He cares for us (see 1 Pet. 5:7). This verse means that we should DEPOSIT our cares with God and *never pick them up again.* That was my problem. How could I "deposit Larry with God" once and for all?

As I came over the top of the viaduct, I thought of an answer. Perhaps I could take a hammer out of my imagination and just NAIL him to the foot of the cross. That would do it. I had to find some way to really deposit this horrible burden on the Lord and not keep carrying it around myself. If I nailed that burden down, I couldn't pick it up again. It was an appealing idea because, to be truthful, I was exhausted.

As I started down the other side of the viaduct, that's exactly what I did. In my mind, I took out a hammer and nails, and mentally nailed to the cross my burden of worry and anxiety over my son.

"Lord," I prayed, "this time I'm really giving Larry to You. By nailing him to the cross, I'm giving him to You once and for all. If he never comes home, it doesn't matter. If I never see him again, it doesn't matter. It's all in Your hands. WHATEVER, LORD—whatever happens, I'm nailing that kid to the cross and giving him to You!"

I've never been much for miracles—at least in my own life. I have the gift of joy but not of faith. (It's comforting to know that none of us is expected to have *every* gift.) So what happened next wasn't typical of me at all. It was as though those words, "Whatever, Lord," opened some hidden chambers inside. The heavy depressed feeling I had carried for so long evaporated. I felt a million tiny splashes of joy bubbling up inside me. I sang all the way home—the first singing I had done in a year—then ran into the house and telephoned Bill.

The excitement in my voice made him think I had totally lost it. I tried to explain about "nailing Larry to the cross," but after I made several attempts Bill finally told me not to call anybody else or to tell anyone ANYTHING. He was coming right home. Bill was the one with brain damage from the accident. He was the one who hadn't known anything for two years, and now HE was telling ME not to call anybody or talk to anybody until he got there.

Bill made it home in record time and I went over the whole thing once more, while he tried to see what had transformed me from a zombie back to a happy, joyous person. Eventually he seemed to understand that talking about "nailing Larry to the cross" was my way of saying that I had finally let go of Larry and given him ENTIRELY, TOTALLY, and COMPLETELY to God.

Bill was relieved. He had learned that day that his insurance wouldn't have covered me anyway.

Then the Phone Rang

The next day the miracle continued. For the first time in almost a year I felt like cleaning the house, and as I was vacuuming the phone rang. It was Larry wanting to know if he could come home to bring me a hamburger as he always used to do. If he had called the day before, I would have said, "You little creep, don't you know that they are ready to put me in the Home for the Bewildered?" But yesterday I had nailed Larry to the cross; today I was able to say, "Come on home, Honey." All I could feel for him was overwhelming love.

The next hour was a mixture of joy, apprehension, and curiosity. As Larry and I ate our hamburgers, I could see he was nervous, so I didn't ask him questions about his life or his lifestyle. He did tell me he was going to school at UCLA, working, and living alone. After a while, Larry left, promising he would be back to see us the next week. After he left, I sat there thinking, *Isn't this just like God? The minute I really let go of my son, he is returned to me.*

It turned out, however, that Larry wasn't really back. He stayed in touch with us for a couple of years and then he was gone again, this time with more anger than ever and more determination to live the gay lifestyle. But I felt at peace because I had finally learned what it means to let go of, or relinquish to God, the one you love.

In the rest of this chapter, I want to talk about relinquishment—and forgiveness. When you can say, "WHATEVER, LORD," and really mean it, depression loses its power to gnaw at your insides. When you let go, life no longer drains everything out of you. When I let go of Larry completely, my heartache turned to JOY.

What Does It Really Mean to "Let Go"?

One of the best things I've ever seen on the subject of relinquishment was done by some good friends in an organization called "Love in Action." The following is excerpted from an article by Bob Davies and Lori Torkelson who are happy to share these thoughts with people in pain:

One of the most frustrating pieces of advice one Christian can give another is to "just give your problems up to God." Most people aren't sure what "giving up" really means. Three basic dictionary definitions of "relinquishment" are:

1. To surrender a right
2. To put aside a plan
3. To loose one's hold on something or someone

This lays out what we're talking about in more concrete terms. The kind of relinquishment we're dealing with usually involves all three of these actions!

All of us in some way are involved in relinquishment. Daily we must make choices. Things that separate us from God must be given up. We can understand this when it concerns things, but when it comes to people, there is often confusion as to our Christian responsibility. Also, relinquishment is so difficult because it often involves someone we are closest to, just the last person we would want to let go of.

When God asks us to let go of someone close to us, the pain of letting go may feel like punishment—but it's NOT! Relinquishment is not the act of God removing from our lives someone we're sinfully attached to. Real "giving up" is a mature decision we make in response to God's request. Abraham saw his surrender of Isaac as an act of worship (Gen. 22:5). When God asks this of us, He is testing our loyalty, perfecting our ability to trust Him with that which is most precious to us. The fact that God requests us to relinquish someone is an encouraging sign that He knows we already have established a relationship of trust with Him. He doesn't ask us to relinquish above the level of our capacity.

Aspects of Relinquishment?

- Facing our limitations. Eventually we reach the point of acknowledging our own helplessness in relating to our loved one, realizing we've reached the limits of our human love and wisdom. We are ready to acknowledge our need to let God take over.

- Acknowledging God's ownership. Like Hannah, we realize that the person we love belongs to God—not to us. Though we may have been entrusted with a position of care and responsibility toward them, they ultimately belong to God and are His responsibility.

- Letting go of our expectations. We may have had many things we hoped would be fulfilled by the person we love: hopes that our children would marry and raise families, exciting plans for the future we made with our husband or wife when we married. And it's certainly not wrong for us to have these hopes! But part of relinquishment is coming to terms with the fact that these things may not happen. We surrender our expectations, realizing that God will still bring fulfillment to our lives, though maybe not in the way we had planned.[5]

To Find Complete Closure You Must Let Go

No matter what may be depressing you, *relinquishment is a key to getting well.* In chapter 2 we looked at dealing with the death of loved ones and the need for CLOSURE—completely letting go of the one who has died, letting the wounds of grief heal, and getting on with your life. I often hear from parents who have a very difficult time doing this. They want to know:

HOW can I let go of my loved one?

Some parents don't seem to want to let go. I got a long letter from a mom who had lost her "favorite son." She wrote to me at the end of the year, after losing her boy the previous spring in a fiery car crash. She admitted that some days she relived that horrible day and pleaded for her son to be "given back" to her. She knew this was foolish, but she couldn't help it.

She wrote about not being able to sleep without taking medication and how she wished she could dream of her son but the dreams never seemed to come. She wanted to see his handsome face and hear his giggle. He had always been an inspiration and the clown of the family. Everyone had a good time around her son. As she said, "He was our lifeline and we failed so many times to tell him."

This mother was also haunted by feelings of guilt because she was not able to spend much time with her son during the three or four weeks preceding his death. She had to be in another city spending time with her daughter and new grandson. When she did get back home, he was busy with college classes. The night before he died, he came in very late and even though the mother was up, he was tired and went immediately to bed. Not a word was spoken between them. She wrote:

> Oh, if I could go back to that night.
>
> The accident happened around 7:30 A.M. Friday morning. By the time we arrived at the scene, we couldn't see the vehicles for the black smoke. I can't believe I left the scene as I was asked to do by the State Police. I should have stayed til my son's body was removed from the scene. Another mistake I can't correct. . . .
>
> My youngest daughter, who is 14, says I do everything for my son. He is the only one I think about. Everything I do should have been done when he was alive. She asks when is her time with me, when she is dead also? I think her grief is as great as mine because she and my son were very close and a lot alike. . . .
>
> Barbara, I don't know what to do. I can't function as I did. I am consumed with trying to keep the memories of my son alive. He was never any trouble and asked for so little. If ever I had a perfect son, it was this boy. Why does God seem to call home the best? He was only 20 and trying so hard to educate himself and make us proud of him. We failed so many times to tell him that he didn't have to prove anything to us, and we were proud of him all the time. . . .
>
> You, yourself, know the suicidal thoughts that cross our path and how hard it is to quench the thoughts. I have a spouse, three daughters, and a grandson born one month before my son's death. I have plenty to be thankful for. But so many times I'm blinded to all of this because my boy is alone in heaven and needs his mama to be with him. I pray the Lord will come tonight!

I have deep concern for this mom, not only because she lost her only son, but because she simply can't seem to accept what she already knows—that he is in heaven with God and very happy there. He is content to wait for her, but she spends each day wanting him to be returned or wanting to join him.

When I contacted this mother, I gently tried to share with her that I know I have two boys in heaven, but they aren't alone at all. For one thing, they are with Jesus, and that is more than enough. They don't need me to be with them. They are rejoicing and happier than they ever were on earth.

As we try to find closure over the death of a loved one, perhaps we can ask God to give us a FROZEN PICTURE of that person in heaven. We can imagine the beauty of what God has prepared for those who love Him. We can take comfort in the Scripture's promise that "eye hath not seen, nor ear heard" what lies ahead for us (see 1 Cor. 2:9). We can have an image of our loved one in a glorious place where there is never-ending joy.

When Tim was killed and I had to go to the SAME viewing room with the SAME carpeting and the SAME wallpaper in the SAME mortuary and stand there next to the SAME mortician in the dark blue suit to identify ANOTHER boy in a box, the grief rolled over me in waves until I thought I would drown.

But when I walked out of that mortuary into the August heat, five years *to the day* after I had identified Steven's body, I had an experience that gave me the frozen picture of Tim that I needed. As I walked to the car, I could smell freshly cut grass and could hear crows cawing in the trees. Then I looked up and there in the sky was an image of Tim's smiling face! He was surrounded with a bright shining light and I heard him saying, "Don't cry, Mom, because I'm not there. I'm rejoicing around the throne of God."

As I said before, miraculous experiences aren't familiar to me. I had never had that happen before and haven't had one since, but perhaps God knew I needed something extra that would help me find closure after losing a second son in violent death.

Letting Go of the Living Is Harder

After reading *Stick A Geranium in Your Hat and Be Happy*, a mother wrote to share how her seventeen-year-old son, unable to handle the stress, turned to drugs after cancer had struck down her husband. The father of the family endured five years of hospitals, radiation, surgeries, and terrible pain as the bones in his back disintegrated and broke. The mother described what happened:

> Our 17-year-old son, who was a dream of a young man, a body builder, a fanatic about eating right and working out and couldn't stand cigarettes, within six months after my husband was hospitalized, was a drug addict. He freaked out. He became skinny and so pitiful. He fought—carried guns and knives. He stole from us. He quit school his senior year.
> I couldn't believe what I was seeing with my eyes, my husband dying slowly—no cure—and my son was killing himself with the drugs. Our home was like hell on earth. . . . It was like the devil himself had moved into our home—once a loving happy family, a Christian home. Was this real, was I dreaming? I'd go to my bedroom and beg God to let us have our other life back.

This mother and wife knew exactly what churning, burning, and yearning are all about. After her husband had been ill about eighteen months, the woman's mother began running into walls and was soon hospitalized and dying, herself. She was given radiation treatments and had to be fed and bathed. Thus, the woman had to endure a terminally ill husband, a terminally ill mother, and a teen-age son who was killing himself with drugs. On one occasion her son overdosed and, while being taken to the hospital, pleaded, "Mama, pray that I'm dying." He survived and now, in his mid-twenties, is "still fighting the demons of hell." Her letter continues:

> My son is getting better, but his anger is so great—it's a giant only God can deal with. As a mother I deal with it daily.

I've got to nail it to the cross and say "Whatever!" just as you did.

This precious mom's words apply to anyone who is facing ongoing grief, the kind that can drive you all the way to despair. Finally, when there is no recourse, no cure, and seemingly "no hope," you have to nail it all to the cross and say, "Whatever, Lord!" I was glad to see that this mother closed her letter with two verses of Scripture that give her the strength to go on:

> For I know the thoughts that I think toward you, says the LORD, thoughts of peace and not of evil, to give you a future and a hope. (Jer. 29:11 NKJV)

> For God has not given us a spirit of fear, but of power and of love and of a sound mind. (2 Tim. 1:7 NKJV)

Being Deserted Can Become a Living Death

Many letters come from depressed wives whose marriages have gone sour. Their husbands want to leave or perhaps have already deserted them. Their questions always come down to:

My husband has left me—how can I go on when life doesn't seem worth it?

There is something about the pain of being rejected, or even a spouse's threat to leave, that can drive the other marital partner to the brink of suicide. Following is a typical letter from a wife who's on that brink:

> I'm 31, with a 2 ½-year-old little boy, and my husband has filed for divorce. As a Christian I was told to let this ungodly man go. The church told me to leave him. I can't begin to tell you how painful this is. I don't know how to survive this! I want Jesus to take me home. Barbara, please pray for me. This life is now a living hell. I don't have money for proper legal

counsel, let alone for counseling for this guilt, pain, condemnation, I'm so-o-o sad. I feel so alone.

This man I married for life is now a monster and threatens to take my child away from me. I can't bear this anymore. What do I do? Can one be given more pain than one can bear? I've thought of taking my life but I love my son too much to do that—but I even question that at times. Sometimes I think I'll do it!

When the pain and depression become overwhelming, we can be plagued by thoughts of how wonderful it would be to "be free of all this." But as I said back in chapter 2, suicide is a permanent answer to a temporary problem. My advice to this deserted wife, and anyone in a similar situation, is this:

Yes, it is dark for you, but suicide is never the answer. The devastation it makes for loved ones cannot even be counted. Even though you feel as if you are in a bottomless pit, there is a way out. Your suffering will not last forever. You will work your way through the maze if you tackle each day counting on God to give you grace to make it through.

It is much easier to think about handling one day at a time and not the whole future at once. Put one foot in front of the other and plod through one day. Before long, you will have made it through a week and then a month. Soon you will have made it through several months, and you will see a bright light ahead that isn't just another train coming!

Instead, you will discover there is a lighthouse out there for you. That lighthouse is the Light of the world and He never changes or moves. He is always there to seek out His own. Only through Christ can you make your way through the heavy fog to safety. Christ is the lighthouse who will always help you get your bearings IF YOU LOOK FOR HIM.

One of my favorite verses is 1 Corinthians 10:13:

. . . God is faithful; he will not let you be tempted beyond what you can bear. But when you are tempted, he will also provide a way out so that you can stand up under it. (NIV)

In Scripture, the Greek word for "tempted" can also be translated "tested." The idea is that of going through a trial. Read 1 Corinthians 10:13 again, inserting the word "tested" for "tempted" and you can see why it's one of my favorite verses.

Is It Better to Have Loved—and Lost?

It's hard enough to have your husband leave you after years of marriage, but it's even more of a blow when it happens while you're still a bride. This wife wrote:

> I have been married for three months and three days. Well, a month ago my husband expressed to me that he made a mistake and no longer wanted to be married to me. It's not like we rushed into this. We've been together since high school, eight years in October. The last month I've been so hurt and confused I came close to killing myself and/or him.

The first thing this dear gal needs to do is become familiar with the laws of her state. She should contact an attorney who might advise her about the possibility of filing for an annulment. On the other hand, she says they had "been together since high school, eight years." If "together" means that they lived together, asking for an annulment might not work.

Even more important, however, is her emotional state. She should try to find a good counselor, someone at her church perhaps, who can guide her through these months of complete upheaval until she can get her balance again.

Also, she may need to contact a professional counselor who can provide her with psychological insight into her emotional needs as she grows through this rejection time.

Here is one other piece of advice. It may not be just what everyone wants to hear, but in this case I do think it contains some food for thought. Any time you get so depressed you are tempted to kill yourself, it's time to do some hard thinking. Someone once told me:

'TIS BETTER TO HAVE LOVED AND LOST—
MUCH BETTER!

I am sure there are many ex-wives and ex-husbands who may disagree with this idea, but it does provide another way of looking at the problem. Any time we have the opportunity to love someone else, we have a great privilege and a great responsibility. To have fulfilled our end of the responsibility is all God really asks.

Occasionally I hear from someone who planned a wedding but it never happened. For example, one disillusioned young woman wrote:

> I was supposed to get married in June, but it didn't happen. The wedding was postponed. Now we don't communicate at all. It's like a whole year of my life has been wiped out or didn't happen—it's still just so <u>unbelievable</u>. It's truly a living nightmare! It has not been easy trying to bounce back. Sometimes the life of a hermit looks very appealing.

I would answer this hurting young woman by saying I'm sure being jilted is no fun, but it can be one way to find God's best for you. The pain is intense for you now, but eventually you will heal. Later, you may even be able to appreciate this paraphrase of the idea I shared earlier:

IT'S BETTER TO HAVE LOVED AND LOST
THAN TO BE CHAINED TO A CHUMP FOR GOOD.

The one who left you behind may not be a chump, but it's obvious that he wasn't the one for you. Some place farther down the road you will look back at all this and be able to THANK GOD for sparing you from what could have been. Also, while it hurts now, remember that this experience can make you a wiser and more discerning person, better equipped to make choices.

Letting Go Always Includes Forgiveness

Many folks write to tell of how they were rejected, abused, and "treated like dirt." Their stories may differ, but the bottom line is that they want to know:

HOW can I forgive and forget what was done to me?

For example, I received a letter from a young woman who hinted at being sexually abused by her father, but she really spoke more of the mental abuse that parents can be guilty of as their children are growing up. This single mother wanted to know:

> What about parents who disappoint their children?
> I have been very disappointed in my father for many years. From . . . mental harassment, to physically beating us, for not standing up for his family, for always making me feel I was the one who was—and consequently still feel like—I am the one who is wrong.
> He had or implied to me (and by my mother's reactions appeared to have had) an extramarital affair. Treated my mother like second-hand merchandise, was never there to cheer me on at my softball or basketball games. Washed my mouth out with soap if I ever said a swear word, but used them liberally himself. Didn't go to church regularly, despised the idea of family devotions, and many other things that have all had an influence on who I am and how I respond to things in my life now.
> Gives me no verbal or monetary support as a single parent. Oh, I suppose I disappointed him by becoming pregnant. Would it have been better to have had an abortion and never said anything because I might have disappointed him? I have taken offense at your statements of children disappointing their parents. Maybe someday you may see that those disappointments were as a result of parents disappointing their children.

My word of encouragement to this young single mom is not to let "if only" eat her alive. It would be so easy for her to play the "if-only game": *If only* he had been there for her when she was growing up. *If only* he had treated her mother better. *If only* he had been a devoted Christian dad. And now that she struggles as a single parent, *if only* he could give her *any* kind of support, verbal or monetary.

But none of that is happening. No wonder this dear single mom takes offense at my statements about children disappointing their parents. In her case, *she* has been disappointed and the shoe is on the other foot! That doesn't make the shoe any easier to wear; in fact, it is probably more difficult.

This single mom can dwell on the past with her father's failures, but it will do no good. Life has dealt her a lousy hand but she has to decide how to play it out. As Robert Louis Stevenson said:

LIFE IS NOT A MATTER OF HOLDING GOOD CARDS,
IT'S PLAYING A POOR HAND WELL.

It always comes back to the same thing: attitude. Your attitude can be so cemented into your life that you make your current problem an absolute that can never be changed. You dwell on it, saying, "I had lousy parents," or "I had a weak and neglectful father who was a hypocrite. I'm stuck and there is no way out . . ."

Or you can take the other view, which says *no problem has to be an absolute*. Everything can be studied, observed, applied, and evaluated. That's how we learn to adapt. Adapting is a continuing process because life is ever-changing. Challenges arise and detours loom up. Our goals have to change. The only healthy answer is to be flexible.

Recently a friend of mine came over to bring me several packages of bubble bath. She knew how much I delighted in having all this wonderfully luscious smelling stuff to revel in while taking a bath, but she had to say, "I am definitely a SHOWER person. I never could stand taking a bath, and in all my years I've only taken showers. If I go to visit someone and they don't have a shower, I can't wait to get home because I cannot adjust to taking a bath at my age."

A red flag went up in my mind. My friend can't adjust to something like taking an occasional bath? What was causing her to be so adamant? Was she experiencing hardening of the attitudes?

Just to make sure I wasn't being cemented into my own preferences, I deliberately took a SHOWER for the next few days, just to remind myself that we have to be adaptable, flexible, moldable—able to "go with the flow," as the kids say.

Becoming resigned to the fact that "life did me wrong in the past" is the path to feelings of hopelessness. Adaptability, however, provides hope that we will reach our destination at some point. If I could put my arms around the single mom whose father had been so neglectful, I would tell her this:

I know it hurts. You have been treated as no daughter should ever be treated, and your dad is continuing that dirty treatment by not giving you any kind of support. But don't just accept this as your fate. ADAPT. You are on a journey, just as I am. I've had to adapt many times and I want to tell you that as you learn to adapt you learn to enjoy and not just endure.

As we go through life, we all suffer emotional fractures. Yours happen to be very splintered, but you can learn from your past and you don't have to WASTE YOUR SORROWS. Be sure to love your own child and try to keep her emotional tank full to the brim. Loving your child will release some of the pain within you. It will help you forgive the one who hurt you. Remember that forgiveness is an incredibly healing force. It's like a salve smoothed on the places in your memory that are still stinging with pain.

Use this experience for the good so that you can instill in your daughter the emotional security that you were robbed of, yourself. You might try imagining God reaching down and wrapping YOU in a special comfort blanket and saying, "There, there, it's all going to be better."

When you are alone and in need of a lift, try singing songs to yourself, for example:

Father loves me, Father loves me,
Father loves me, Father loves me.

This simple phrase, repeated over and over to a rhythmic tune as though you're singing "Allelujah" will be a comforting reminder that YOU ARE LOVED. You are special. You will feel whole again.

To Let Go—Forgive

Ask any psychologist and he or she will tell you that many patients are depressed because they can't bring themselves to forgive. Someone they trusted has hurt them badly. They keep chewing on that hurt and never letting it heal. According to Lewis Smedes, author of *Forgive and Forget: Healing the Hurts We Don't Deserve*, you have three choices for handling unfair pain: (1) You can try to deny it and make believe it never happened. (2) You can try to get even, but as Smedes says, "getting even is a loser's game." (3) You can forgive, which is hardest by far, but it's the only healthy way to cope with the situation. Smedes wrote:

> Forgiving is love's toughest work. But you can make it easier if you don't confuse forgiving with forgetting. You do not have to forget in order to forgive. Besides, some things should never be forgotten, lest we let them happen again.[6]

To really forgive someone, Smedes advises us to go ahead and feel the pain. And when pain is undeserved, we tend to feel it even more deeply. At the same time, we may feel resentment, even hatred. We shouldn't be afraid of these feelings, but we shouldn't dwell on them either. These are the feelings that can lead straight into depression.

To begin to heal yourself, start seeing the person who hurt you as weak and needy. Don't excuse the person, but begin to try to understand. This brings you to what may be the most important step of all:

TO FORGIVE,
SURRENDER YOUR RIGHT TO GET EVEN.

One of the most creative ways to forgive I've ever seen comes from a woman whose letter said:

I have strengthened my prayer life by weeding my flower bed. I used to have names on all the weeds and really would hoe, chop, and mutilate people who had frustrated me. Now my weeds are still named, but instead of chopping them, I gently pull them and pause and pray for them. I call it the love approach instead of the angry approach. I also have added to my list those who need extra encouragement through prayer and not just my "hit list."

You may want to try this mom's approach to weeding resentment, dislike, and even hatred out of your life. In addition, here are some more tips from Dr. Smedes:

It helps to be concrete. Don't try to forgive someone for being what he or she is. Forgive people only for what they do. Forgive in verbs, not nouns, one thing at a time.

And remember, forgiveness only works when you are ready. It's good to remember this when we want someone to forgive us. You'll forgive when you decide that you've had enough pain. . . .

There is no easy way to forgive. Forgiving is a type of spiritual surgery. You slice out of your past a cancer that shouldn't be there. And surgery is never easy. In short, forgiveness reverses the flow of hurt pouring silently but painfully out of your past.[7]

Forgiving Yourself Can Be Hardest of All

Sometimes the hardest person to forgive is yourself. Recently I spoke to a Rotary Club and during my talk I emphasized that yesterday is a canceled check, tomorrow is a promissory note, and today is cash. I reminded them that we shouldn't crucify ourselves between two thieves, regret for yesterday and fear for tomorrow. I also quoted 1 John 1:9: "If we confess our sins, He is faithful and just to forgive us our sins and to cleanse us from all unrighteousness" (NKJV).

Afterward, a man of about forty-five came up to tell me how much the talk had meant to him. In fact, he said it had literally changed his life. At the age of nine, he had accidentally killed a fifteen-year-old friend, and he had carried that burden of guilt and inability to forgive himself right up to that very day. His guilt had destroyed his first marriage and now it was threatening to ruin a new relationship with a woman he wanted to marry. The only problem was, she had a fifteen-year-old son, the same age as the friend he had killed. Her son also had the *same first name* as his friend.

"I really can't explain it," he said, "but hearing you talk today helped me understand that I could forgive myself, that I can look ahead and find a light. I know the past is over and I don't need to whip myself any longer with my guilt."

That's the key—realizing that what has passed is in the past, and it won't do any good to whip yourself any longer.

On the day I "nailed Larry to the cross," I carried my heavy burden up on that viaduct, intent on killing myself, but I came down the other side free of the pain, the depression—and the hatred. Letting go of Larry also meant forgiving him for all the hurt he had caused. For months I had tried to tell myself that I had forgiven Larry, but all that time I had still been nursing the hurt. It festered deep inside until it drove me to the brink of suicide.

But at the moment I said, "Whatever, Lord," I not only forgave Larry, I forgave the whole world. In fact, I had been mad at God for almost a year. Now I decided to forgive Him too! And as I forgave, I felt forgiven! The joy flooded into my heart and a song came to my lips.

Perhaps we could argue about what comes first: forgiving or

letting go. Maybe you do them both at the same time. As the poet says:

> To let go doesn't mean to STOP CARING,
>   it means I can't DO IT for someone else. . . .
> To let go is not to try to CHANGE or BLAME another,
>   I can ONLY change myself. . . .
> To let go is not to JUDGE, but to allow another
>   to be a human being. . . .
> To let go is not to REGRET the past,
>   but to GROW and live for the future.
> To let go is to FEAR LESS,
>   trust in Christ more,
>   and freely give the love He's given to me.[8]

Gloomee Busters

> Every now and then, without warning,
>   each of us has a good day;
>   Please, Lord, it's my
>   turn today,
>   ain't it?
>
> Maybe tomorrow?
>   next Tuesday or Wednesday?
>   . . . half a day Thursday?
>   (8:30 to 9:15 Friday morning?)

☐ ☐ ☐

EVEN IF IT BURNS A LITTLE BIT LOW AT TIMES,
THE SECRET OF LIFE IS
TO ALWAYS KEEP THE FLAME OF HOPE ALIVE.

☐ ☐ ☐

Honest Hymn Singing

If I were entirely honest every time I sang a hymn or gospel song, here's how some of the old titles would come out:

> I Surrender Some
> Oh, How I Like Jesus
> He's Quite a Bit to Me
> Take My Life and Let Me Be
> There Is Scattered Cloudiness in My Soul Today
> Where He Leads Me, I Will Consider Following
> Just As I Pretend to Be
> When the Saints Go Sneaking In
>
> —Source unknown

□   □   □

YOU ARE NOT WHAT YOU THINK, BUT WHAT YOU THINK, YOU ARE.

□   □   □

> May those who love us, love us.
> And those who don't love us,
> May God turn their hearts.
> And if He doesn't turn their hearts
> May He turn their ankles,
> So we will know them by their limping.
>
> —Source unknown

□   □   □

RUB IT OUT, DON'T RUB IT IN.

Perhaps you have heard of the little boy who prayed, "Father, forgive us our trespasses, as we give it to those who trespass against us."

At least the little boy was being honest. It's just like many of us to want to lash back instead of love back!

It's human to want to pay back those who offend us; but it's God-like to forgive.

We don't forgive to be forgiven, but if we're forgiven by God, we will forgive others.

When we forgive others, we promise to do three things:

(1) not to take it out on others,

(2) not to talk about it to others,

(3) and not to brood about it any more.

Let's rub it out, and not rub it in.

—Adapted. Source unknown

☐ ☐ ☐

FAITH, HOPE, AND CHARITY . . .
IF WE HAD MORE OF THE FIRST TWO,
WE'D NEED LESS OF THE LAST.

☐ ☐ ☐

The good Lord never gives you more than you can handle
unless you die of something.

☐ ☐ ☐

WHAT TO DO IN CASE OF EMERGENCY

1. Pick up your hat.
2. Grab your coat.
3. Leave your worries on the doorstep.
4. Direct your feet to the sunny side of the street.

☐ ☐ ☐

What happiness for those whose guilt has been forgiven! What joys when sins are covered over! What relief for those who have confessed their sins and God has cleared their record! (Ps. 32:1 TLB)

7

Pack Up Your Gloomees in a Great Big Box, Then Sit on the Lid and Laugh!

If Noah had been truly wise,
he would have swatted those two flies.[1]

Collecting poems brings me almost as much joy as bumper snickers and one-liners. The other day I found a bit of verse that sums up my philosophy for dealing with life when pain and trouble bring on the GLOOMEES:

> Build for yourself a strong box,
>   Fashion each part with care;
> When it's strong as your hand can make it,
>   Put all your troubles there;
> Hide there all thought of your failures,
>   And each bitter cup that you quaff;
> Lock all your heartaches within it,
>   Then sit on the lid and laugh.

179

Tell no one else its contents,
Never its secrets share;
When you've dropped in your care and worry
Keep them forever there;
Hide them from sight so completely
That the world will never dream half;
Fasten the strong box securely—
Then sit on the lid and laugh.

—Bertha Adams Backus[2]

When Jell-O Ran Red on the Wall

Long before the four horsemen of pain descended on our home, I always enjoyed a good laugh and would do my best to turn problems into something we could all chuckle over. For example, there was the time I sometimes call "the Johnson kids and their crazy Jell-O caper."

One day I came home from shopping and heard all four of my boys out in the kitchen, shrieking with laughter. Tim was about sixteen at the time, Steve was fifteen, Larry was eleven, and Barney was eight. But Tim was the ringleader who was engineering the whole show.

I couldn't imagine what they were doing until I walked in and saw them sitting around the table, dipping tablespoons into a big bowl of red raspberry Jell-O with bananas in it. They were FLICKING big spoonfuls of the red gooey stuff against the white brick wall at the far end of the kitchen, and then watching it ooze down as the pieces of banana caught on the bricks.

Oh, what fun they were having, but I had to decide how to react: Faint? Scream? Spank? (KILL?) Here was an opportunity to make memories for life. This was a moment all of us would never forget, so I decided to make the most of it.

At least half of the big bowl of red Jell-O was still there, waiting to be eaten—or fired at the bricks. *The kids are going to have to clean all this up anyway,* I mused to myself. *So why not have some fun?*

Sitting down at the table next to Tim I asked, "Where's my spoon?"

Tim was so glad I was going to shoot the Jell-O instead of him that he grabbed a big cooking ladle and handed it to me. After all, why fool with mere tablespoons when you're trying to have fun? I loaded the giant ladle with a glob of red Jell-O and slung it against the brick wall. I started to laugh, got another load, and let it fly. I could see why the kids enjoyed Jell-O slinging so much.

At first they didn't know what to make of me, but then they got the message—especially when I told them between chuckles that they would have to clean it up anyway so we might as well all have a good time first.

So, there all five of us sat, firing red Jell-O at the bricks as fast as we could and laughing so hard we were almost hysterical. Soon the wall was a red dripping mess. There wasn't a white brick left anywhere.

I suppose some child-rearing experts could say I was modeling irresponsibility for my kids, but I don't think so. After we used up all the Jell-O, it took them almost two hours to scrub down the wall and clean up the floor. But the memories we all made that day were UNFORGETTABLE. Even now whenever Barney or Larry see Bill Cosby advertising Jell-O on TV, they remember the day Mom caught them firing raspberry missiles at the white brick wall and how she joined in on the fun.

Jell-O Memories Are Good for My Health

That Jell-O scene is a frozen picture in my mind and I still thaw it out now and then when life gets stressful. What better way to alleviate stress than to be aware of the humor in day-to-day living! For example:

You can get humor from your memories, as I do by thinking of the word *Jell-O*, but you can also be ready to laugh about even mundane things. Next time you see a sign in a cafeteria that says, "Shoes required to eat in cafeteria," ask the person you are with, "I wonder where the socks have to go to eat!"

Always be ready to laugh at yourself. Recently I traveled to Grand Rapids, Michigan, where I had been invited to hold a two-day conference in the very church where I had been a member as a child. Some generous folks loaned me a lovely new car to use while I was in town, and my sister, Janet, became the "official driver."

On at least two occasions while using the car, we had to stop to ask people on the street for directions, and both times we couldn't figure out how to get the car window open. Instead, we had to OPEN THE DOOR in order to talk to people. For some reason, we couldn't find the window-opener button. We pushed all the buttons on the dashboard, but only succeeded in turning on the radio, tape player, air conditioner, atmosphere control, etc. I remember telling Janet, "How dumb for a wonderful computerized car like this not to have a way to get the windows down!"

The next day we returned the car and I happened to mention to the owner, "This is a beautiful car, but how do you get the windows down?"

He pointed to a crank on the door and said, "You just turn the crank."

Janet and I looked at the side of the door, and there it was— the "old-fashioned" crank handle that *all* cars used to have a few years ago. For a second, we gasped with embarrassment. Then Janet looked at me and we began to laugh. How stupid could we be not to think that the car might have a crank on the door to roll down the windows? Somehow, all the other computer instruments, lights, and buttons on the dash had totally fooled us. For the rest of the day, we laughed at ourselves so much the tears often flowed down our cheeks. Obviously, neither one of us is "mechanically inclined."

Memorize Proverbs 17:22 and practice it often: "A cheerful heart is good medicine" (NIV). More and more medical researchers are actually admitting that there is a "physiology of happiness" that not only affects our hearts but the rest of our physical bodies as well, especially the immune system.

When tragedy strikes, many folks tend to become physically ill. For example, after losing a loved one they may let their minds become full of negative thoughts and the ensuing "chemical stew" inhibits the immune system, which leaves them much more susceptible to disease. On the other hand, when we can unload our troubled memories and find relief in laughter, our immune function improves.

Dr. Paul McGhee, a psychologist and president of The Laughter Remedy, has been conducting laughter research for twenty years. He was recently quoted in a newspaper as saying, "There really is something to this idea that one's frame of mind has an impact on the body's health system." McGhee went on to say that during the nineties we'll be hearing more and more about a whole new area that he calls "managing your mood for better health."[3]

Norman Cousins helped revolutionize the approach to getting well when he used old movies of the Marx Brothers and Laurel and Hardy to treat himself for a terminal disease. He wrote *The Anatomy of an Illness* to share what he had learned. During the following ten years, many in the medical community followed Cousins's lead. For example, Clemson University did a study of nursing-home patients who had watched "The Honeymooners" and other old comedies. Their aches and pains vanished and as a rule these "old folks" felt better.

In recent years, grants have been awarded to 125 hospitals, nursing homes, and other agencies to start humor programs for their patients. Specifically, here's what a little laughter can do for you:

Laughter helps you relax and unwind. Just try lifting anything heavy when you're enjoying a good belly laugh. You can't do it because your large muscles are totally relaxed. The only ones working are some muscles in your face and your abdomen.

Laughter strengthens the immune system. Research shows that when you have a really good laugh, the body produces more immunoglobulin A, the body's warrior against upper respiratory infections.

Laughter improves your circulation by increasing the heart rate and boosting the oxygen supply to the brain. This is part of what helps you relax and calm down.

Lynn Erdman, coordinator of nursing services in a large cancer treatment center, was quoted in the same article as McGhee. Of laughter, she said, "You feel like the burdens of the world have been lifted from you." At her hospital, Erdman likes to pass out prescriptions for laughter that warn patients of *"humoroids."* And what is the cure for humoroids? "A mild *laughsitive* each day."[4]

Laughter is a way to live an enriched life instead of just maintaining your existence, getting through each day somehow. Laughter is a key to finding pleasure and, when you have to endure mental and emotional pain, you need all the pleasure you can get. I'm not talking about being "lovers of pleasure rather than lovers of God" (2 Tim. 3:4 NIV), or "enjoying the fleeting pleasures of sin" (Heb. 11:25 TLB). Those verses describe the kind of hedonism that leaves God out, but there are unlimited legitimate pleasures you can enjoy by letting God in. For example:

. . . enjoying a tasty meal . . . listening to favorite music . . . watching the embers of a fire . . . marveling at the leaves turning color in the fall . . . AND SEEING THE HUMOR THAT IS ALL AROUND US.

All of these are pleasure-moments God wants us to enjoy, and we can do so if we learn to fine-tune the pleasure channels of our lives to His frequency. For me, the greatest pleasure comes from writing books and speaking to encourage downhearted people. My greatest satisfaction comes from telling SAD hearts how to become MERRY.

Chuck Swindoll, who loves to laugh as much, if not more, than anyone, wrote an excellent book called *Living on the Ragged Edge*, which is based on Ecclesiastes, King Solomon's observations about finding a meaningful life. If anyone knew the difference between seeking hollow pleasure and the right kind of pleasure, it was Solomon, who said:

Go, eat your bread with joy,
And drink your wine with a merry heart;
For God has already accepted your works.

Let your garments always be white
And let your head lack no oil. . . .
Whatever your hand finds to do, do it with your might.
(Eccles. 9:7–8, 10 NKJV)

As Swindoll comments, God wants us to get on with life, not
groan over the past. In other words:

HAVE A BLAST WHILE YOU LAST!⁵

Olive Oil—and Pet Shampoo

Solomon's words in the verse above about letting our heads
lack no oil took on special meaning for me not long ago. Bill
and I were planning to leave Friday noon for a weekend conference near Denver, where I was to speak several times. I had
made an appointment to have my hair done early Friday
morning, giving us plenty of time to get to the airport. The
night before, however, I had decided to give my hair my super
home-conditioning treatment by saturating my scalp with
heavy olive oil. Yes, I know you can buy oil treatments at the
store, but I guess I'm a little frumpy (and also cheap!). After
applying the oil, I wrapped my head in a towel and went to
bed, confident that in the morning my hair would be sleek and
glossy—after it was washed, of course.

Just as I was about to leave for the beauty shop early Friday
morning, Judy, my hairdresser, called and said, "Barb, our
power is out. We have NO hot water and NO hair dryers."

"But my hair and scalp are soaked with olive oil—I gave
myself an oil treatment and I have to get it OUT!"

Judy suggested I find some shampoo that had coal tar in it,
wash my hair thoroughly a couple of times, and then call her
back to see if their electricity had been restored. I said, "Okay,"
but after hanging up I wondered, *Where will I find shampoo with
coal tar in it at 7 A.M.?*

I rewrapped my oily head in a towel and dashed down to the
7-Eleven store on the corner where I found a shelf containing

lots of plain shampoos, but none of the labels mentioned coal tar or pine tar. As I turned away from that shelf, my eye fell on a bottle of SARGENT'S PET SHAMPOO that was supposed to be good for getting rid of fleas on dogs. In bold letters the label read: "WITH PINE TAR." And farther down on the label, in smaller words, it also said, "Coal tar added, will kill lice."

"THAT'S IT!" I almost shouted aloud. "I've gotta have it!"

I dashed home and soaped up twice with the dog shampoo, rubbing it in "real good," just as Judy had instructed. Then I called her, only to learn that the electric power was still out. My appointment was down the drain, so to speak. What to do now? I was on my own, equipped only with dog shampoo and NO HAIR DRYER. Because I have my hair done weekly at the shop, I never had use for one.

Then I remembered our good old Electrolux vacuum cleaner, the same vacuum with the super suction power I've described in a prior book. I dragged the vacuum out of the closet, plugged it in, and reversed the suction to turn it into a mighty blower. Then I lay down on the rug, hoping the warm air would do the drying job.

Eventually, my hair did dry but I had two problems: (1) Now I smelled like tar or naphtha or whatever it is they put in pet shampoo, and (2) Instead of looking shiny and glossy, my well-blown hair made me look like a porcupine caught in a high wind.

There was also one other problem. Time was running out. We would have to leave within minutes to make the plane.

WHAT WAS I TO DO? I could tie a turban around my head and possibly try to get my hair done in Denver before I had to speak, but that wasn't likely since the schedule didn't really allow for it. Then I remembered a special box out in my Joy Room where I keep assorted toys for the grandkids when they come to visit. In that box was an old beat-up blonde wig that the kids love to wear to play dress-up. The crown of the wig had been thinned and refashioned by a puppy somewhere along the way, and it was full of cracker crumbs and Crayola wrappings my grandchildren had dropped in the toy box. I shook it out thoroughly and pulled it down on my head, shoving my hair up under the wig and pulling out a few strands through the holes in the crown. My hair was dark brown and the wig was ash-blonde, but no matter. By this time, I was DESPERATE.

Bill was calling me, so there was no more time to make any improvements. I grabbed my purse and dashed out to the car where he was waiting. During all the time I had been going through my hair crisis, he had been completely oblivious to any problem. He had been chatting with a neighbor, packing, taking out the trash, adjusting the thermostat—lost in his world of details and completely unaware of my near-frantic condition. As I got in the car, I checked myself out in the visor mirror and almost cried as I saw the frayed, chewed-up ash-blonde wig with wisps of my own dark hair peeking out at the sides and at the crown.

"What's the matter?" Bill asked as we turned onto the freeway.

Almost tearfully I explained what had happened and how pathetic I looked for the trip. But Bill continued driving in his same unjangled way. Glancing at my hair, he just smiled and said, "You don't look any different to me!"

Laughter Is in Nation-Wide Demand

According to my mail, a lot of people are looking for joy and laughter. Here are a few of their comments:

I pray for more joy in my attitude that I can laugh more and enjoy life more. I tend to be too serious, so your book has been a breath of fresh air.

□ □ □

We have lost a six-year-old daughter with leukemia and know from experience some of the pain and grief you write about. It certainly has given us the credentials to help others in similar situations. It took eight years to work through our experience before we could talk about it to each other. Thank God we stuck together rather than separate as so many couples do when situations so hard come into their life.

There is a great need in our area for people to find some joy in life. People have bottled up the springs of joy and God forbid if they should laugh at anything silly, let alone let anyone know that humor does have a place in life.

□ □ □

Parents with broken dreams, broken families, and broken hearts need a special touch as often as possible. God is using you and your ministry to give us "joy-aid."

☐ ☐ ☐

I just finished reading your book and received a tremendous blessing. I'm reminded each day to look for a laugh as I'm a very serious negative individual and realize God has deliverance that can glorify Himself in being a help to others.

☐ ☐ ☐

I did receive a copy of your book and began reading it when I really was in need of a lift. But I recommend the publisher put on the following label:

WARNING
For women with bladder weakness,
wearing your DEPENDS is recommended.

☐ ☐ ☐

Your book came at a very needy time in my life as I had just lost my husband very suddenly after 31 years. . . . I was having a very difficult time handling my loss and trying to be brave for my children, making decisions alone, living alone, going to bed alone, waking up alone, living the life of a marble rolling around on the linoleum, no direction, just existing. Then I started your book and realized I sure had nothing to kick about. I had 31 good and wonderful years with very few bumps in the road. I had always used humor in my life to ride over the bumps, but humor had left me, and your book and lessons helped me to get it back.

These letters are only a sampling of the mail I get from folks who haven't laughed in months or even years. A basic question many people have is:

Will I ever laugh again? How long does this intense pain last?

One of my favorite bumper snickers says, "Pain is inevitable, but misery is optional." (In fact, I like it so much I used it on the cover of my book, *Stick a Geranium in Your Hat and Be Happy.*) But sometimes, when you're in pain because of a loss or someone is driving you to the Home for the Bewildered, you think misery is NOT optional. You may feel as if you will NEVER be normal again.

A heavy mantle of grief will enclose you in the thick fog of despair, but shedding tears, talking, and the passing of time will work wonders. One morning you will wake up and realize suddenly that you're not thinking about your pain. You will actually be able to hear the birds sing or see a fluffy white cloud drift across the sky. One day you will have that glimmer of hope and begin to realize there is something more to life than your SPECIFIC PROBLEM.

To put it another way, the night of grief will end, and, as Psalm 30:5 promises:

JOY COMES IN THE MORNING.

The intense pain will ease up, flatten out, and not be so encompassing. I cannot give any specific time as to how long anyone's pain will last. It depends on what you are doing to accelerate yourself through your grieving period. All kinds of resources are within your reach: helpful audio and video tapes, support groups, recovery systems, or just opening your heart to a trusted friend.

Keep in mind that, while tears and talking help, *time is your most trusted friend.* Scar tissue may remain from the hurt you suffer, but your deep wounds will heal. One way to get through this is to keep telling yourself:

ONE DAY I'LL LOOK BACK ON ALL
THIS AND LAUGH.

EXTRA- STRENGTH DEODORANT

Sometimes life is the pits.

If you think that sounds crazy, I understand. I believed that I would never laugh again, much less be able to tell audiences about the experiences our family went through, and be able to do it with humor. For example, I've found many a laugh in my ignorance of homosexuality and now as I retell stories of how I learned about Larry, I put in plenty of examples that make audiences chuckle.

For example, in 1975, who knew what *bisexual* meant? I sure didn't. I had to learn the hard way that it doesn't mean having sex twice a month! Another good laugh always comes out of my sister's purple luggage and my naive (totally erroneous) fear that Janet was a lesbian because lesbians supposedly love the color purple. In truth, lesbians like all kinds of colors, depending on personal taste.

Several months after my "Whatever, Lord" experience and Larry's return, I visited Janet in Minneapolis, where I confessed my "purple paranoia" problem with her luggage. I was glad when Janet laughed harder than anyone at my story. These days I like to tell folks that purple is the color of royalty, and I love purple myself because I'm a daughter of the KING!

Over the years my story, which began with the utter devastation that struck four times in nine years, has been turned into an account sprinkled with humor and joy, but it didn't happen overnight. I hope it shows people how, as we look back, we can poke fun at ourselves and see humor even in tragic moments. We can see how God can use the fractures in our lives to bring restoration to others. That is why I appreciate the way God has taken the painful episodes in my life and used them to infuse others with the joy He has given me.

Will you ever laugh again? OF COURSE you will! You will feel better. You will smile and eventually laugh out loud. Hang in there. Tomorrow could bring that shining moment—in fact, it might even happen TODAY!

Parents Need All the Laughs They Can Get

Because I deal with so many hurting parents, I'm always

looking for something to help them see the funny side of life. Believe me, if you've ever been a parent, you know you can use all the laughs you can get!

Somebody sent me the following instructions on "How to Eat Like a Child" and, as so often happens, no source was given. But whoever wrote the following directions knew something about kids and how to laugh at being a parent. (Even if you've never had a kid, you have probably seen one eating somewhere, so don't skip this because you'll miss some good chuckles.)

PEAS: Mash into thin sheet on plate. Press back of fork into peas, hold fork vertically, prongs up, and lick off peas.

MASHED POTATOES: Pat mashed potatoes flat on top. Dig several little depressions. Think of them as ponds or pools. Fill pools with gravy. With your fork, sculpt rivers between them. Decorate with peas. Do not eat. Alternate method: Make a large hole in center of mashed potatoes. Pour in ketchup. Stir until potatoes turn pink. Eat as you would peas.

SANDWICH: Leave the crusts. If your mother says you have to eat them because that's the best part, stuff them into your pocket or between the cushions of the couch.

SPAGHETTI: Wind too many strands on fork and make sure at least two strands dangle down. Open mouth wide and stuff in spaghetti; suck noisily to inhale dangling strands. Clean plate, ask for seconds, and eat only half. When carrying plate to kitchen, hold tilted so that remaining spaghetti slides onto the floor.

ICE CREAM CONE: Ask for double scoop. Knock the top scoop off while walking out the door of the ice cream parlor. Cry. Lick remaining scoop slowly so that ice cream melts down outside of the cone and over your hand. Stop licking when ice cream is even with top of cone. Eat a hole in bottom of cone and suck the rest of ice cream out the bottom. When only cone remains with ice cream coating the inside, leave on car dashboard.

SPINACH: Divide into little piles. Rearrange into new piles. After five or six maneuvers, sit back and say you are full.

CHOCOLATE CHIP COOKIES: Half-sit, half-lie on bed, propped up by pillow. Read a book. Place cookies next to you on sheet so that crumbs get in bed. As you eat the cookies, remove each chocolate chip and place it on your stomach. When all cookies are consumed, eat chips one by one, allowing two per page.

MILK SHAKE: Bite off one end of paper covering straw. Blow through straw to shoot paper across the table. Place straw in shake and suck. When shake just reaches your mouth, place a finger over top of straw—the pressure will keep the shake in straw. Lift straw out of shake, put bottom end in mouth, release finger, and swallow. Do this until straw is squashed so you can't suck through it. Ask for another. This time shoot paper at the waitress when she isn't looking. Sip your shake casually—you are just minding your own business—until there is about an inch of shake remaining. Then blow through straw until bubbles rise to top of glass. When your father says he's had just about enough, get a stomachache.

Kids' antics are so funny because we work so hard to "raise them right" but they seem to have a sixth sense empowering them to know just how to drive us crazy. Despite this, most parents I know wouldn't trade those funny, crazy times for all the cruise ships in the Caribbean. If your kids are still at home, keep the following thoughts in mind:

The best thing that you can give your children, next to good habits, are good memories.

Children need models more than they need critics.

Childhood is like the old joke about a small town—one blink and it's gone.

Appreciate every moment with your kids. Don't wish their childhood away. One hundred years from now it will not matter what kind of car you drove, or what kind of house you lived in, or how many books you wrote, or what your clothes looked like; but the world may be a little better because you were important in the life of a child.

She Gave Her Own Birthday Party

Because I'm always urging people to put laughter into their lives, you can imagine how tickled I was when I got the following letter:

> Today is my birthday. Yesterday I attended a women's conference you did in San Bruno, California. I was so filled with joy afterwards I went to Mervyn's and put $100 on my charge card.
>
> You see, I am married to one of those very strange only children. He thinks so much of himself that I have to help him celebrate my birthday in the "proper" manner. So I bought myself some birthday presents. I also bought myself a cake and made myself some signs that state, "We love you. Happy Birthday, Mom!"
>
> You told us to look for ways to make joy happen. I'm having a wonderful day, thanks to me. In fact, this is about the best birthday I've had since I was with my mother last. I will be seeing her soon as I am going to be taking off for my homeland in about 24 hours. I'm the one who flies a lot. Thank you for all the laughter and the words of wisdom.
>
> P.S. I went for a walk today and saw the diamonds in the sidewalk. They were beautiful.

About a month later I got another letter from this same lady after she took her trip overseas to see her mom. When she came back, she found even more joy, but this time her family played a big part in it:

> I left for a two-week stay with my daughter, sister, and Mother the day after my birthday. This was the longest time I have ever been away from my family my entire married life. I had a good time being pampered, etc., by my mom.

When I returned here my eldest son, who was on his way out (in fact, he was literally driving away in a car and turned around when he saw me coming), opened the car door for me and gave me a very tender hug. He is 21 years old—I was blown away.

When I entered my home, they had made signs, "Welcome home, Mom. We missed you." The floor was clean, the rugs were recently vacuumed, the dishes done, as well as the wash. The wash was not folded but at least it was clean.

This was all done by my three sons ages 21, 16, and 15. Is this a miracle? And I didn't even pray for one. God really answers prayers that are not even uttered. . . .

Have a wonderful day. Remember that diamonds are a girl's best friend. Isn't it wonderful to have so many???

Laughter Lifts a Tired Spirit

A good laugh can lift your spirits when you're tired and a little cranky. Recently, my good friend, Lynda, and I were driving to Yucaipa, California, about ninety miles away, for a weekend conference at a Baptist church. I had gotten up feeling a little weary that morning and was thinking how much fun it would be to just have a weekend off for a change, when Lynda asked me, "Do you ever get tired of spreading your joy and sharing your story?"

"Well, yes, I sure do," I admitted. "Sometimes I think I can't go over the SAME story, the SAME events, the SAME details, ONE MORE TIME. In fact, I'm so tired of spreading joy I just wish I could stay home and never have to tell my story again."

As we turned off the freeway onto the road to Yucaipa, Lynda and I discussed what it was like to have the symptoms of burnout. I felt as if I had been experiencing just about ALL of them. Then, as we rounded a curve, a huge highway billboard loomed up on the right-hand side and on it were printed only three words in gigantic letters about twenty feet high:

SPREAD YOUR JOY!

In smaller letters near the bottom of the sign was the notation, "Paid for by First Baptist Church, Yucaipa"—the very place where I was going to speak! Talk about SOMEONE sending me a message! We both burst out laughing simultaneously and then drove on down the road to the church where we had one of the best conferences ever.

My joy was abundant that day and the results were 110 percent. Many women came forward for prayer, and several decisions were made to come to the Lord. Some might say the sign appeared when it did by pure coincidence; but isn't it strange how "coincidences" happen? Afterward, I realized again that in spreading my joy, God had restored ME. MY JOY WAS FULL! As soon as I had a moment to myself, I told God I was sorry for my petulant outburst and I thanked Him for His reminder that as we pour out ourselves for others we ourselves are renewed!

I found a little poem called "Boomerang" that sums up my "spread your joy!" experience perfectly:

> When a bit of sunshine hits ye,
> After passing of a cloud,
> When a fit of laughter gits ye,
> An' yer spine is feelin' proud.
> Don't fergit to up and fling it
> At a soul that's feelin' blue,
> For the minute that ye sling it,
> It's a boomerang to you![6]

Eight Ways to Put Laughter in Your Life

Dr. Paul McGhee, president of The Laughter Remedy, suggests eight ways to put more laughter in your life:

- Make a list of fun things you enjoy doing—and do them. Hang around positive people.

- Immerse yourself in humor. Watch cartoons or funny movies, spend Saturday night at a comedy club, your lunch hour at a costume shop, weekends with kids.

- Learn jokes—and tell them. Start with one and people will tell you their favorites.

- Focus on seeing and creating ambiguity, forming puns. Sometimes you see these in newspaper headlines ("Grandmother of Nine Shoots Hole in One") or in signs ("Use Stairs for Restroom").

- Look for humor in everyday situations. And if you overhear something funny, write it down so you can remember it and tell it to others.

- Just laugh—more often and more heartily. Work on great big belly laughs, not just chuckles.

- Learn to laugh at yourself in a kind way. Make a list of things you don't like about yourself, then just start poking fun at them, exaggerate them.

- Learn to find humor in difficult situations, in the midst of stress. This is when you really need it and when your sense of humor abandons you most often.[7]

That last suggestion by Dr. McGhee reminds me of a stressful situation I faced not long ago, when my sense of humor stayed intact, fortunately, even though my dignity suffered a little.

Happy Birthday on the Saw

While I try to make an effort to be dignified, I sometimes wind up in situations that are anything but. I grew up in a very musical family where my mom was a piano teacher, my dad played the violin and sang, and my sister played the vibraharp and piano. I played the piano accordion and sang too.

When I was about ten years old, my dad thought I should learn to play "the saw." Yes, I'm talking about an actual carpenter's saw.

If you bend it back and forth at just the right angle, you can get a screechy, whining sound out of it by using a violin bow—sort of like a sick cat howling on a fence.

Daddy asked one of the men in our church to come over to teach me this unusual "art." As I began to make progress, my father was thrilled because he thought it would be great for me to go along with him to play the saw when he did evangelistic speaking at jails or prisons. (I guess he thought the saw would be more portable than my heavy piano accordion and that the inmates would be so desperate for music they wouldn't mind listening to my amateur efforts.)

As I practiced on my saw, my mother served as my accompanist on the piano, which helped drown out some of the sour notes. After awhile, I could get through a few old songs, and even make them recognizable. My saw repertoire included "I Come to the Garden Alone" and "At the Cross, At the Cross, Where I First Saw the Light."

Mom thought my learning to play the saw was ridiculous, but she went along with the whole thing and pulled together a special outfit for me to wear and still look ladylike. In order to play the saw, you must hold it between your legs and a dress wouldn't work very well. In those days they didn't have slacks or pantsuits, so Mom made something like beach pajamas— today they'd probably be called culottes.

My saw-playing career didn't last long, but it did come back to haunt me years later. Not long ago, I went out to dinner with friends to celebrate the birthday of Mike, one of the young men in our group. As we were sitting in this lovely, conservative restaurant eating dinner, Mike reminded me that I had once told him I could play the saw and that I had promised I would play "Happy Birthday" on the saw for his next birthday!

Because it was Sunday night and I had just spoken at a local church, I had on a dress, and playing a saw was out of the question. Besides, I didn't have one handy so I thought I would get away scot-free. I placated him by saying that I surely would play it for him some other time, but he wasn't about to be put off. Then and there, he pulled out a carpenter's saw and a violin bow and insisted I keep my promise!

So there I sat in a restaurant booth, where we had to push the table away so I could get the saw between my legs, while I managed to screech out a few bars of "Happy Birthday" for the guest of honor.

We were all laughing and having fun when two men who had been in the church service that evening and had bought copies of my book came over to our table and asked me to sign their books. Terribly embarrassed, I quickly straightened my dress and tried to pretend that autographing books after playing the saw was nothing unusual at all, but I wonder what THEY thought!

I was just thankful no one had brought a camera and snapped a picture of me trying to play a saw while wearing a dress in a crowded restaurant. Later, on the way home, I admonished myself, *Barbara, that wasn't very mature!* But then I laughed out loud, because IT SURE WAS FUN!

A Joy Box Full of Sparkling Pinwheels

Back in chapter 1 I mentioned using a Joy Box to cope with the stresses of life. Lots of folks have taken me up on my idea over the years. Just about anything will do for a Joy Box. One lady wrote to describe using a lovely hat box covered with pictures of beautiful red apples. But perhaps the most common container is a plain old shoe box. It doesn't matter what the box is; it's what's inside that counts: cards, letters, curios, cartoons, pictures—anything to make you smile or laugh, particularly when the GLOOMEES attack.

One lady who lives in constant pain with joint disease and weekly migraine headaches admitted she loses joy when the pain makes it difficult to even want to be alive. She wrote:

> The last couple of months I have been "forgetting" to practice joy. . . . I know the Enemy wants me to spend as many days as possible with a big sour face muttering grumblings and complaints. I hope to smile as many days as possible despite the hurt and pain. And I know I get to *choose*

to smile and make an effort to surround myself with what is good and wonderful.

After I first read your book, I had so much fun gathering pleasure things for my Joy Box. I love shiny anythings and I found some sparkling, glittering, rainbow-ee pinwheels I purchased for my front yard. When my kids and husband asked why I was buying pinwheels for myself in the middle of winter, I just smiled and said, "Because Barbara said so!" (just kidding). Actually we had a talk about God's love and doing things that remind us of His many gifts. Sparkling pinwheels make me think of all the beautiful things we will see in heaven.

I started my first Joy Box after Larry disappeared. As I began sharing my story with folks, they started sending me contributions and soon I had several Joy Boxes. Eventually, my Joy Box grew into a twenty-by-sixty-foot JOY ROOM that today is filled with hundreds of signs, sayings, and novel gimmicks of every conceivable description. Everything in my Joy Room has one quality in common: it's bound to make someone smile or chuckle.

New contributions to my Joy Room come practically every week. In the last year or two, I've received more than twenty geranium hats from women who heard me speak about *Stick a Geranium in Your Hat and Be Happy*. These hats now adorn the walls of my Joy Room, but I do save one to put on my latest life-sized doll, who I call Miss Joybells. She's at least five feet tall, wears rolled-down stockings and granny glasses, and carries a purse containing real dentures, denture adhesive, and some corn pads. Oh yes, she also has a mole on her chin with a hair right in the center of it.

Miss Joybells has replaced Long Lena, another huge doll, as my traveling companion in the car, and she accompanies me on trips to conferences that are within driving distance of my home. I get a lot of weird looks from other motorists, but I don't mind. Sometimes I tell folks Miss Joybells is very helpful, particularly when I want to use the Diamond Lane, which, in California, is reserved for "commuter" cars with two or more passengers (just kidding, of course).

Although I love the feeling of a fireplace, we have no fireplace in our home now, and I have often missed it—until recently. To add to my joy collections, someone sent me a twenty-minute video of a roaring fire, complete with the crackling, popping sounds that only a fire can make. So now I just sit back in a nice easy chair and for twenty minutes I watch a roaring fire start up, burn merrily, and then diminish into glowing embers. I can almost SMELL the wood burning.

People often ask me, "How do you unwind after a busy day?" Now I tell them I not only use my bubble bath, but I can always "play my fireplace."

The Sound of Rain Refreshes My Soul

One other recent arrival in my Joy Room is what is called a "rain stick." It's a hollow tube about five feet long that contains cactus seeds. When you rotate it, the stick makes a perfect imitation of rain on the roof.

According to the instruction pamphlet, the rain stick is made from the fallen stalks of the normata cactus. Thorns from the cactus are pressed into the hollow staff so that when the stick is rotated the seeds fall on the thorns to create the sound of light showers or driving rain. The rain stick was used by the Diaguita Indians of Chile to call on the rain spirits. I'm not interested in contacting the rain spirits, but it is nice to tilt my rain stick at a 40 degree angle and thank the Lord for His showers of blessing.

While growing up in Michigan, I loved the sound of rain on the roof, but since living in Southern California (where it supposedly NEVER rains), I've missed that pleasure. So now I'm really happy, because I have my bubble bath, my fireplace, AND my rain sounds to comfort me. Whenever I listen to my rain stick, I think of a stanza from a poem written by my good friend, Betty Henry Taylor:

> I love to hear the sound of rain
>   splashing on my windowpane
>   or pounding on a roof of tin.
> 'Tis music to my ears.
> The sound of blessing from the Lord;
>   showers He has sent my way.
> Refreshing to my soul.[8]

On nights when I can't sleep, I wander out to my Joy Room to enjoy myself and pause to pray for people who've sent me certain items. The other night something stopped me and I had to laugh. I have this little mirror with a picture painted on it of a little boy furtively picking an apple off a tree, as if he hopes he won't get caught. Below the picture the sign says, "Look who God loves!"

As I looked into the mirror at the picture, of course I saw myself and then thought, *Why, yes, He DOES love me, even when I'm like the little boy and doing things I shouldn't.*

I went to bed, smiling as I thought of how God loves us all and He sends His enjoyment in every kind of package—even a piece of hollow cactus full of seeds that makes a sound like rain.

I'm sure you'll see why, then, I especially treasure a letter from a mom with an openly gay son who is a policeman in a large city. She wrote me recently to share her gloomees, but I love her P.S., which says:

> One last thought! Last night at midnight I was awakened to the sound of rain falling. What a wonderful sound to our drought-stricken land. As I lay there listening to the rain, it was like God saying to me, "I'm washing away some of your pain. I'm washing away your pain." Today I laughed—I actually was able to laugh! I can almost see the light.

Gloomee Busters

(Because this chapter is about fun and laughter, I've included some extra Gloomee Busters—just for fun, of course!)

REASONS TO SMILE

Every seven minutes of every day, someone in an aerobics class pulls a hamstring.
Really rich people are much more likely to drown in yacht accidents.
Mechanics' cars break down, too.
Thin people are not really happy.

☐   ☐   ☐

Laughter for the Here-After!

An inexperienced preacher was conducting his first funeral. As solemnly as he knew how, while pointing to the body, he declared, "What we have here is only a shell. The nut is already gone."

Laughter cannot be buried. Consider these headstones:

Here lies Col. Brown.
Shot in battle by an enemy soldier.
"Well Done Thou Good and Faithful Servant"

Here lies Tom Stone
Drowned in the waters of the sea.
"By a Few Affectionate Friends"

Here lies Lucy Mann
(Unmarried)
She lived an old Maid
She died an old Mann

If you haven't purchased your headstone yet, you might be interested in this one. A local classified ad read, "For sale, one used headstone. Good buy for anyone named Murphy."[9]

☐   ☐   ☐

LIFE IS AN ENDLESS STRUGGLE
FULL OF FRUSTRATIONS AND CHALLENGES
BUT EVENTUALLY YOU FIND A HAIRSTYLIST YOU LIKE!

☐ ☐ ☐

Q: What do you get when you cross an insomniac, an agnostic, and a dyslexic?
A: A person who lies awake all night trying to decide if there really IS a doG.

☐ ☐ ☐

Creative Ways to Handle Stress

1. Forget the diet center and send yourself a candy gram.
2. Put a bag on your head. Mark it "Closed for remodeling."
3. Brush your teeth vigorously with Cheez Whiz.
4. Pound your head repeatedly on a pile of lightly toasted Wonder Bread.
5. Find out what a frog in a blender really looks like.

☐ ☐ ☐

A young lady went to heaven. Saint Peter met her and asked if she knew God's Son. She said, "Yes."
"Do you know His name?" Saint Peter inquired.
"Yes," the young woman said, "His name is Andy . . . You know, Andy walks with me, Andy talks with me, Andy tells me I am His own. . . ."

☐ ☐ ☐

Every woman KNOWS that one special
way to drive a man WILD . . .
(Hide the TV remote control.)

☐ ☐ ☐

DIFFERENT DEFINITIONS

HIGHBROW—A person who can listen to the William Tell Overture without thinking of the Lone Ranger.

MOONLIGHTER—A man who holds day and night jobs so he can drive from one to the other in a better car.

RINGLEADER—First one in the bathtub.

☐ ☐ ☐

Examples of Unclear Writing

From actual letters received by a large city's welfare department:

1. I am writing the Welfare Department to say that my baby was born two years old. WHEN do I get my money?
2. Mrs. Jones has not had any clothes for a year and has been visited regularly by the clergy.
3. I cannot get sick pay. I have six children. Can you tell me why?
4. This is my eighth child. What are you going to do about it?
5. Please find for certain if my husband is dead. The man I am now living with can't eat or do anything till he knows.
6. I am very much annoyed to find you have branded my son illiterate. This is a dirty lie as I was married a week before he was born.
7. In answer to your letter, I have given birth to a boy weighing ten pounds. I hope this is satisfactory.
8. I am forwarding my marriage certificate and three children, one of which is a mistake as you can see.
9. I have no children yet as my husband is a truck driver and works day and night.
10. In accordance with your instructions, I have given birth to twins in the enclosed envelope.

☐ ☐ ☐

Unsolved Mysteries of Anatomy

Where can a man buy a cap for his knee,
Or the key to a lock of his hair?
Is the crown of your head where jewels are found?
Who travels the bridge of your nose?
If you wanted to shingle the roof of your mouth
Would you use the nails in your toes?
Can you sit in the shade of the palm of your hand?
Or beat on the drum in your ear?
Can the calf of your leg eat the corn off your toe?
Then why not grow corn on the ear?
Can the crook in your elbow be sent to jail?
If so, what did he do?
How can you sharpen your shoulder blades?
I'll be darned if I know, do you?

□   □   □

There is a right time for everything: . . .
A time to cry;
A time to laugh. . . . (Ecc. 3:1, 4 TLB)

At Day's End, I Turn
All My Problems Over to God . . .
He's Going to Be Up Anyway

Thank You, dear God
For all You have given me,
For all You have taken away from me,
For all You have left me!

Sometimes when you try to run away from your problems, you only run smack into more. I can remember a stressful time when two of our boys were in their teens and giving us difficulties. Steven, in particular, had started running with a crowd we didn't approve of; he also wanted to leave school to join the Marines. Tim had a girlfriend we weren't too happy about either. After dinner one night, Bill and I left the boys at home watching TV while we went for a walk to sort things out.

We walked down to the park at the corner and, because it was a warm evening, we decided to sit on one of the benches

209

located in a pleasant spot well off the street. As we sat there trying to sort through our problems, Bill began tying and untying his shoelaces, a nervous habit he engages in while thinking. (Bill wears out lots of shoelaces that way.)

We had laid out our alternatives and were realizing our options seemed rather limited when suddenly it seemed that Old Faithful had erupted on us. Actually, it was the park sprinkler system, which the automatic timer had activated at full force. We sprang to our feet, and with our shoes sinking deep into the wet grass, we dashed through the sprinklers to reach the safety of the sidewalk.

Soaking wet, we hurried home where we found all four of our boys still watching TV in the living room. They looked up to see their parents, clothes dripping, hair matted down and soggy, and they began roaring with laughter. Tim knew where we had gone and why, and he quipped, "Well, you've got it all solved now, eh? Were you baptized with the answer, or is it raining out right now?"

I had been laughing all the way home and continued laughing at Tim's remark. But Bill didn't laugh. With his melancholy disposition, what happened only dampened his spirits. But I learned something about problems. I was reminded that the best thing to do is lighten up, laugh at your misfortunes, and trust God a lot more.

So that's why the title of this chapter is really more than just facetious fun. Turning your problems over to the Lord is a very good idea that has been confirmed for me by one of my favorite theologians, eight-year-old Danny Dutton, who wrote the following "Essay on God."

> One of God's main jobs is making people. He makes these to put in place of the ones that die, so there will be enough people to take care of things here on earth. He doesn't make grownups. Just babies. I think because they are smaller and easier to make. That way He doesn't have to take up His valuable time teaching them to talk and walk. He can just leave that up to mothers and fathers. I think it works out pretty good.

God's second-most important job is listening to prayers. An awful lot of this goes on, because some people are like preachers, and pray other times besides bedtime. God doesn't have time to listen to the radio or TV on account of this. Because God hears everything, not only prayers, there must be a terrible lot of noise going on in His ears, unless He has thought of a way to turn it off.

God sees everything and hears everything and is everywhere. Which keeps Him pretty busy. So you shouldn't go wasting His time by going over your parents' heads and asking for something they said you couldn't have.

Atheists are people who don't believe in God. I don't think there are any in our town. At least there aren't any who come to church.

Jesus is God's Son. He used to do all the hard work, like walking on water and doing miracles and trying to teach people about God who didn't want to learn. They finally got tired of His preaching to them and they crucified Him. But He was good and kind like His Father, and He told His Father that they didn't know what they were doing and to forgive them, and God said O.K.

His Father appreciated everything He had done and all His hard work on earth, so He told Him He didn't have to go out on the road any more. He could stay in heaven. So He did. And now He helps His Father out by listening to prayers and seeing which things are important for God to take care of and which ones He can take care of Himself without having to bother God. Like a secretary, only more important, of course. You can pray anytime you want and They are sure to hear you because They've got it worked out so One of them is on duty all the time.

You should always go to Sunday school because it makes God happy, and if there's anybody you want to make happy, it's God. Don't skip Sunday school to do something you think will be more fun like going to the beach. That is wrong. And besides the sun doesn't come out at the beach until noon.

If you don't believe in God, besides being an Atheist, you will be very lonely, because your parents can't go everywhere with you, like to camp, but God can. It's good to know He is around when you're scared of the dark or when you can't

swim very good and you get thrown in real deep water by big
kids.

But you shouldn't just always think of what God can do for
you. I figure God put me here and He can take me back
anytime he pleases.

And that's why I believe in God.[1]

Do You Still Believe the Way You Used To?

Many older and more learned theologians have written a lot
about God, but I am not sure they have always matched the
wisdom in little Danny's words. I have no idea where Danny
Dutton's essay came from, or how long ago he wrote it. Danny
is probably a grown man by now, and I'd love to meet him. The
first thing I'd ask him is, "Do you still believe in God the way
you used to? Do you still trust Him with that childlike faith?"

Those are basic, bottom-line questions for all of us, and, although my mail is full of pain, it reflects the ability many folks
have to turn their problems over to God. Often it seems the
more problems folks have, the stronger their faith becomes. For
example, one lady wrote to say that she lost her father, then two
days later her mother died, and five days later her husband of
thirty-two years came in and told her that she should be getting
a lawyer because he was leaving her for another woman. She
added:

> By the grace of God my 16-year-old son and I are "making
> it." On top of all that, we lost our only cat! Your book, as I
> said before, really helped.

Another mother tells me she has always had stress. Married
at seventeen to an alcoholic husband, she had six children in ten
years but lost three of them through death. On the week of her
twenty-fifth wedding anniversary, she and her husband
planned to have a church wedding and rededicate themselves.
Just a few days before, however, he was in an explosion at work

and burned over 65 percent of his body. He survived and when things started to look up a little, she learned she had lupus.

Next, her daughter, who has three children, was divorced by her husband, who remarried just a few weeks later. Her latest news came from her son, who wrote a letter on his birthday thanking his parents for all their love, and then adding that he was gay. Her letter continues:

> I wrote and told our son that we loved him and would pray for him. My first inclination was to preach how wrong he was, but I stopped long enough to ask what Jesus would do. I was saved from much remorse. I'm still grieving but Satan no longer has power to taunt me over this. I have put on God's armor, Ephesians 6:13, but I am a war-torn, battle-scarred mom trying to hang in there. Please send me any information you can. . . .

A Spatula friend took along a copy of my book, *Splashes of Joy in the Cesspools of Life*, while waiting for her husband to be examined by the eye specialist for what he thought might be a very serious problem. She wrote about enduring the stressful moments as they waited for the doctor's verdict:

> I have to tell you as I looked at my big strapping hubby in that doctor's chair I prayed. I saw the chair as the palm of God's hand holding on to him!! I kept repeating, "I gift-wrap you and hand you to the Lord." My worries were erased and a feeling of peace was in that examining room!!!

Later, the doctor came in and told the woman there was no need for laser surgery on her husband's eye. There was some swelling, but the retina was intact and conventional therapy would do the job.

Everyone has different pain to deal with, and it's your attitude that makes the difference. That's what one wife wrote to me as she explained what had happened to her and her husband:

Presently, my husband and I own half of a convenience store/gas station. We're in the midst of a partner split and the realization that our partner misappropriated funds that were to be used for paying taxes, as well as the realization that all we've put into this business is owed to the IRS . . . BUT . . . the Lord has this situation in His hands and after all, it will come to pass!

Another sparkle came in the mail from a mom who had some good news to tell me about her son:

We're so proud (in the "humble" way) that our son is doing so well, out of drugs and alcohol and the gay life. He has a good job. . . . He lives alone. One thing I do know: we must love and care about our kids, no matter what. And pray and pray and God will do it! Life is sure "no bowl of cherries" but our hope is in the Lord. I just say, "Hang in there and love 'em the best we can."

Lord, I Believe, But I Need to Believe MORE

Letters like those above are a real sparkle for me because they help build MY faith. As I admitted earlier, I have an abundance of joy but I'm slim on faith. I know that doesn't make sense because most Bible teachers will tell you that joy comes out of faith. But I can identify with the lady who wrote to say:

The special thing I learned from you is that I can have joy but still be low on faith. I always thought faith had to be with joy. It caused me to feel guilty because my faith is not always strong.

And I also appreciate the mom who wrote to say:

Barbara, I've just finished reading two of your books back to back. I now feel like I have a full coat of armor on. However, I have located the nearest <u>dump</u> just in case.*

---

*When a drunk driver killed our son Tim I spent a lot of nights grieving at a nearby dump. See chapter 2.

Like the father of the paralytic boy, I know what it's like to tell God, "I do have faith; oh, help me to have *more!*" (Mark 9:24 TLB). I probably shouldn't admit it, but I even kind of like the old Moroccan proverb:

TRUST IN GOD,
BUT TIE YOUR CAMEL TIGHT.

And yet God has rewarded the little mustard seeds of faith I've planted by restoring my son to us after he had disowned his family and disappeared into the gay lifestyle. Today Larry and I are best friends, so it was very special for me this past Mother's Day when he came over and brought me a necklace that says, "FIRST RATE MOM."

A lot of folks receive jewelry that says "First Rate Grandma," or "First Rate Friend," but to receive "FIRST RATE MOM" from the boy who had disowned us, changed his name, and never wanted to SEE us again really has a special meaning. I will always treasure this little necklace because it stands in such contrast to a relationship that was broken for eleven years.

Maybe one reason Larry and I are good friends is that we both cope with needing stronger faith—at least on certain occasions. It seems that the longer you're a Christian, the harder it is to have faith because you have more opportunities to be disappointed, more prayers that appear to go "unanswered." I've often thought it's easier for new Christians to have faith because they haven't had time to become a little cynical yet. It reminds me of the bumper sticker that says:

IF YOU CAN REMAIN CALM,
YOU JUST DON'T HAVE ALL THE FACTS.

Don't Worry, Mom, the Keys Are Safe with Us!

Not too long ago Bill and I were invited to use a friend's condo for a couple of weeks on the island of Maui in Hawaii.

Larry and his friend, Tom, who was a new Christian, were going to come over for the second week to enjoy Maui with us. As that second week came to a close, Bill and I had a flight that left the day BEFORE the boys were to depart.

Playing my role of cautious mom to the hilt, I painstakingly instructed Larry about locking up the condo and being SURE not to lose the keys to the condo or to our rental car, which he was to turn in for us. The owners of the condo had told us if the key to any unit got lost, it would mean re-keying the whole complex at a cost of several hundred dollars.

After talking to Larry and stressing the importance of all this, I also tacked written instructions on the refrigerator to remind him to be sure to guard those keys with his life, and to put gas in the rental car before returning it.

Larry drove us to the airport to catch our plane home and on the way, I AGAIN reminded him to be careful about returning all the keys, locking up securely when he left the next day, returning the rental car with the gas tank filled. By now I had moved across the line from REMINDING to NAGGING, but Larry good-naturedly assured me he would take care of it and we flew back to California. The boys returned home a day later and we assumed all had gone well.

Several MONTHS after our Hawaiian vacation, I had occasion to borrow Larry's car. According to my usual custom, I opened the ashtray to put in all my loose change so Larry would have parking-meter money if he ever needed it. There inside the ash tray was a brand-new, shiny gold car key. I could tell the key wasn't to his car and I couldn't help but ask him what the new key was for. He looked rather sheepish, then laughed and told me what had happened.

Evidently, on the same day Bill and I had left, Larry and Tom drove the rental car up to a beautiful beach called Kapalua where snorkeling is terrific. You can swim way out into the bay, where the crystal clear water is filled with coral, shells, and beautiful fish. Larry locked up his wallet and clothes in the car and then put the keys to the car and the condo in the back pocket of his swim trunks.

Remembering all of my instructions, Larry buttoned the pocket of his swim trunks securely—he thought. For an hour or two, Larry and Tom had a terrific time, snorkeling about a mile out in the bay. Finally they decided to grab some lunch, so they swam back to shore. As Larry reached for the keys to the car (and the condo) he realized THE KEY RING WAS NOT IN HIS POCKET. The keys were gone!

Larry and Tom swam back out into the bay and for over an hour they searched almost hysterically, peering down into the water, trying to spot the keys on the ocean floor. Back and forth they swam, retracing all the places they thought they had been—but no keys.

Exhausted, they returned to the little shack on the beach where they had rented their snorkeling equipment.

"Has anyone turned in any lost keys?" Larry frantically asked the proprietor. He promptly pulled down a huge glass jar of car keys, obviously collected over many months from many similar tourist mishaps. But as he pointed to the jar he said, "I've got a whole jar full of lost keys, but none were turned in today."

Larry was desperate. Because his wallet was locked up in the car, he had no money to even make a telephone call to the car-rental agency to see if they could make him another car key. He finally hiked up to a hotel about a half a mile away and explained his situation. A kind hotel clerk let him use a phone to call the car-rental agency, which told him a spare key could be made but he would have to come and get it. That made no sense to Larry since he had NO WAY TO GET THERE. The car-rental agency suggested he could take a taxi to their office.

Larry reminded them he had no wallet; then he suggested, "Why don't you send me a duplicate key with a taxi cab driver? Then I can open the car, get my wallet, and pay the cab fare."

The car-rental agency said that would be acceptable, but it would take a couple of hours to have the duplicate key made and then have it driven over to him.

Larry paced up and down, waiting for the cab and wondering how in the world he could explain the loss of the condo key to the manager of the condominium complex. Meanwhile, Tom, a comparatively new Christian, just kept saying, "Hang on, Larry, just trust the Lord. Those keys will show up."

"Are you kidding?" Larry replied. "Don't you know that I lost them at least a mile out in the OCEAN? How would you expect we could ever get them back? My mom will just die when she finds out we have lost those keys to the condo, not to mention the car. And how will we get in the condo? I don't even know the owner's name, and it's a big place with lots of units— the manager won't know who we are."

Relax, All We Need Is a Miracle

Tom persisted in believing that miracles do happen and God would answer their prayers. But all Larry could say was, "Get REAL! Do you think some guardian angel is going to fly those keys back here from the bottom of the ocean? What if they really do have to re-key the whole place, just as my mom said they would? I'm telling you, this is big trouble and it's going to be expensive . . ."

Larry kept fretting about his loss, waiting for the cab to come with the key to the rental car. At that moment he would have agreed with the motto that says:

THINGS AREN'T AS BAD AS THEY SEEM . . .
THEY'RE WORSE!

The hours dragged by with frustrated, stressed-out Larry pacing in circles and confident Tom just "trusting the Lord." There was no money for lunch, no money to call anyone, no nothing—only their beach towels and Tom's firm conviction that God would answer their prayers to find the keys.

As time ticked slowly on, the boys waited near the rental shack on the beach, anxiously watching for the cab to come with the key to the rental car. Suddenly Larry heard a guy hollering, "Hey, aren't you the guy who lost your keys in the ocean this morning?"

Larry looked up and saw the proprietor of the rental shack leaning out his window, and shouting toward them. He ran quickly over to the office where the man dangled a set of keys— THE KEYS THAT LARRY HAD LOST OVER A MILE OUT IN THE OCEAN!

Larry was so amazed he could hardly talk. "How . . . how . . . how did you get THESE?"

"Well, some people who rented scuba diving gear found them on the ocean floor. They just now turned them in and I had a feeling they might be yours. They found them about a mile out from the beach."

Larry thanked the man profusely, took the keys, and went back over to where Tom was waiting. He admits he was tempted to tell Tom that a big fish had swallowed the keys, that a lady in a restaurant was eating the fish and had found them and . . .

On second thought, he decided against that kind of fish story and just held up the key ring. When Tom saw the keys, he smiled and said, "See? I knew the Lord would answer our prayers . . ."

Next Larry tried to call the car-rental agency to cancel the spare key, but they told him the cab was already on the way. The cab pulled up just a few minutes later and Larry paid for the key as well as the taxi—a total of $75.

The cost of getting the key (which he no longer needed) was one thing, but the bigger cost was the anxiety he had experienced all afternoon, worrying about what would happen. Meanwhile, Tom had kept calm. He waited for his miracle and it WAS, indeed, a miracle.

So that's why Larry kept that shiny new gold key in the ashtray of the car, just to remind him of that day when a guardian angel was looking over his shoulder and something he knew was lost forever had come back to him. Now when he gets in stressful situations—heavy traffic, for example—he just takes out that key and remembers it's far better to say a prayer, trust the Lord, and relax. It is a symbol of God's care for him.

When Hope Is Deferred, Pray Harder

Larry's car key adventure makes a good point about trusting in God's care, but at the same time, for many folks there are times when the keys AREN'T found, when the miracle DOESN'T happen. Actually, however, that's when we REALLY need to turn our problems over to God. That's when we need to pray EVEN MORE than we ever have before.

When Larry disappeared into the gay lifestyle and was gone for years with no word, I went through what I call a "hope-deferred" period. As King Solomon said, "Hope deferred makes the heart sick" (Prov. 13:12 TLB). I could have driven myself and everyone around me crazy if I thought each day was supposed to include a miracle. But day after day went by, and nothing seemed to happen. It took eleven years for our hopes to be realized and to experience the joy of having our son return home to ask forgiveness for the pain he had caused us. Then the rest of Proverbs 13:12 was ours: "when dreams come true at last, there is life and joy."

While living in a hope-deferred set of parentheses we have to realize that it often takes years before our prayers are answered, but that doesn't stop us from living expectantly through each day knowing God is still in control of it all. He will answer our prayers in His perfect timing. When our hope is deferred, we must remember:

GOD NEVER HAS TO SAY, "OOPS!"

Did you ever think of your life, with all the mistakes and sins of the past, as being much like the tangles in a ball of yarn? When hope is deferred, it's a comfort to know we can get up and face each day by putting ourselves and our loved ones in His hands, knowing that in His loving mercy He will untangle it all.

You could never hope to straighten out a mess you're facing, but you don't have to. If there is one message I have tried to communicate in this book, it is this:

PLACE YOUR CHILD IN GOD'S HANDS
AND RELEASE THE LOAD TO HIM.

John White is the author of many fine books, but perhaps his most heartfelt writing is *Parents in Pain* because Dr. White is a parent who knows what pain is like. When one of his sons wound up in jail, he wrote an article that contains many good points, including the disturbing thought that you must allow your children to face tragedy and even death by allowing them to live with the consequences of their own actions. White believes relinquishment means trusting God with your children, rather than relying on your own ability to manage their lives. Relinquishment means giving up your delusions about your own power to determine the destinies of your children.

Turning to the parable of the Prodigal Son, White observes that we must be to our children what God the Father is to each of us. We must let our children go and then never give up loving them. He writes:

> Hardest of all is to share the pain with the Father, to let our puddle of sorrow flow into His great ocean of woe. It is (in the case of our finite minds) to allow faith, hope, and love to go on living. This is what the father of the prodigal did.
>
> How do I know? Listen to what Jesus tells us:
>
> But while he was still a long way off, his father saw him and was filled with compassion for him; he ran to his son, threw his arms around him and kissed him (see Lk. 15:20).
>
> You don't identify your son when he is "still a long way off" unless you happen to be looking for him, staring at the horizon in hope. Either you give up trying, because the pain is too great, or else faith, hope and love refuse to die in you, and you go on looking, looking until you spot the prodigal in the distance. And then you run—run until you have him safe in your arms.
>
> That is how God is with us. He lets us choose. Then He swallows His pain and waits.
>
> Let's fall on our faces before Him. Let's ask Him to search our parental hearts and make them like His own.[2]

Only God Can Untangle Your Threads

John White's thoughts about the parable of the Prodigal Son remind me that God alone can untangle the threads of our lives. What a joy and comfort it can be for us to drop all of them into His hands and then LEAVE them there! A mother with a son in the gay lifestyle wrote:

> I have come in this past year to a better acceptance of my 24-year-old son and I would like to share this with you. It is a different kind of acceptance, perhaps based on my teaching of all kinds of physically and emotionally handicapped children and my work with their parents.
>
> I have come to accept homosexuality as a handicap. For the past four years, I was just angry that my son had chosen this path and only wanted him to CHANGE. I now feel that just as some physically handicapped people are able to conquer or rather rise above the handicap, so SOME homosexuals are able to. But many of the children I have worked with were also weak emotionally and just not able to handle their infirmities. As a teacher, I have worked around the problem to try to give the child as normal a life as possible. In time, I didn't even see the outward child but related to the humanness which is God-given to all.
>
> While I still often yearn for normal sexuality in my son, this is, in reality, a rejection of him. Because, like it or not, this is his present orientation. This must be a very difficult "place" for him to be and my role as his mother is not to make his life any harder. I no longer look for the miracle each time I'm with him, and I feel better when I do spend time with him. Perhaps these thoughts might be helpful to some other parents.

Note that this mom talks about her son's "present orientation." Isn't that true of all of us? We are all in some kind of present orientation, and we are all in a change process that means growing and becoming what God wants us to be. I especially like this mom's concept about learning how to enjoy pleasant times with her son and not constantly straining to see some sign of change. After all, only God can bring about any shift of behavior anyway. And, as she says, she might as well relax and enjoy the time they have together.

How to Pray for a Rebel

Another question I often get from folks who are struggling with a son, daughter, close relative, or friend involved in a self-destructive lifestyle, is:

How are we to pray about this? We pray and God doesn't seem to answer. We wonder if God even cares.

The following thoughts about prayer are adapted from a paper by my good friend, Bob Davies, of the Love in Action organization in San Rafael, California. If your loved one is in rebellion, remember:

- There is a natural law of cause and effect that all of us take for granted. This law means that every action we take has some kind of consequence. If our action is in agreement with the way God created us to live, we reap good results. If it is contrary to God's plan, the effects can be painful. This principle is so obvious, and yet so many times we actually work against it.

- In His love, God allows painful consequences to occur in a person's life as a result of his rebellion. Sometimes, it simply takes time until rebellious actions begin to bear sour fruit. We must be patient, and allow that time to pass. There is NOTHING that we can do to hurry this process, except to recognize what is happening and to allow the Lord to work.

- The built-in results of sinful actions are one of the strongest deterrents to continued sin. So don't pray that God will remove the consequences of your loved one's rebellion! And don't thwart God's purposes by removing them yourself. For example, the worst thing you can

do for your wayward son (or daughter) is to send him
all the money he wants when he has wasted his finances
on weekend parties for all his gay friends.

- God may work in totally unexpected ways to bring an
  end to rebellion. Probably the way God will work in the
  situation is not any way that you have thought of. "For
  My thoughts are not your thoughts, neither are your
  way My ways," declares the Lord in Isaiah 55:8. We can
  only see a minute fraction of the whole situation; God
  sees all of it.

- Pray that God will work supernaturally, but be prepared! The weeks, months, even years that the person
  you are praying for is in rebellion may seem like forever.
  So pray for God's supernatural protection during your
  friend or relative's rebellion. God may still bring some
  hair-raising consequences into their life. Their health
  may suffer dreadfully. . . . But God is still at work—
  trust Him!

It is vitally important to realize that the final choice
whether to serve God or self is up to the person involved in
sin. God has given us a free will, and no one has ever been
dragged into submission to the Lord against his will. You
cannot make that choice for your child. To really grasp this
principle will relieve you of much misunderstanding and
frustration with God's ways.[3]

After I let go of Larry by praying "Whatever, Lord!" up there
on that viaduct, God took me at my word and tested me to see
if I really meant it. Letting go is one thing, but then you discover
you have to keep turning it over to God in faith *every day*.

After Larry left a second time, I threw myself into my Spatula
ministry with renewed energy. Folks would come up to me and
ask, "And how is your family now?"

And I would answer, "Well, my two sons have not risen from
the dead and my third son has disowned us, changed his name,
and never wants to see us again. That doesn't sound like much

of a victory, but two years ago when I said, 'Whatever, Lord!' I really meant it. So I'm still trusting God to bring our son back. God only gives the score on a life when the game is over, and the game ain't over *yet* with my kid."

Although my hope was deferred, I NEVER LOST HOPE. I clung to the belief that someday the values I had built into Larry would surface, and God would bring conviction to his heart. After eleven years that is just what happened.

During all those years, God was fine-tuning me for the ministry He has given me to do. While I was in that deferred-hope situation, I learned much about developing a "TURN-IT-OVER" attitude. And in His good timing, He brought us through to life and joy.

What Is a Turn-It-Over Attitude?

Recently a friend sent me a tape of a message preached by the Reverend Bruce Larson based on his best-selling book, *There's A Lot More to Health Than Not Being Sick* (Word, 1981). In his message Larson mentioned visiting the Menninger Foundation and asking members of its staff, "What is the single most important ingredient in your treatment here?"

The doctors answered, "We know it's hope. We don't know how it comes or how to give it to people, but we know that when people get hope, they get well."

"What does hope look like?" Larson asked next.

These skilled medical doctors told him they could tell almost immediately when patients suddenly turned the corner and realized they did not have to go on as they had before. As Larson put it in his message:

HOPE MEANS YOU ARE NO LONGER A PRISONER
OF YOUR TRACK RECORD.

I continually get letters from folks who have learned the meaning of hope. Their track record may sound depressing, but they know they are not prisoners. Instead, they are free. One mom put it this way:

> You came into my life when my 18-year-old son attempted suicide in November. I'm glad to report that he's doing fine. The Lord made it clear to me that this is not <u>who my son is</u> and that we must not let this spontaneous act define him. Everybody hits bottom, but it's what happens next that's really important. The Lord has shown me that I can be proud and thankful for the toughness he showed in healing, instead of focusing on the fact of what happened.
>
> I still have "panic attacks" but try to stand on raw faith and just decide to trust both him and the Lord.

Turning It Over Doesn't Mean You Quit Trying

In that same message, Larson went on to ask a provocative question: "Do you have the courage to be happy?"

I hear from so many folks who understand that a turn-it-over attitude doesn't mean you put your feet up and quit trying. Two of my favorite verses are Philippians 2:12–13:

The secret to success is to stay cool and calm on top and paddle like crazy underneath.

"Therefore . . . work out your own salvation with fear and trembling; for it is God who works in you both to will and to do for His good pleasure" (NKJV). That sums up a principle for living that is a sure-fire combination for success:

PRAY AS IF EVERYTHING DEPENDED ON GOD
AND WORK AS IF EVERYTHING DEPENDED ON YOU.

There is an old story that illustrates this principle very well. It seems that two frogs were playing on the rafters of a dairy farm one night and they fell into adjoining pails of cream. Both frogs scrambled for survival, but one fought longer and harder, and stayed the course.

When the farmer came in the next morning, he found one frog floating on the top of a pail of cream, dead; and the other frog standing on a cake of butter—exhausted, but happy to be alive.

Moral: When we let problems overwhelm us, when we stop jumping and hopping and scrambling for survival, we stop living. But when we hang in there and fight the good fight we end up on a cake of butter.

One mom whose gay son causes her all kinds of hurt is a beautiful illustration of this frog story. In a letter to me, she admitted that things haven't been so good lately. Although her son lives in the next block, she sees him seldom. For the past year, he has missed her birthday and Easter, although he did manage to send a Mother's Day card that arrived the following week.

But this mother hasn't let it get her down, as her letter described:

> I want to share something that the Lord led me to see in the Bible. So often, holidays are ruined for me because I want a family like other people have. Nonetheless there are a lot of caring people in my life: a wonderful young mother who lived here as a student many years ago and is like a daughter to me, and people from a Bible study who have become very close to me and many others. But, like David in 2 Samuel

18:33, I continued to grieve for the lost life of my son while I made my friends feel that no one was as important to me as he was.

Then God, like Joab did to David, made me see, as you said in your book, that the sin of one person was ruining my life. That made all the difference in my Mother's Day. I sent cards to all the first-time mothers I knew and to my young friends who care about me when it hurts. I accepted a dinner invitation, took lilacs and candy to my hostess, a lady in her eighties, and had a great day. It was the nicest Mother's Day in many years.

Hope Equals Endless Possibilities

According to Bruce Larson, hope also means being excited about your future because you believe God sets you free from your past mistakes. Hope has you saying, "I can't wait to get up in the morning." In fact, if you have the habit of turning all your problems over to God at day's end, you will be ready for whatever tomorrow may bring. As Larson puts it:

WHEN JESUS CHRIST IS THERE
LIFE HAS INFINITE POSSIBILITIES.

I'm big on optimism and thinking positively, but those aren't the real ingredients of hope. Hope comes out of knowing to whom you belong and knowing that He is in control.

When Tim was in college, he worked for one of the most prestigious mortuaries in Southern California. One of his chief duties was driving the grieving family to the grave site in a rose-colored limousine and, if they had no minister to preside, he would also conduct a brief service by reading some words of comfort from a prepared text.

One day I came home and found the limousine, with the familiar mortuary monogram on the side, parked in our driveway. Tim was supposed to be working, so I wondered what had brought him home during that hour of the day. I went into the house, and found him sitting forlornly at the kitchen table. When he saw me, he jumped up, ran over, and hugged me tightly.

I wondered what on earth had prompted all this attention, but then Tim explained. He had been conducting a funeral service that morning and, as he read from his prepared text, he looked down and saw the "loved one" in the casket. She looked so much like me—same coloring and same appearance—that he could hardly continue with the service. Even though he knew it wasn't his mother, he still had a lump swelling up in his throat.

As soon as the service was over, he dashed home to be sure "Everything was okay." I'm not quite sure why this made such an impression on Tim. He had been brought up in the church and had made a decision for Christ while still a very young child. He had been to many summer church camps and had attended church all his life, but he always concerned us because his faith just didn't seem real to him. He wasn't rebellious; he was just sort of "flat" and never very excited about being a Christian.

Perhaps seeing someone who looked like his mother lying in a coffin caused Tim to stop and realize that death would touch his own family someday—that life is fleeting and none of us lasts forever.

It could well be that this unsettling experience helped prepare Tim for the encounter he would have later with a man named Bill Pritchard, whose counsel helped him reach a new level of spiritual understanding and commitment that he'd never had before. A few months later, Tim went into training with the sheriff's department, and part of that training included spending time guarding prisoners at one of the "honor farms" north of Los Angeles. One night he penned a letter to Bill Pritchard, part of which said:

> This place reminds me of a Marine boot camp, and every officer is a drill instructor. You can't really sit down and talk

with these inmates, but I knew God would provide a way for me to witness to some of them. I got a couple of dozen booklets (*The Four Spiritual Laws*, etc.) and distributed them among the barracks. It gave me a good feeling when I walked into the barracks after reveille to see Hell's Angels and Black Panthers lying on their bunks reading these booklets. I could get fired for passing out literature, but it would be well worth it to know that another person received eternal life. . . .

Less than six months later, Tim's own life was snuffed out on the Alaska Highway. The bodies of Tim and his friend, Ron, were shipped home, and a few days later we held a memorial service that was attended by nearly a thousand people. We printed bright green bookmarks, about a thousand with Tim's picture and another thousand with Ron's picture, and beneath the photos was the poem "Safely Home," which says, in part:

> I am home in Heaven, dear ones;
>   All's so happy, all's so bright!
> There's perfect joy and beauty
>   In this everlasting light.
>
> All the pain and grief are over,
>   Every restless tossing passed;
> I am now at peace forever,
>   Safely home in Heaven at last.
> . . . .
> Then you must not grieve so sorely,
>   For I love you dearly still;
> Try to look beyond earth's shadows,
>   Pray to trust our Father's will.
>
> There is work still waiting for you,
>   So you must not idle stand;
> Do your work while life remaineth—
>   You shall rest in Jesus' land.

When that work is all complete,
He will gently call you home;
Oh, the rapture of the meeting!
Oh, the joy to see you come![4]

Why Tim had to die just when his own faith was at a new level is one of the secret things I'll have to leave with God, but even in his death he left many folks with new hope for their lives. Someone has said, "Hope is not the conviction that something will turn out well, but the certainty that something makes sense, regardless of how it turns out."

Ralph Waldo Emerson wrote:

One of the illusions of life is that the present hour is not the critical, decisive hour. Write it on your heart that every day is the best day of the year. He only is rich who owns the day, and no one owns the day who allows it to be invaded with worry, fret and anxiety. Finish every day and be done with it. You have done what you could.

And for the Christian I would add, "Trust God with what was undone or even done incorrectly. In His good time, He will make it right."

Gloomee Busters

The measure of success is
not whether you have
a tough problem
to deal with, but whether
it's the same problem
you had last year.
—John Foster Dulles

□   □   □

You are struggling . . .
I see it,
I feel it,
I hurt for you.
But I must tell you, dear friend,
I believe with all my heart
that you will emerge
somehow wiser, stronger,
and more aware.
Hold on to that thought,
tuck it away in a
corner of your heart
until the hurt melts enough
for the learning to have
meaning.[5]

☐   ☐   ☐

Worry Defined

Worry is the senseless process of using today to clutter up
tomorrow's opportunities with leftover problems from yesterday.

☐   ☐   ☐

When someone
says,
"Life is hard,"
ask them,
"Compared to what?"

☐   ☐   ☐

I believe the nicest and sweetest days are not those on
which anything very splendid or wonderful or exciting
happens, but just those that bring simple little pleasures,
following one another softly, like pearls slipping off a string.[6]

☐   ☐   ☐

STEADFAST HEART

I've dreamed many dreams that never came true.
I've seen them vanish at dawn.
But I've realized enough of my dreams, thank God,
To make me want to dream on.

I've prayed many prayers when no answer came,
Though I waited patient and long,
But answers have come to enough of my prayers
To make me keep praying on.

I've trusted many a friend that failed,
And left me to weep alone,
But I've found enough of my friends true blue,
To make me keep trusting on.

I've sown many seed that fell by the way
For the birds to feed upon,
But I've held enough golden sheaves in my hands,
To make me keep sowing on.

I've drained the cup of disappointment and pain
And gone many days without song,
But I've sipped enough nectar from the roses of life
To make me want to live on.

—Source unknown

□ □ □

GOODNIGHT, DEAR GOD

The sun has gone down from the sky
    And peace of night is drawing nigh.
I pray, Dear God, my soul You'll keep
    While in Your loving arms I sleep.
Forgive the things I did today
    When from Your glorious path I'd stray.
And as I slumber through the night
    Please take my hand and hold it tight.
And when I awake to a bright new morn,
    Restored, refreshed, renewed, reborn,
I'll try again, Dear God, to be
    The person You would hope of me.

—Source unknown

□ □ □

I run in the path of your commands,
for You have set my heart free.
(Ps. 119:32 NIV)

Always Take Your Rainbow with You!

After the darkness,
  the daylight shines through
After the showers,
  the rainbow's in view
After life's heartaches,
  there comes from above
The peace and the comfort
  of God's healing love.
                    —*Kristone*

Before closing the lid on the gloomees box, I want to share some final thoughts with you that I came across as I was straightening my Joy Room the other day. I ran across a little sign that says:

AMUSING GRACE . . .
HOW SWEET THE SOUND OF LAUGHTER.

The more I thought about that, the more I realized we need all the *amusing* grace we can get from God's amazing, inexhaustible supply. If you're like me, you've learned that some days you can be confident you will get through it, but on other days, you're back to square one. As somebody said,

CONFIDENCE IS WHAT YOU HAVE
WHEN YOU DON'T REALLY UNDERSTAND
THE SITUATION.

The Case of the Missing Cotton Picker

Several years ago I received a call from a lady with a problem and I was "confident" I knew the answer—until I realized I didn't understand the problem!

This darling mother called me from Arizona, exasperated because her gay daughter had promised to come to their ranch and feed the animals and watch over the place while she and her husband were going to another ranch to pick cotton. Instead of minding the ranch for a few days as she had promised, the gay daughter wanted to go off with her lesbian friend, and the parents had no one who could take her place on such short notice. Furthermore, the mother said it was imperative that they take all nine of their cotton pickers to the other ranch to make sure the cotton got picked.

Well, it all sounded OBVIOUS to me. I told this mom that it would be simple to just leave one of the cotton pickers there to tend the ranch and use the other eight cotton pickers to do the job. Wouldn't this solve the problem rather easily?

Fortunately, the woman was gracious and, realizing I was not a farm girl, she patiently explained to me that cotton pickers are not PEOPLE; they are MACHINES that cost ninety thousand dollars apiece!

Oh well, win a few, lose a few! Having a sense of humor is a requisite for working in this ministry, or for just living in this zoo we call the world today. So I hope you'll keep yours in working order—your sense of humor, of course, not the zoo. There is no better way to keep your sense of humor than to remember that God's grace—His love, mercy, and help—is ALWAYS available.

Grace Is God—in the Flesh

Grace is one of those "theological" words that we say we believe in and even count on, but sometimes it's good to consider what grace really *does* mean in a world where the gloomees are always out to get you. As Lewis Smedes says, God's grace can make life all RIGHT despite the fact that everything is obviously all WRONG . . . Grace is the reality of God entering history—and our lives—to make things right at the very center:

> He came as a living Person called Jesus, talking and hurting and dying and coming to life again; His mission was to bring grace to the world, and so in deepest reality to make it All Right precisely when things are all wrong. Grace? It is shorthand for everything that God is and does for us in our tired and sinful broken lives.[1]

Grace does not stand for an escape mechanism, some kind of all-expense-paid trip to Disneyland because God knows we can't afford to go ourselves. Grace has nothing to do with Disneylands, Fantasy Islands, magical cures, or instant solutions. As Smedes says,

> Grace is rather an amazing power to look earthy reality full in the face, see its sad and tragic edges, feel its cruel cuts, join in the primeval chorus against its outrageous unfairness, and yet feel in your deepest being that it is good and right for you to be alive on God's good earth.[2]

You may have seen the acrostic on grace that puts it all in perspective:

God's
Riches
At
Christ's
Expense

PACK UP YOUR GLOOMEES

Jesus never used the word *grace*. God left that for Paul, but if you want to describe grace in one word it is *Jesus*.

Grace (Jesus) is the answer for our guilt and failure.

Grace (Jesus) is the strength we need to cope with life.

Grace (Jesus) is the promise that gives us the hope that keeps us going.

The Gloomees Thrive on Guilt

Most dangerous of all the gloomees that lie in wait to drag us down is guilt, that pervading feeling that we haven't measured up to our own standards, not to mention God's. Almost daily I hear from parents who are downhearted and guilt-ridden. Their children, usually grown adults themselves, have disappointed them and they don't understand what happened. For example:

> Our 17-year-old son just decided he couldn't go to high school here because (in his own words) ". . . the teachers hate me and you don't stick up for me and, and, and . . ." He went to live with my brother and his family in North Dakota. He is the baby and I am feeling like a failure. He has two older brothers. The 25-year-old moved out with our blessings in May, but now he is keeping company with a married woman and quit church.

Now, it would be easy to look at a situation like this one and say, "Oh, I see the problem—these parents were TOO STRICT." Or perhaps we could quickly surmise, "Yes, it's obvious what happened here—PERMISSIVENESS. They were far too lenient."

It's simple to see the answer to someone else's problem. We can wrap up our "solution" in a neat little package of slick answers and present it to them with smug assurance.

But when you're IN that hurting family, there are no slick answers. I pray with hurting parents and I hurt with them, as well. I feel their frustration and their pain. I speak and write for hurting parents who haven't found any Band-Aid solutions. Often they have sought help from the experts, the specialists, and the authorities, but they have found no answers that meet real needs. They've heard all the cozy Christian phrases such as, "Just praise the Lord," or "You can give it all to Jesus." Please understand, there is nothing wrong with praising God or giving it all to Jesus, but it's all too easy to push pat answers on others without being sensitive to their problem. I have done it myself and I have learned to use extreme care in dealing with hurting folks. I am sure that sometimes I still miss the mark, but I can only ask forgiveness and throw myself at the mercy of God's grace.

When everything goes wrong and the bottom drops out, we are overwhelmed with a barrage of emotions: panic, frustration, anger, fear, and shame, all of which are just the beginning of the final death blow called guilt. You condemn yourself and then you begin to hate yourself as you watch your family spinning out of control. One guilt-burdened mom says it with words that are so gut-level honest they speak for many parents I know:

> It has only been a month since our son sat and defended homosexuality. He would never come right out and say he was involved—but my husband and I agree he might as well have. . . . Did we just think we were a happy family with normal problems? I ask myself. I cannot get past the guilt. I always loved my children—but I was too domineering, too outspoken—my husband says I am focusing only on my faults and magnifying them. . . . I don't see how mothers/ fathers (mostly mothers) get out from under the cloud of guilt—and why should we—if we have had anything to do with it? If mothers help cause this—then we deserve to suffer forever. I've read your books—I still don't know how you got away from the guilt enough to be happy. My heart is like lead in my chest.

How can this dear mom get rid of her lead-heavy load of guilt? She doesn't even have positive confirmation her son is a homosexual, yet she is condemning herself and wondering how I got free from guilt over my own son. When a parent feels this overwhelmed, there is only that one, positive answer: *God only knows*—and what God has to offer is His grace.

I can only hope this mother won't multiply her guilt feelings by lashing out at her son as I did at mine. I said many harsh things to Larry in the beginning; my words were sharp and cutting. I didn't listen to him as he tried to tell me what his hurts were. I just blasted him with a recital of my own feelings.

Our kids don't need our condemnation. What they do need is our encouragement to be open and honest with us. They need to know that, yes, we are hurt, and yes, we are disappointed, but we can honestly share these feelings without being destructive. Jesus met people right where they were, whatever their condition. He didn't show them sympathy. He didn't necessarily show them mercy. But He ALWAYS showed them grace.

Amazing Grace from the IRS

Not long ago I saw grace demonstrated in a most unlikely setting—the INTERNAL REVENUE SERVICE. Julia had a son in trouble, and in desperation she came to our Spatula support group for help. We became good friends and shortly thereafter she came to know Christ. Overnight we saw big changes in her life.

Then one hot summer day she called with the news that she was to be audited by the IRS! Tearfully she confessed to me that she had lied on her prior year's income tax return, saying she had given large amounts to an orphanage in Mexico. Now they were calling her in to a local IRS office to document her records. There was only one problem: this orphanage didn't even exist!

As we talked, she asked me to go with her when she was audited. What good could I possibly do except give moral support? I agreed to go, however, and when we got to the IRS office, we just sat in the car a moment and prayed together. I prayed that whoever we talked to would show MERCY. Julia was not expecting any kind of pardon, but a little mercy would be most welcome. She was truly repentant for what she had done. It had all happened before she had become a Christian, but now her past sins had caught up with her.

Julia's sweet prayer for forgiveness was touching. This was right where the rubber meets the road, no wobble room here. Julia definitely repented of that deception and wanted to make things right.

We walked into the IRS office and sat waiting until Julia's name was called. The income-tax examiner who would handle her case ushered us into a tiny cubicle. As I looked around, I noticed a fish sign on her calendar. Could it BE? Was this lady a Christian?

Julia had already decided to come clean and she didn't hesitate: "I wasn't a Christian last year, and when we filled out the tax form I lied. I put down that we gave money to this orphanage in Mexico. But that was all a lie because the orphanage is nonexistent, and I am truly sorry and I have asked God to forgive me. I felt heavy conviction about it even before I got your notice to come in and be audited, but I am here to tell the truth. Actually, all the deductions for contributions I claimed are false; I never gave anything to any charity last year."

Julia choked out her confession between tears, then continued to sob quietly.

The IRS examiner had listened without interrupting. Now she reached out, patted Julia on the shoulder, and said, "God forgives you for that. Now, let's see how we can work all this out . . ."

She began to go over Julia's income tax report for the prior year and carefully asked questions about other areas where there might be deductions. Her questions brought out some things Julia hadn't even thought were legitimate. Before we knew it, the woman had it all worked out. Julia did not owe a dime, even though the trumped-up deductions had all been removed from the tax report.

We both thanked the woman profusely. I gave her a hug and said, "I noticed the little fish sign on your calendar. We're Christians, too, and we're so glad God led us to you today."

Our IRS friend smiled, but maintained her official government decorum. She said she understood, but that she had another appointment soon and that our time was up. I think perhaps she would have liked to have talked longer, but she knew her supervisor could look in and wonder what all this hugging and crying was about.

Julia and I left the IRS offices rejoicing. We sat out in the car while Julia wept tears of joy for several minutes. I couldn't help but note the difference. Before we had gone in we had sat in the car, praying for MERCY, and now we were sitting there thanking the Lord that Julia had received GRACE.

The best part about Julia's story is not that she "got off" and didn't have to go to jail or pay some huge fine. The best part is what the lady said after Julia sincerely confessed what she had done wrong:

"God forgives you . . . now let's see how we can work all this out . . ."

Isn't that just like the Lord? When we come to Him in true repentance, asking for forgiveness, He says, *"Of course* I forgive you. Now let's see what we can do—*together."*

Grace Gives Us a Helping Hand

Before Christ gave grace its full meaning through His death on the cross, the Old Testament referred to grace with the Hebrew word *hen*, meaning ". . . the compassionate response of one who is able to help another person in need." Whenever we are unable to deal with life, we ask for help in one way or another. The Psalms can give us a great example of how this works as we see the psalmist crying out for help because of:

Distress—Psalm 4:1; 31:9
Agony—Psalm 6:2
Persecution by enemies—Psalm 19:13; 56:1
Loneliness and affliction—Psalm 25:16
Disaster—Psalm 57:1
The contempt of others—Psalm 123:3
Weakness and trouble—Psalm 41:1; 86:16
Sin itself—Psalm 51:1

All of the above are only a part of what theologians call the "human condition" that holds all of us in bondage. As Bible scholar Larry Richards put it:

> Only God can act to release us and enable us to overcome the foes within us and around us. But God is Who He is. He is compassionate and loving. We are confident that when we call on God, He will respond. He will act, not because we merit help, but because He recognizes our desperate need and love moves Him to exercise His power to meet our need. This indeed is grace![3]

The Mail Is Full of God's Grace

The postman continues to bring me stories of how people find themselves facing distress, disaster, loneliness, and all those other gloomees faced by the psalmist. But somehow God's grace sees them through. They find the strength to handle the situation. One mother wrote to say:

> I have two adopted sons, and the 20-year-old is having homosexual feelings. My husband and I are really appalled by the whole thing but we are trying to work with him and help him in every way we can. This is kind of like our worst nightmare come true.
>
> Our 15-year-old is going through a rebellion that is very scary. He has run away from home, broken nearly every window in our house, lived with friends for a short time and is now at home doing quite well, I think. We have taken him out of public school and I am now home schooling him, as he was failing everything in school and getting mixed up with the wrong crowd. We are working together and with the Lord to work out our family problems, but books like yours really help, it's great knowing what I am feeling is shared with others.

Sometimes grace can be found in the strangest places, even on a foggy highway. My friend, Evelyn Heinz, who is an author and poet, shared a fabulous episode of grace she had experienced. She faced a very difficult trip of 125 miles one way to visit her dying mother. The weather was supposed to be clear, but the night before it changed radically, and the next morning she had to start out in the rain and fog. Her letter continued:

> The night before, I read one meditation from a little book . . ."I am sending an angel ahead of you to guard you along the way. . . ." That verse eased my thoughts for the morning ride. To my surprise, my angel (angels) came in human form under a white Winnebago camper. God put him ahead of me to keep my speed down and I followed his camper through the fog. Then, before he turned, another angel in human form came ahead of me, this time in a black van with three initials on its out-of-state license, EMH. Barbara those are mine! Evelyn Marie Heinz! The fog was clearing, the van turned and the rest of the 60-some-odd miles were clear!
>
> My visit with my mother went very compassionately, the time moved too swiftly, but I felt the "JOY" of being with her. Hiding my tears, I held her hand and kissed her forehead and we exchanged "I love yous" before it came time for me to go. Her last words were, "Be careful on the drive home. I'll be praying for you!" I smiled and said, "Mom, I'll be praying for you too."

We Live from Hope to Hope

I've given away several copies of Lewis Smedes's fine book, *How Can It Be All Right When Everything Is All Wrong?* because I love how he helps his readers discover hope through the gift of grace. In his introduction, Smedes says he wrote this book for people who are still trying hard to believe in God even though a hundred voices inside are telling them to stop believing. He confesses that, at times, his faith has waned and that his words are filtered "through many years of believing against the grain."

Believing doesn't come easy for Smedes because many people he cares about hurt too much. People close to him have died of cancer "too soon," despite his fervent prayers to take away the pain. He's had friends whose marriages have turned into battlefields as their children have gone through all kinds of "mini-hells." Smedes admits, "God does not do many miracles for my crowd."

There are folks in the Spatula crowd who are short on miracles too. I received an eight-page letter from a mother who apparently just can't take any more:

> Why has my life been so awful? I accepted Christ when I was twelve. I have now so many hurts, so many injustices— Why? I would commit suicide, but God would condemn me to hell. I sometimes wonder if hell wouldn't be better than this life. Our finances are a wreck, my health is a wreck, I don't believe my husband really believes or comprehends my pain. I don't feel loved. God may say all those great things in our Bible, but He doesn't really carry them out to all. . . . I'm happy for you. You are one of the chosen ones—I'm not—I really am not a pessimist, just have become realistic.
>
> You don't have to pray for me, God has dealt all the blows I need. . . . I just don't know how much longer I can *continue to function.* Please don't promise happy futures for everyone who believes. It just doesn't happen. I'm afraid I don't fit anywhere.

This precious mother sounds like she can't be sure if life is passing her by or running her over. She says she believes I am one of the "chosen ones," but I am no more chosen than she is. I HAVE chosen to *trust in God's grace,* and THAT is what has brought me through the fiery trials. As Lewis Smedes puts it:

> Grace does come. . . . Grace happens to me when I feel a surge of honest joy that makes me glad to be alive in spite of valid reasons for feeling terrible. . . . Grace is the gift of feeling sure that our future, even our dying, is going to turn out more splendidly than we dare imagine. Grace is the feeling of hope.[4]

I have mentioned hope several times in this book because, when the gloomees close in *hope is really all we have*. As Jean Kerr put it,

HOPE IS A FEELING YOU HAVE
THAT THE FEELING YOU HAVE ISN'T PERMANENT.

As I was working on these final chapters, I received a letter from a mother whose words so nicely describe how grace is the feeling of hope:

> It seems our last ten years have sort of been one situation on top of another. In that time God has taught me a great deal. For one thing I learned to thank Him for "all things" and MEAN it (something I had tried to do, but never was quite able to carry off). He taught me what it means to really, truly, totally trust Him! I have always trusted Him, but never with the kind of trust I now have. He taught me that I can endure many things I would have never dreamed I could do without losing my sanity, and He showed me how to be happy while I was going through the trial.

This mother closes her letter with the assurance that she knows that God holds her hand and walks day by day through each circumstance with her. Then she adds a thought that we all need to burn into our hearts:

FAITH NEVER KNOWS WHERE IT IS BEING LED,
BUT IT LOVES THE ONE WHO IS LEADING.

God's Grace Paints the Rainbow

Have you ever thought of how a rainbow is a perfect picture of God's grace? Life's storms may buffet us, ripping apart our plans, and flooding us with multiplied problems, many of which are of our own making. But grace is God's promise that we will not be destroyed, just as a rainbow was His promise that He would never again send a flood to devastate the earth.[5]

The following poem puts that promise in perspective.

> In life's daily walk
> There are drops of rain,
> In life's ever flowing journey
> There often is some pain.
>
> But, my friend,
> We need not fear,
> For your loving Savior
> Is always near.
>
> He gives us grace to bear
> The problems that pass our way.
> Yes, even on that very rainy day.
>
> Sometimes when the rain of life
> Comes to each one,
> We feel for a moment
> We cannot see the sun.
>
> But God's promise to you is
> Look up and see,
> The Love He shares with both you and me.
>
> For, my friend,
>   A rainbow will appear
> After the storm clouds of life have cleared.
>   —Donna Larkin

Because rain is in such short supply in Southern California, we don't see many rainbows, but when one does appear, I try to take full advantage of its beautiful hues and colors. Phyllis Eger tells a lovely little story about how a phone call interrupted her dinner preparations as a neighbor told her to hurry outside to see the most beautiful rainbow in the eastern sky. She turned off her stove and dashed outside, and there it was—a double arc of lovely colors, pink, lavender, blue, and gold.

She quickly called her mother who lived on the other side of town to tell her about the rainbow, and her mother in turn passed the word to a neighbor. Other families saw them look-ing up at the sky and came out to see what was going on. Soon, more than a dozen people were appreciating that beautiful rain-bow—all because one lady made a phone call. Eger observes:

> Why is it that bad news travels fast? We habitually keep one another updated on the latest burglaries, jet crashes and divorces. But how often do we tell a friend or neighbor about a nest of robins, a baby's first steps, a new kitten or an inspira-tional book we've read? It's the little things that add color and texture to our days, so why not share the Rainbow?[6]

Yes, why not, indeed? Share life's simple pleasures with oth-ers and always remember to share life's greatest pleasure—God's grace.

After the Storm—the Rainbow!

Do you remember the all-American family whose story of multiple tragedies became the first letter to be shared back in chapter 1? As I was preparing to ship this manuscript to the publisher, another letter from the same mother came in, not describing more tragedy, thank God, but with GOOD NEWS:

> In these—our glorious Christian lives—the "Paschal cycle" of dying and rising goes on and on. The trials ("dyings") we experienced from '86 through '91 are now giving way to some wonderful risings. We have a grand new son-in-law. Our anorexic daughter grew into a beautiful young woman, valedictorian of her class with a four-year scholarship to a great university. We are grateful for the progress of modern psychiatry coupled with an expert knowledge of pharmacol-ogy. The depressed daughter has been helped. The alcohol-addicted son has gone to AA and by the grace of God has enjoyed, so far, six months of sobriety.
> There's even more, but that's enough to confirm how all things work together for good for those who love God. (Romans 8, right?)

I guess the best thing is what I'll use to close. After my son's suicide, one of the recommendations on a list of "grieving techniques" was, "Ask God to give you a sign that your loved one is with Him." This was not my usual way of praying, but I felt led to ask for the resolution of an incredibly difficult situation. Last November (two years and one month after his death), the sign came bright and clear and the situation has been clearly <u>sustained by the grace of God!</u>

P.S. Thank God <u>a much brighter day</u> has dawned for us!

This joyful mom's letter is a special sparkle I just had to tuck in before closing this book. She knows from experience the wisdom in a cross-stitch that hangs on the wall of my Joy Room. It says:

> THE SOUL WOULD HAVE NO RAINBOWS
> IF THE EYES HAD NO TEARS.

One of my favorite poets is Joan Anglund, who does bits of gentle verse with lovely illustrations. One of her collections is called "Rainbow Love," and in it she reminds us that though the days may be dark and full of gloomees we can still "keep a Rainbow in our hearts." We can choose to stay under a cloud, or we can busy ourselves in finding our rainbow.

Yes, the rainbow is God's gift to us to remind us of His greater gift—His amazing grace. His grace is ALWAYS THERE to draw upon *when we remember to do so.* So, pack up your gloomees in that great big box, then sit on the lid and laugh and . . .

> ALWAYS REMEMBER TO TAKE
> YOUR RAINBOW WITH YOU.[7]

Discussion Guide

Because many readers use my books in Spatula groups and other sessions, I've included these questions to help you get your discussions started.

Introduction   If It's Free, It's Advice;
If You Pay for It, It's Counseling;
If You Can Use Either One, It's a Miracle!

1. Why is it important to share your problems with others?

2. What has been the most difficult part of your problem to accept?

3. Where have you already looked for help and comfort? Which sources helped and which ones didn't?

Chapter 1   We're All in This Together . . .
You're Just in a Little Deeper

1. How has your current situation helped you look at your life from a new perspective? How have your priorities changed?

2. How can you look at your problem with a positive attitude? Can you find something to be happy about or thankful for without becoming a "Pollyanna" who hides from reality?

3. Look at different translations of Ps. 69:1–3 and see the different words used to symbolize David's problems. What

words would you use to symbolize your own problems? Now use symbolic words to describe your continued trust in God.

4. Ask yourself the questions Larry Crabb asks his seminar participants: Do you use God to solve your problems? Or do you use your problems to find God? Why is it better to use our problems to find God?

Chapter 2   **If You Can't Go Around It, Over It, or Through It, You Had Better Negotiate with It**

1. How has humor helped accelerate your trip through the grief process?

2. Which stage of grief are you in—shock, suffering, or recovery? Describe the progress you've made through the grief process, and how you see yourself a year from now.

3. How have others impeded or assisted you in moving through the grief process?

4. Now that you have "credentials," how will you help others who are hurting?

Chapter 3   **There's One Place You Can Always Find Me . . . At the Corner of Here and Now**

1. Can you see yourself as "desert-sweetened grapefruit"? In what way is your current situation bittersweet?

2. Describe your own experiences in some or all of the five steps of emotional pain:

    a. Churn
    b. Burn
    c. Yearn
    d. Learn
    e. Turn

3. Are you ever tormented by the "if onlys" or the "blame game"? How have you overcome those regrets or accusations?

4. Do you see Proverbs 22:6 in a new light now? How has your understanding of this verse changed?

Chapter 4   You're a WHAT?!?

1. On a scale of one to ten, where do you rate the problem of having a homosexual child? If you have a homosexual child, has this rating changed since you first learned of his or her homosexuality? What caused the change?

2. How have you "handled" your child's homosexuality: critically? acceptingly? harshly? lovingly? How would you do things differently if you could start over again after learning of his homosexuality?

3. How can you show unconditional love to your homosexual child without accepting his behavior?

4. Imagine Jesus scooping up a hurting child in His loving arms. Can you also imagine that this hurting child is a homosexual? How do you think the Lord would treat one of His followers who was homosexual?

Chapter 5   Life Is a Sexually Transmitted, Terminal Disease

1. Many AIDS victims, knowing they don't have long to live, often come to grips with who they are and what is going to happen to them. How would your life change if you suddenly learned you had only a short time to live?

2. How would Jesus respond to AIDS victims?

3. Many parents have trouble letting their homosexual children with AIDS come home for care and treatment. What would it say about you as a Christian if you allowed your homosexual child with AIDS to come home?

4. How can you refute the argument that AIDS is God's punishment on homosexuals?

Chapter 6   **Where Do I Put My Hatred While I Say My Prayers?**

1. What has caused you to feel anger or hatred as you've wrestled with your hurt?

2. What signs of depression have you experienced? What has helped you overcome these symptoms?

3. Have you been able to "let go"? If so, what helped you release your problem and turn it over to God? If not, what is keeping you from giving it up?

4. Look at 1 Cor. 10:13. How does this verse apply to you?

Chapter 7   **Pack Up Your Gloomees in a Great Big Box, Then Sit on the Lid and Laugh!**

1. What are some of your "Jell-O" memories?

2. How have laughter and humor helped ease your hurt? How has God taken painful episodes in your life and used them to infuse others with joy?

3. One of the suggestions in this chapter is to "learn to laugh at yourself." Think of three things you don't like about yourself, then poke fun at them and exaggerate them.

4. I found comfort in a bubble bath, my video fireplace, and the soothing sounds of my rain stick. What brings you comfort?

Chapter 8   **At Day's End, I Turn All of My Problems Over to God . . . He's Going to Be Up Anyway**

1. Do you still believe in God the way you used to? Have your trials increased or diminished your trust in God?

2. How does this Moroccan proverb apply to your life: "Trust in God but tie your camel tight"?

3. In what ways are you to your child as God is to you?

4. How has God worked in unexpected ways to help you deal with your problems?

P.S.   **Always Take Your Rainbow with You!**

1. How can God's grace make life all RIGHT despite the fact that everything is obviously all WRONG?

2. If your child has disappointed you, how has that caused you to feel guilty? How can you overcome that guilt?

3. Look at your relationship with your child. How is it a condemning relationship? How is it an encouraging relationship?

4. What does a rainbow mean to you?

Endnotes

Chapter 1 We're All in This Together . . . You're Just in a Little Deeper

1. Henry Asher, "Attorney's Large Family One That Stays Together," *New Orleans Times-Picayune* (10 June 1984).
2. Margaret Clarkson, *Grace Grows Best in Winter* (Grand Rapids: Zondervan, 1972), 55.
3. Psalm 42:5 KJV.
4. Michael Malloy, *Christian Counseling Services Newsletter* (Spring 1992).
5. Ibid.
6. Robert Fulghum, *Uh-Oh* (New York: Villard Books, 1991), 6.

Chapter 2 If You Can't Go Around It, Over It, or Through It, You Had Better Negotiate with It

1. Robin Williams, quoted in *The Fourth 637 Things Anybody Ever Said*, Robert Byrne, comp. (New York: Fawcett Crest, 1990).
2. Ashleigh Brilliant, Pot-Shot No. 1510, © Ashleigh Brilliant Enterprises, 1979. Used by permission.
3. From a card published by Morris Printing Company, 326 West Park, Waterloo, Iowa 50701. Used by permission.
4. Granger Westberg, *Good Grief* (Philadelphia: Fortress Press, 1962, 1971). This small book is based on a chapter

from Granger Westberg, *Minister and Doctor Meet* (New York: Harper and Row, 1961).

5. Westberg, *Good Grief*, 7.
6. Westberg, *Good Grief*, 13.
7. Gini Kopecky, "Have a Good Cry," *Redbook* (May 1992), 109.
8. Paul R. Van Gorder, *Daily Bread*, July 1988.
9. From a card printed by David M & Company, 6029 Etiwanda Avenue, Tarzana, California 91356, © 1986.
10. Westberg, *Good Grief*, 46.

Chapter 3   There's One Place You Can Always Find Me . . . At the Corner of Here and Now

1. As seen in a Dear Abby column by Abigail Van Buren. Copyright 1992 Universal Press Syndicate. Reprinted with permission. All rights reserved.
2. Barbara Johnson, *Stick A Geranium in Your Hat and Be Happy* (Dallas: Word, 1990), 66–67.
3. Robert Fulghum, *Uh-Oh: Some Observations from Both Sides of the Refrigerator Door* (New York: Villard Books, 1991), 30.
4. Planet Greetings, Box 410, Fresh Meadows, N.Y. 11365.
5. Charles Swindoll, *You and Your Child* (Nashville: Thomas Nelson, 1977), 20.
6. Fritz Ridenour, *What Teen-Agers Wish Their Parents Knew About Kids* (Waco, Tex.: Word, 1982), 64.
7. This line is part of the dialogue between actresses Jessica Tandy and Cathy Bates in the movie *Fried Green Tomatoes*. Produced by 20th Century Fox, 1991.
8. Alan Francis, *Everything Men Know About Women* (Austin, Tex.: Newport House, 1990).
9. See Margaret Nelson, "Too Tough to Die," *People Weekly* (3 February 1992), 30. Later reports revealed that the surgery had been successful and the reattached arms were beginning to work (see Margaret Nelson and Karen S. Schneider, "Comeback Kid," *People Weekly* [25 May 1992], 44).
10. Psalm 107:35 RSV.

11. Source unknown.
12. © Recycled Paper Products, Inc. All rights reserved. Original design by John Richard Allen. Reprinted by permission.

Chapter 4   You're a WHAT?!?

1. "Most Gay Readers Glad About Orientation," Ann Landers, *San Gabriel Valley Tribune* (26 April 1992), D6. Permission granted by Ann Landers and Creators Syndicate.
2. Anita Worthen, "Guess Who's Coming to Dinner," *Love in Action* (1988).
3. Herbert Vander Lugt, "How to Love Unconditionally," *Discovery Digest* (July-August 1982): 48–51.
4. From a message presented by Stephen Arterburn in February 1991 at Biola College, La Mirada, California.
5. "From This Moment on . . . Love!" *Moment Ministries*, 235 E. Chestnut, Monrovia, California 91016.
6. Ashleigh Brilliant, Pot-Shots No. 1027, © Ashleigh Brilliant Enterprises, 1977. Used by permission.
7. Ashleigh Brilliant, Pot-Shots, No.2212, Ashleigh Brilliant Enterprises © 1991. Used by permission.

Chapter 5   Life Is a Sexually Transmitted, Terminal Disease

1. A slogan of Love & Action, 3 Church Circle, Annapolis, Maryland 21401. Used by permission.
2. See Revelation 6:8.
3. Statistics on AIDS reported in "Straight Talk About HIV/AIDS," *Staying Current* 4, No. 2 (March/April 1992): 1. This is the newsletter of AIDS Information Ministries, P.O. Box 136116, Fort Worth, Texas 76136.
4. Ibid., 2.
5. Harold Ivan Smith, "Christians! AIDS Victims Need Your Help," *Charisma* (September 1987), 38.

6. Philip Yancey, "Jogging Past the AIDS Clinic," *Christianity Today* (7 March 1986), 64.

7. Ibid.

8. Wayne E. Caldwell, "Moments with Readers," *Wesleyan Advocate* 149, No. 7 (July 1991).

9. Jerry Arterburn with his brother, Stephen Arterburn, *How Will I Tell My Mother?* (Nashville: Oliver Nelson, 1988), 126–27.

10. Ashleigh Brilliant, Pot-Shots No. 295, © Ashleigh Brilliant Enterprises, 1971. Used by permission.

Chapter 6   Where Do I Put My Hatred While I Say My Prayers?

1. Source unknown.

2. Carl Sherman, "Is It Just a Mood or Real Depression?" *Family Circle* (1 April 1992), 65.

3. Frank B. Minirth and Paul D. Meier, *Happiness Is a Choice* (Grand Rapids: Baker, 1978), 124–28.

4. Ibid., 125.

5. Bob Davies and Lori Torkelson. Reprinted with permission from "Love in Action," P. O.Box 2655, San Rafael, California 94912.

6. Lewis B. Smedes, *How Can It Be All Right When Everything Is All Wrong?* (New York: Pocket Books, a division of Simon and Schuster, 1982).

7. Ibid.

8. From the poem "Letting Go." Author unknown.

Chapter 7   Pack Up Your Gloomees in a Great Big Box, Then Sit on the Lid and Laugh!

1. Source unknown.

2. Included in *Poems That Touch the Heart*, A. L. Alexander, compiler, (New York: Doubleday, 1956), 304.

3. Diane Suchetka, "Laughter . . . Is the Best Medicine," *The Orange County Register* (10 March 1992), E-1.

4. Ibid., E-1, E-2.

5. See Charles Swindoll, *Living on the Ragged Edge* (Dallas: Word, 1985), 262. Swindoll thanks his friend, Dr. Ken Gangel, for the remark, "Have a blast while you last!"

6. Source unknown.

7. Dr. Paul McGhee, quoted in Diane Suchetka, "Laughter . . . Is the Best Medicine," *The Orange County Register* (10 March 1992), E-1.

8. Betty Henry Taylor, "Sound of Rain," *Opening Up Closets and Dumping Out Drawers* (New York: Chrysalis Publishing, 1991), 98. Used by permission.

9. George Goldtrap, *Laughter Works* newsletter, 3, no. 2 (Spring 1991).

Chapter 8   At Day's End, I Turn All of My Problems Over to God . . . He's Going to Be Up Anyway

1. Danny Dutton. Publishing source unknown.

2. John White, "Relinquishment of Adult Children," *Equipping the Saints* 5, No. 2 (Spring 1991).

3. Bob Davies, Love in Action, San Rafael, California.

4. Source unknown.

5. Source unknown.

6. From L. M. Montgomery, *Anne of Avonlea* (New York: New American Library, 1987).

P.S.   Always Take Your Rainbow with You!

1. Lewis B. Smedes, *How Can It Be All Right When Everything Is All Wrong?* (New York: Pocket Books, a division of Simon and Schuster, 1982), 17.

2. Ibid., 18.

3. Lawrence O. Richards, *Expository Dictionary of Bible Words* (Grand Rapids: Zondervan, 1985), 317.

4. Smedes, 11.

5. See Genesis 9:8–16.

6. Phyllis Eger, "Share the Rainbow," *Sunshine Magazine* (May 1989).

7. Adapted from poetry by Joan Walsh Anglund, "Rainbow Love," Determined Productions, P.O. Box 2150, San Francisco, California 94126.